WHAT HAPPENED TO HUMANITY?

Samina Rose

& The Truth Teller Collective

ISBN: 979-8-9882468-4-8
Allegra Publishing

CONTENTS

Preface

There are moments in life when the world stops making sense. Not because of what happens in the shadows, but because of what happens in plain sight. The places that promise safety. The institutions that claim to heal. The professionals trained to listen. The systems built to deliver justice. And yet, you find yourself living in a world where those very institutions betray you, harm you, and gaslight you into believing it is somehow your fault.

If only you had the right degree.
The right body.
The right car.
The right house.
The right mind.

But it is none of those things.

Everything comes down to money and greed.

I made a simple rule for myself: whenever I am unsure whether to blame myself or the system, I ask one question— *Could fair access to resources have changed the outcome?* The answer is almost always yes. And when that is the case, the blame does not belong to the individual; it belongs to a system that distributes resources unjustly.

This is not deflection. It is clarity.

Poverty creates profound trauma that we have normalized as "just the way things are." The scarcity mindset produced by capitalism is a lie we collectively participate in, even as we go to work each day and follow rules we know will harm other human beings—rules justified in the name of policy and law. In our effort to cling to small pockets of safety and control, we slowly let our souls wither. And when the soul dies, the body eventually follows.

This book was born in the space between two traumas: the harm done to me in interpersonal relationships—particularly within my family—and the harm inflicted by a system that manufactures scarcity and precarity. A system that does not care whether I live or die, or perhaps sees me only as a data point, a cost, or a line in a spreadsheet rather than as a human being.

The second trauma is compounded, cumulative, chronic, and nearly impossible to escape because we are forced to live inside the very structures that reduce us to numbers and cash value. It happens everywhere, every day. To survive, our nervous systems adapt by normalizing the violence.

This is exactly what happens in abusive families. Most children do not recognize the abuse they endure until years later, often when they grow up and try to love their own children differently. As children, we form trauma bonds. As adults, we develop trauma-bonded compliance with systems that harm us. We fear questioning them—even when we are gasping for survival.

The silence of the world around us is not neutral. And yet, most of us remain passive in the face of harm. The system is structured, enforced, and justified through mythical logic—stories about merit, worthiness, productivity, and deservingness. We internalize that logic and allow it to dictate whose needs matter and whose suffering is acceptable. Who deserves care—and who is left to die a slow, extractive death.

I learned that bureaucracy can wound with the same precision as an individual perpetrator. I learned that institutions can be asleep—even while insisting they are awake. I have experienced two oppressive systems, first in Iran, and then in the USA. Each was different because in Iran I experienced poverty as a child, but eventually my family could mobilize their class to upper middle. While in America no matter how much effort I put in, what degrees I get, or if I change my name to something more acceptable and erase many parts of my identity, still the system decides who gets to be seen, heard and stay alive. The cruelty in Iran was overt, while in the US it is covert and thus harder to detect the patterns.

For years, I tried to navigate the labyrinth of hospitals, clinics, schools, agencies, licensing boards, and legal offices that were supposed to help me seek justice. I called. I wrote. I begged. I tried again. Twenty lawyers turned me away—not because the truth was unclear, but because the law had decided that truth has an expiration date. Statutes of limitation replaced compassion. "Insufficient evidence" replaced belief. And the humanity I kept searching for remained out of reach.

In my previous work, I wrote about CRC-PTSD and how the absence of authentic care—especially within institutions—produces the same symptoms we recognize in depression, anxiety, and complex PTSD. CRC-PTSD is a universal human adaptation to chronic institutional betrayal, but its visibility varies by vulnerability, buffering resources, and normative conditioning toward cruelty. This book continues that inquiry, but with a broader lens: not just asking what happened to me, but asking what happened to all of us.

What happened to humanity?

That is the question at the heart of this book.

How did we fall asleep to each other's suffering?
How did systems that claim to protect us become mechanisms of denial, minimization, and institutional betrayal?
How did compassion become an inconvenience?
How did people lose their ability to recognize and sit with their own pain?

And perhaps most importantly—
How do we wake up?

This book is not a memoir, though it is shaped by the scars I carry. It is not only a sociological analysis, though it is grounded in theory, structure, and the patterns that repeat across society. It is a truth-teller's account of what it means to confront a world that has lost touch with itself. Humans don't learn safety alone. We learn it **with someone**, and then we carry it forward.This book is a place to learn safety.

There are others like me—people who refused to go numb, who saw the cracks, who felt the collective sleep but could not join it. This book is for them. For the ones who live with moral injuries the world cannot name. For the ones who have seen behind the curtain. For the ones who carry more humanity than the systems that tried to diminish them.

If you are reading this, perhaps you are one of them.

My hope is not to save the world, but to contribute to its awakening. Not through grand gestures, but through clarity, honesty, and the courage to name what so many are afraid to name. Because humanity is not lost—it is buried under layers of compliance, fear, and denial. And the first step toward reclaiming it is simply telling the truth.

This is my truth.
This is our truth.
And this is the beginning of waking up.

Finally, I want to ask you to research every claim made in this book. My knowledge as a human is extremely limited compared to the vastness of our universe. Always do your own research—it's much easier today with access to the internet. Think critically, and don't accept every word you hear without taking time to process it. Remember that our world is filled with psychological operations and manipulation, so asking who benefits from any piece of information we're offered can be a guiding light.

1 — The World Asleep: A Crisis of Consciousness and Forbidden Descent

"We are born awake. It is the world that teaches us to sleep."

— Samina Rose

Most people don't realize when something inside them has gone quiet. I didn't either — not for the first three decades of my life.

I was awake in every functional sense: I worked hard, followed the rules, smiled when expected, excelled academically, showed up, and survived. My eyes were wide open. But my heart? That part had been trained to stay closed — not out of choice, but out of necessity.

What I'm describing isn't "sleep" in a mystical or insulting way. It's a **state of emotional and moral shutdown** that develops slowly, invisibly, and predictably under structurally traumatogenic conditions. Conditions that sort us into an arbitrary value system, based on our body, country, gender, size, financial ability, and greed. It's not natural selection. It's a design bought by humans devoured by greed. It's not that all people don't care. It's that the system teaches them to mute the parts of themselves that would hurt too much to feel fully. And just like that, they are running a cruel program of depopulating the earth to %10 of its population.

We don't see it or think about it every day because it is psychologically unbearable. But we feel it every day. We feel it through institutions designed to erase impact—through arbitrary, human-made policies and laws that justify harm while pretending neutrality. Harm doesn't need to look violent to be lethal.

A murder is still a murder.

Whether someone dies because insurance denied care.
Whether someone burns out so completely they can no longer care for themselves.
Whether someone becomes so depressed they no longer want to feel anything at all.

All death is a life lost.
All of it counts.

What we are living through is dehumanization—people reduced to expendable collateral damage in systems that measure profit, efficiency, and control, not life. The precarity we experience is not accidental. It is evidence of a slow, lonely, painful ending built into the design—one where no rescue is coming from above.

Unless we change direction.

Unless we open our eyes and hearts and allow ourselves to grieve what has been done to us.
Unless we begin to see and hold each other's pain instead of numbing it away.
Unless we refuse systems that extract from our suffering and start valuing kindness over money, care over ownership, people over land and profit.

They want us to believe we are powerless.
But they are the minority.
Ten percent at most.

We are the ninety percent.
And healing—like harm—is collective.

Human meaning doesn't disappear under pressure — it gets buried. "Greed addiction" creates the noise that buries it: endless extraction, competition, and manufactured urgency that keep people distracted from what matters. In this economy, success often depends on forgetting — forgetting care, forgetting limits, forgetting one's own soul — and that forgetting is not only tolerated, it is rewarded. Greed is rewarded and labeled as success. Not balance and harmony with earth.

The counterpart of greed addiction is **CRC-PTSD (Compounded Relational Complex PTSD).** In my work on **CRC-PTSD** , I write about how emotional numbing, hypervigilance, internalized shame, fawning, and withdrawal from one's moral instincts are not personality traits — they are adaptations. They emerge when you grow up or function in environments where authenticity is punished, vulnerability is unsafe, and honesty is inconvenient for the people in power.

These patterns look internal, but their cause is external.

People aren't disconnected because they're lazy or unaware;
They're disconnected because the system rewards compliance and punishes awareness.

And I say this not as an observer looking down, but as someone who lived inside that shutdown for years — eyes open wide, heart sealed for safety, navigating life with all the metrics of external "success" but none of the internal freedom.

What I call "sleep" is really **over-adaptation**: the body learning to survive in places that never learned how to care for us. This kind of sleep is not an accident. It's learned. Not just as something we pick up in childhood or school, but as a **condition of survival** inside systems that demand obedience to human-made constructs.

People are trained into this shutdown through:

- **chronic stress**
- **institutional gaslighting**
- **shame-based socialization**
- **scarcity narratives**
- **perfectionism and the "myth of perfect"**
- **trauma-bonded compliance**
- **and a lifetime of pressure to "act normal," stay pleasant, and**

not make others uncomfortable

But here's the deeper truth:
This entire framework—what counts as "normal," "good," "professional," "successful," "strong," "deserving"—is a human construct.

A set of rules invented by earlier generations, shaped by power, privilege, and dominance. As I argue throughout my work, none of these norms are universal truths. They are **scripts** created to maintain social order, economic hierarchy, and emotional conformity. Yet we carry them as if they were laws of nature rather than stories passed down through fear.

Power created this dynamic out of convenience and control. When a society is organized around:

- productivity over personhood,
- compliance over curiosity,
- hierarchy over humanity,
- extraction over care,
- and image over truth,

It needs its people to stay in a manageable emotional range. A cage simply made of language and words.
It needs them to be predictable, self-blaming, self-regulating, and afraid to step outside the lines — afraid to trust their feelings, their intuition, or their inner compass as real senses, just as valid as the five physical senses we teach children in school.

CRC-PTSD develops in that forgetting.

Because when people internalize constructed norms as "the way things are," they stop questioning the harm those norms cause. They learn to contort themselves into shapes demanded by power structures, even when those shapes suffocate the self and lead to burnout.

Waking up is not rebellion; it is remembering.

Remembering that the rules shaping our lives—our emotional expressions, our worth, our identities, our futures—were invented by humans, not handed down by the universe. And if humans made them, humans can replace them with systems grounded in care instead of control.

The result of being asleep is a society full of people who follow rules, meet expectations, achieve milestones, and yet rarely stop to ask the most basic question:

Is this who I am, or is this what the system conditioned me to be?

Most people don't ask because asking hurts.
It threatens the survival strategies they built to get through their childhoods, their workplaces, their schools, and their relationships. It threatens the story that "everything is fine" and that suffering is a personal failure instead of a structural problem.

And so we sleep — eyes open, hearts closed.

What we are experiencing is not unprecedented suffering — it is unprecedented **denial of suffering**. Ancient societies like the Sumerians lived with scarcity, illness, and instability as givens of existence, yet they did not pretend otherwise. Hardship was named, ritualized, and shared. Pain was not treated as personal failure or individual pathology, but as part of a fragile human condition embedded in nature, time, and fate. Their gods were imperfect, their world uncertain, and their lives finite — and meaning arose not from control, but from participation, continuity, and mutual obligation.

By contrast, modern society produces an illusion of mastery while systematically dismantling the conditions for dignity. We promise safety, progress, and abundance, then punish those whose bodies reveal the cost of maintaining that illusion. Where ancient civilizations expected instability and prepared culturally for loss, we insist on endless growth and pathologize anyone who cannot adapt to its violence. The result is not resilience, but fragmentation — people breaking quietly while institutions continue functioning as if nothing is wrong.

The Sumerians feared excess because they understood it destabilized the social order. They practiced limits, debt forgiveness, and visible redistribution not out of moral purity, but out of survival wisdom. Today, excess is abstracted, hidden, and celebrated. Hoarding is framed as intelligence. Exploitation is called efficiency. Debt is moralized and made permanent. What was once understood as dangerous imbalance has been rebranded as success — and this inversion has profound psychological consequences.

This is why modern trauma feels uniquely disorienting. It is not only that harm occurs, but that it is denied, minimized, and reframed as personal inadequacy. Ancient people endured suffering together in a world that admitted its harshness. We endure suffering alone in systems that insist there is nothing wrong. That denial — not hardship itself — is what erodes the soul. It fractures narrative, disrupts trust, and teaches the nervous system that reality itself cannot be spoken.

In this sense, what we have lost is not comfort, technology, or longevity — it is the permission to be human in the face of vulnerability. We have replaced shared meaning with metrics, care with optimization, and wisdom with control. And yet, as history reminds us, meaning does not disappear when systems fail. It waits — buried beneath noise, fear, and extraction — until we remember that survival without dignity is not survival at all.

What this sleep actually is?

It is what I describe in my CRC-PTSD framework: a condition in which the nervous system is shaped not only by personal trauma, but by **repeated denials, delays, gaslighting, and bureaucratic erasures across every institution a person depends on**—from birth until death.

The training starts early.

From the moment we're born, we're **assigned a number**—a legal identity that replaces our personhood before we are even capable of understanding we have one. That number follows us everywhere. We become data before we become selves.

We learn our first lessons about love from caregivers who themselves were shaped by **old rules of productivity-as-worth**. They teach us—without intending to—that love is conditional, care is inconsistent, and connection must be earned. This is not because our parents were unloving; it's because **they inherited a system that demanded exhaustion, obedience, and suppression long before we ever**

arrived.

Then we go to school, where imagination is slowly squeezed out of us.
Curiosity becomes "disruption."
Authenticity becomes "immaturity."
Asking "why" becomes "misbehavior."
Exploration becomes "lack of focus."

We learn to sit still, stay quiet, fit in, perform.

As we grow older, we see more and more examples of people being punished for honesty, vulnerability, and difference. We internalize this pattern. We swallow it. We braid all these experiences together:

- childhood misunderstanding
- parental overwhelm
- peer cruelty
- institutional dismissal
- workplace silencing
- social disapproval
- cultural shame

And eventually, the braid becomes heavy enough to pull our heads down—not in submission, but in **self-protection**.

CRC-PTSD is what happens when these personal betrayals merge with **institutional betrayals**.
When the echo of childhood "not enough" meets adult "case denied."
When the old wound of "be quiet" meets the present-day "you don't qualify."
When early abandonment meets modern bureaucracy and endless holds on the phone.
When the body finally understands that safety cannot be found in systems that were never designed to nurture us.

And yes, there are people who exploit this darkness. They are those of us

addicted to greed.
They benefit from a population that is too tired to resist, too ashamed to speak, too overwhelmed to question the rules. These people—individuals, institutions, corporations—know that **fear shrinks a soul faster than hunger**. They know that if you can convince someone their pain is personal, you never have to look at the system that caused it.

They kill love before it can grow into a full tree.
But here's the truth they cannot erase:

Love never dies.

The first act of love is to wake up to our own pain. We must see ourselves before we can truly see anyone else. We need to recognize—and honor—how hard we have worked just to survive. I firmly believe no human enters this world intending anything other than goodness. Children want to be good. Adults want to be good too. The problem is not our moral compass; it is the way society invented mythical measurements of goodness and success based on performance, productivity, and paper value.

The system gaslights us into forgetting our inner knowing—the real human values of kindness, love, sharing, care, and harmony with the earth and one another. When we become tangled in these false value systems, we lose the ability to truly see others, because we have lost sight of ourselves.

When I am criticizing and unkind to myself, when my CRC-PTSD is triggered and I feel like nobody cares, I sometimes slip back into capitalism's story of unworthiness. Reconnecting with the truth that I have value simply because I exist is not easy. By being in the world, I've been brain washed too. But when I do reconnect—when I remember—it feels as though I am living in a different dimension from the one most people inhabit. That the only reason enough for me to exist with dignity, is that I exist.

It is a dissonant divide. And my wish is to find more and more people who can see it too—and who can stay in that dimension not ruled by survival, but grounded in love and our intrinsic worth just because we exist.

According to the CRC-PTSD manuscript, the symptoms of compounded relational harm include:

- **Toxic shame and self-blame**
- **Trustphobia and relational withdrawal**
- **Fear of happiness and self-sabotage**
- **Internalized anger**
- **Never feeling safe**
- **Exhaustion/Burnout from the Double Shift** — surviving and translating yourself into an acceptable version at once
- **Loss of identity and role confusion**
- **Hypervigilance**
- **Loss of meaning and suicidal ideation**
- **Debilitating perfectionism / all-or-nothing mindsets**
- **Shutdown/numbing ("the flat gray")**
- **Emotional flashbacks (feeling like a helpless child)**
- **Fawning/compliance/self-sacrifice**
- **Masking and camouflaging**
- **Dissociation and depersonalization**
- **Distrust of institutions** — expecting dismissal or retraumatization.

None of these symptoms point to laziness or personal failure.
As the CRC-PTSD book explicitly states:

"What looks like a symptom is actually a record/evidence."

A record of:

- each moment we were minimized

- each time we were told we were "too sensitive"
- each dismissal from a school counselor
- each invalidation by a doctor
- each bureaucratic delay
- each institutional betrayal
- each time our truth cost us safety

Hypervigilance is not paranoia — **it's evidence.**
Shutdown is not laziness — **it's evidence.**
Numbing is not apathy — **it's evidence.**
Fawning is not weakness — **it's evidence.**
Distrust of institutions is not cynicism — **it's evidence.**

CRC-PTSD teaches us that these so-called "symptoms" are **records of systemic harm**, etched into the nervous system by environments that reward silence and punish authenticity.

Structural PTSD makes this clear:

These symptoms are "population-level dysregulation generated by long-duration exposure to coercive social environments."

Why the truth-tellers wake up first?

Some people cannot stay asleep, even when they try.
These are the truth-tellers — the people who notice the things others ignore, react strongly to harm that others normalize, and refuse to emotionally detach from suffering. They are not oversensitive; they are under-numbed.

Truth-tellers tend to be:

- children who were shamed for noticing dysfunction

- immigrants who see contradictions between cultures
- people who survived trauma and can detect power dynamics instantly
- individuals who ask "why?" instead of "how high?" when someone tells them to jump
- or anyone who lost the ability to pretend everything is fine

Truth-tellers are often the first to wake up because they have the least capacity to tolerate the cognitive dissonance required to stay asleep.

But here's the problem:
In dysfunctional systems, the truth-teller becomes the threat. That's why we all need to become truth tellers. They can punish one person, but what about 8 billion?

What we have lost

Awakening is not just a psychological shift — it is a **political, structural, and relational awakening** to the harms that have shaped the nervous system. It is recognizing the injuries we have absorbed and the ones we continue to participate in **under the name of policy, procedure, and law**. We let people suffer and even die while numbly insisting "there's nothing we can do."
But there is.
There always is.

What is required of us is difficult, but it is profoundly human and universally accessible:
We must sit with our fears and listen. That's the way out of fear; not running from it.
Not react, not run, not numb — *listen*. When we do, we begin to see fear for what it truly is: a shadow cast by other human beings who were once trapped in scarcity, shame, and abandonment. Their lack devoured them — and then, through them, devoured others.

The flaw is not that humans are helpless. Helplessness is part of being human, part of being alive, part of having a soul. We have always been vulnerable to nature—earthquakes, illness, time, death—and that vulnerability is not a failure. It is what binds us to one another.

The real problem is our refusal to accept this shared helplessness. Instead of meeting it with humility, care, and collective responsibility, we try to outrun it by inventing new arbitrary hierarchies of control—systems where some humans dominate others, where power is hoarded, where a few prepare bunkers and escape plans while the rest are treated as expendable.

Nature already holds immense power over us. Adding human-made power designed to preemptively destroy other human lives is not "natural selection." It is not evolution. It is not wisdom. It is a deliberate, organized betrayal of our own species.

What is happening is not survival—it is sanctioned violence disguised as foresight. It is fear masquerading as intelligence. And it leaves behind not progress, but a moral stain: a world where human ingenuity is used not to protect life, but to decide who is allowed to live. A world void of any dignity and humanity.

The gray, three-fingered, big-eyed alien that haunts our collective imagination is not best understood as an external being, but as a **symbolic mirror**. Carl Jung would have described it as a **collective shadow archetype** — a projection of what we fear we are becoming.

It looks unsettling precisely because it is not foreign enough.

Pale skin drained of warmth.
Oversized eyes built for constant watching rather than seeing.
A small mouth that suggests diminished speech, emotion, and connection.
A thin, fragile body optimized for survival, not for touch or joy.

This figure reflects an anxiety about a future shaped by fear: humans retreating underground — into bunkers, screens, systems — adapting not just biologically but psychologically. In this sense, the alien is not a prediction of what we *will* become, but a warning about what we might become **if survival eclipses humanity**.

That is why the image terrifies us.
Not because it is unknown — but because it is recognizable.

It is the shadow of a world where humans endure without relating, see without loving, and live without being fully alive. And like all shadow symbols, it does not arrive from the future — it emerges from the present, asking to be seen, integrated, and transformed.

Still, every one of us holds a flame beneath that shadow. The flame of love. The flame of truth. The flame of the self that was never extinguished, only covered.

If we sit with our fears long enough, we begin to feel the power inside us — the power to see clearly, to speak honestly even when our voice shakes, and to step forward when we witness injustice.
This is what awakening really is: **the courage to feel again and be as innocent, carefree, hopeful and imaginative as a child.**

For many, "sleep" is simply what the body does when the world becomes too cruel to face fully awake. But we do not have to wake alone. If we wake together love can catch like fire, spreading from one nervous system to another, until it becomes **collective clarity** instead of collective numbness.

Waking up is not mystical — it's psychological, ethical, and relational

Waking up simply means becoming conscious again:

- conscious of your own needs,
- conscious of the systems shaping your reactions,
- conscious of the difference between real self and conditioned self,
- conscious of your emotional numbing,
- conscious of the parts of you that learned to stay small for safety.

It also means remembering something essential that the system tries to make you forget:

You are a person, not a product.
A soul, not a statistic.
A human being, not an economic unit.

This is not poetic language.
It is psychological truth.

Humans thrive in connection, not competition.
Humans need meaning to stay alive.
Humans require unconditional acceptance to develop healthy identities.
Humans break under chronic institutional betrayal — and they are not meant to handle it alone.

And most of all we need rest, to restore. Working two jobs and having a side hustle, while you take care of your children, is a constant chase that leaves no time to slow down, and that's how they keep us asleep.

Karl Marx wrote that in a capitalist society people become *estranged* from the products of their own labor — alienated from what they create, from each other, and from themselves. But what he could not have predicted is where we have now arrived:

We are no longer alienated from the products of our own labor — we *are* the product.

The rich and elite, the guardians of capital, groom us gently and violently into modern servitude. They do not need whips or chains; they have efficiency metrics, productivity quotas, and narratives about "success" that keep us obedient. Our lives are no longer our own unless we can afford to buy them back with money — and to acquire that money, we must run endlessly after the dangling carrot of survival.

This chase is not natural.
It is engineered.
A design meant to keep us hooked, desperate, and too exhausted to question the rules.

Over time, the system **turns us into products**:
expendable, replaceable, adjustable, discardable.
People to be "let die" when we become too costly, too ill, too inconvenient, too unproductive — measured against actuarial tables and liability reports rather than human dignity.

And somehow, we adapt.
We bend ourselves into the shapes demanded of us.
We call this adaptation "adulthood," when in reality it is a slow amputation of the self.

We lose sight of the most tragic truth:
humanity was killed in the name of productivity and monetary success long before we realized we were grieving.

And the irony — the bitter, ludicrous irony — is that **money itself is a human invention**. A collective story. A consensus hallucination.

If every person on earth woke up tomorrow and agreed that money had no meaning, the entire machinery of oppression would crumble instantly. Not metaphorically. Literally.

It would be chaotic, yes — but so is every birth.
Every transformation begins as chaos.

From that chaos, we could build a new value system:
One not based on extraction, but on **kindness, sharing, imagination, care, and creativity**.
We would work not because we are forced to, but because humans naturally hunger to shape their environments, to contribute, to create beauty, to be part of something larger than themselves.

The fear that "no one will work" is a fear taught by the capitalism to maintain control.
In reality, humans crave meaning far more deeply than they crave money.
The real crisis is that we were trained to distrust our own goodness.

Returning to our childhood innocence does not mean naïveté;
It means remembering the truthfulness of our original self — the self that knew how to rest, how to play, how to share, how to speak needs honestly.
It means refusing to extract from ourselves in the name of productivity.

A humane society would simply flow:
From those with abilities to those with needs(Marx, *Critique of the Gotha Program*, 1875).

And believe me:
Caring, loving, sharing — these are not luxuries.
They are human needs more vital than material success.
The emptiness so many people feel inside is not a psychological disorder;
It is the **black hole left behind when connection is replaced by competition.**

While I was writing this chapter, I went for a walk to clear my mind. On the sidewalk, I found a fortune cookie. Inside was a quote attributed to Margaret Thatcher:

"No one would remember the Good Samaritan if he'd only had good intentions; he had money as well."

I actually had to Google it because it felt so wrong to me. I don't agree with that at all.
The Good Samaritan wasn't remembered because of wealth —
He was remembered because of **his willingness to feel**, to see another human's pain and respond. Goodness begins in empathy, not in currency. We've been looking at things the wrong way for too long we lost the logic.

The system we live in grants money an almost divine power. But stripped of mythology, money is not inherently valuable. It is a piece of paper or metal—or more accurately, a string of zeros and ones in a digital database. Its power exists only because we collectively agree that it does. And the same collective agreement that created its power could, in theory, withdraw it.

What is rarely acknowledged is this: even the wealthy feel the same hollow center. Money does not spare them from loneliness, distrust, or emptiness. In many cases, it deepens those wounds. They know people are drawn to their resources, not their humanity. And yet they cannot let go of accumulation, because accumulation has become their primary form of control—the only leverage they know for feeling safe in an unpredictable world.

This is the hidden addiction at the core of modern life. The belief that control—over money, over bodies, over others—will produce safety. It is a form of magical thinking. Safety does not come from domination or accumulation. It comes from co-regulation: from being seen, held, and known by others without condition.

When someone has never been loved simply for existing, they never learn what safety feels like. Without that foundation, the nervous system searches endlessly for external substitutes—wealth, power, productivity, perfection. But no amount of external accumulation can fill an internal void created by relational absence.

Safety can be learned. But learning it requires something our culture actively discourages: vulnerability without performance. Being bare. Being honest. Dropping the masks we use to hide our perceived weaknesses. Only then do we rediscover what was never missing in the first place—the innocence, care, and love of the inner child. Those qualities were always there. What was absent was someone to mirror them back to us, someone to show us how to access them.

This is why the current system is a lose-lose for everyone. A structure built on scarcity wounds all who live inside it, regardless of status. The cure for the emptiness it produces is not wealth or control. It is community—one that sees us, believes us, accepts us, and makes space for our truth.

A community patient enough to let people feel safe again.
A community where innocence can reemerge without fear.

Safety was never something to be owned.
It was always something to be shared.

The real cure for that hollow place inside is not wealth.
It is **community** — a community that sees us, believes us, accepts us, and welcomes our truth.

If humanity continues down our current path — a path paved with lies, scarcity conditioning, dehumanization, and institutional abuse — we will be swallowed by the very darkness we created.
Not because we were weak, but because we forgot a simple truth:

Humans built this cage — and humans have the power to dismantle it.

And here is the truth we are meant to remember:

With today's technological capacity, we can produce **more than enough** of every essential resource — energy, water, food, housing, medicine, clean water, transportation. The earth provides more than what we need.
The problem is not scarcity.
The problem is **ownership**.

The problem is that a tiny fraction of humans claimed the earth as their private property.

They hoarded land they do not need.
They extracted wealth they will never use.
They stockpiled resources only to restrict access and force the rest of us into a never-ending survival game — the real-world Hunger Games we are living now.

This is not fate.
This is **design** — a human-made construction.

And what has been constructed
can be dismantled, reimagined, and replaced
by something worthy of the word *humanity*.

What this book is inviting you into

This book is not a spiritual treatise.
It is a psychological and sociological intervention.

It is an invitation to:

- examine the systems that shaped us by analyzing each sector,
- challenge the narratives that harmed us,
- understand the mechanisms behind collective PTSD,
- and reclaim the parts of ourselves that learned to shut down just to survive.

It is an invitation to remember that under all the conditioning, you are still intact.

Not perfect — intact.
Not unhurt — but unbroken at your core.
Not lost — just buried under layers of survival.

And once we peel those layers back, slowly and intentionally, something remarkable emerges:

Not a new self — but the self you were before the world taught you to forget.

The conscious one.
The awake one.
The human one.
The one.

2 — When "Help" Harms: Institutional Betrayal and the Second Wound

The first wound is the originating trauma—violence, exploitation, neglect, or crisis that overwhelms one's capacity to cope. The second wound occurs later, after the original trauma, when the institutions tasked with providing care instead respond with dismissal, minimization, or punitive indifference. This second wound—*institutional betrayal*—produces a distinct pattern of psychological, relational, and physiological harm that cannot be explained solely through individual psychopathology. It reflects a breakdown in the moral contract between person and institution, mirroring the dynamics of betrayal trauma at the interpersonal level (Freyd 1996; Smith and Freyd 2014). In structurally traumatogenic environments, the second wound is not anomalous; it is predictable.

Institutional betrayal emerges through discursive, procedural, and affective mechanisms that converge to erode trust, suppress authenticity, and destabilize narrative coherence. Research on betrayal trauma demonstrates that violations committed by trusted or depended-upon entities produce deeper dysregulation than comparable harm inflicted by strangers (Herman 1997; Freyd 1996). At scale, institutions reproduce these dynamics through denials of harm, bureaucratic opacity, and self-protective decision-making that prioritize liability over care (Ford and Kelly 2015; Harris 2016; Graeber 2015). The result is a paradoxical environment in which individuals seeking safety experience retraumatization, and where "helping systems" inadvertently replicate the power dynamics of perpetrators (Smith and Freyd 2014; DePrince and Freyd 2002).

Discursive Mechanisms: How Institutions Redefine Harm

Institutional betrayal begins at the discursive layer. Institutions often deploy language that reframes suffering as individual failure—echoing neoliberal narratives of personal responsibility and emotional self-regulation (Cabanas and Illouz 2019; Ehrenreich 2009). Requests for help are translated into diagnostic categories, eligibility criteria, or moral judgments ("noncompliance," "insufficient evidence," "unable to verify claim"). These linguistic practices shift causality away from structural conditions and toward the individual, consistent with research on labeling, stigma, and epistemic invalidation (Scheff 1984; Horwitz and Wakefield 2007).

Institutions hide behind what Porter (1995) calls "procedural neutrality," using the ritual invocation of policy as a moral shield. They perform objectivity the way a magician performs misdirection: repeat the rule, point to the form, gesture at the protocol, and hope no one notices the harm happening in plain sight. And it works. Procedural neutrality allows institutions to claim innocence while committing violence through paperwork.

This is not neutrality — it is **institutional gaslighting**.
Not the interpersonal kind where one manipulative person rewrites your reality, and demeans you; but the industrial version described by Sweet (2019): gaslighting embedded in scripts, forms, workflows, and eligibility criteria. Here, the "gaslighter" is the entire apparatus. The individual encounters a coordinated message delivered through emails, case notes, automated denials, and polite voicemail recordings:

Your experience is not valid here unless it fits a checkbox.
And if there is no checkbox for you, then you do not exist.

There is no box for *human*.
But there are boxes for **race**, **disability status**, **income thresholds**, **behavior codes, diagnostic labels**, and every other category used to sort us by presumed worth — White, Black, Hispanic, Middle Eastern, "other." There are strict poverty lines, as though being one dollar above the cutoff suddenly grants stability. There are diagnostic categories, as though pain can be neatly mapped onto DSM pages without context or

history.

We aren't just sorted by these boxes — **we are controlled by them.**

Because in the modern economy, we are not only the product;
our *pain* is the mechanism that keeps the product line moving.

Institutions extract from the sick, the poor, the unsupported, the overworked, and the already breaking — because vulnerability produces cheap labor and silent compliance. They have engineered a world where suffering is profitable and healing is unaffordable. And when we eventually collapse under the weight of the system that outlawed humanity in the name of "efficiency," there is no safety net. There is only the quiet disposal of human beings who were used until they could not produce anymore.

Not discarded with dignity.
Not acknowledged as casualties.
But **erased slowly, quietly, through bureaucratic indifference** —
a form of slow painful death no human being deserves.

Institutional Technologies: Bureaucracy as a Vector of Harm

Following the discursive layer, betrayal becomes visible through what I call **institutional technologies** — the everyday tools of control that get disguised as "procedure." Surveillance, endless documentation requirements, eligibility rituals, service exclusion, and the infamous "start over" culture. Bureaucracy turns into a form of **impersonal violence** (Graeber 2015): delays that stretch for months, phones that never ring back, forms designed to confuse you, and labyrinths so complex that only the most resourced people ever make it through.

People seeking care are forced into long waitlists, denied services on technicalities, or required to retell their trauma repeatedly to new gatekeepers who "just need to verify." This isn't care — it's **institutional extraction**, and research shows these conditions amplify distress, dissociation, and withdrawal (Becker-Blease & Freyd 2007; Ford & Kelly 2015). Of course we fall apart. The system is engineered to wear us down.

Sociology has been warning us for decades: when institutions face resource strain or political pressure, they don't become more humane — they become **more punitive** (Harris 2016). They tighten access, raise thresholds, and double down on rules. Add scarcity mindsets into the mix and you get workers whose cognitive load is so high that empathy collapses (Lupien et al. 2009). Under this pressure, frontline staff — teachers, nurses, caseworkers — often reproduce harm even when they don't intend to. Not because they're cruel, but because the structure trains them to behave like the system, not like themselves.

From a leadership perspective, all of this is the predictable outcome of what sociologists call **audit culture** — organizations obsessed with metrics, liability management, and performance codes (Power 1999; Strathern 2000). Leaders raised in these environments are taught that emotional detachment equals professionalism, and that flexibility is a threat to institutional order. They confuse compliance with competence.

And when compliance replaces care, institutions lose the ability to respond to human beings. They become machines of denial — efficient at data, ruthless with policy, and utterly incapable of compassion.

This is the architecture of betrayal. Not one villain.
Not one bad day.
A whole system designed to prioritize its own stability over our survival.

Relational and Affective Erosion: The Psychological Dynamics of Betrayal

At the relational level, institutional betrayal strikes at the core of our attachment systems. Betrayal trauma theory shows that when a trusted source of safety becomes a source of harm, the survivor experiences heightened shame, self-blame, and profound emotional disorientation (Freyd 1996; DePrince 2005). Institutions function as attachment figures on a collective scale: we depend on them for healthcare, justice, education, safety, and the basic conditions of survival. When these structures respond with indifference, hostility, or punishment, the injury is not merely administrative — it is **affective**, **psychological**, and **moral**.

Unlike personal relationships, which we can—at least in theory—end or leave, our relationship with society cannot be severed. We cannot divorce the government. We cannot walk away from the medical system. We cannot opt out of the laws that govern our bodies or the institutions that gatekeep our needs. Being "part of the system" means being bound to it, even when its practices violate us. This is where the hopelessness sets in: the sense of being **trapped inside a relationship we never consented to but cannot escape.**

Over time, this produces a kind of **learned helplessness**, not because we are helpless, but because the system repeatedly teaches us that resistance is futile. It is a psychological cage built from patterns of dismissal. And yet — our helplessness is a lie. Beneath it lives a truth so powerful institutions are terrified of it: **collective action and collective clarity.** The moment we see the truth together, the spell breaks. The humiliation becomes visible. The direction of change becomes obvious.

Research demonstrates that invalidation from high-power actors evokes stronger physiological stress responses than similar invalidation from peers (Dickerson & Kemeny 2004). This is why hospitals, welfare offices, courts, universities, and immigration systems can destabilize people so quickly. The power asymmetry amplifies the injury. When disclosures are met with disbelief, survivors experience rumination, hypervigilance, emotional withdrawal, and shame spirals — core patterns associated with complex trauma (Herman 1997; van der Kolk 2015).

And then comes the ultimate institutional cruelty:
the moment when everyone listening to your story gasps, nods, or says, "That's horrible,"
but the **institution** hands you a piece of paper claiming they "could not substantiate evidence," or that they are bound by the law to decline your life threatening need.

This is not neutrality.
This is not procedure.
This is **gaslighting in its most devastating form**.

With that single line — "unsubstantiated" — they erase your reality, nullify your injury, and absolve themselves of responsibility. They also weaponize their own incompetence: "We didn't find evidence" really means "We did not bother to look, or we chose not to see." The red flags were not missed; they were ignored.

Betrayal erodes moral integrity, producing **moral injury** — a violation of deeply held values that fractures identity and shatters trust in institutions (Litz et al. 2009) and self. Moral injury intensifies when individuals see leaders act with negligence, cowardice, or self-protection instead of care.

Yet this is exactly where transformation begins.
Leadership is not a title.
It is a posture of truth.

Every one of us has the capacity to become that kind of a leader — the one who speaks up, who sits with the discomfort of truth, who refuses to gaslight or be gaslit, who holds the line between fear and dignity.

It begins with the courage to look at what is happening without flinching. And it continues when we refuse to look away.

Embodied Dysregulation: Chronic Stress and the Physiological Sequelae of Betrayal

The physiological consequences of institutional betrayal do not live in the abstract — they live in the body. Chronic invalidation and bureaucratic cruelty are not merely "stressful experiences." They are **physiological events** that alter the architecture of the brain, the immune system, and the endocrine system.

Research on chronic stress and allostatic load shows that persistent exposure to bureaucratic obstacles, surveillance, evaluations, and threat cues forces the HPA axis into overdrive (McEwen 2006; Lupien et al. 2009). The result is cortisol dysregulation, immune suppression, and neural changes identical to those caused by direct trauma. Survivors often describe this as exhaustion, brain fog, digestive issues, migraines, chronic pain, insomnia — symptoms that traditional psychiatry mistakenly classifies as "individual pathology," even though they are the **biological signatures of structural harm** (van der Kolk 2015).

Being repeatedly judged, doubted, or scrutinized activates the same neural networks involved in physical pain (Eisenberger & Lieberman 2004). This means that an accusatory benefits interview, a hostile medical provider, or a dismissive police officer doesn't just "hurt feelings" — it **hurts the body**. Every denial of care, every accusation of malingering, every demand to "prove" your suffering inflicts measurable physiological injury.

Institutional betrayal also creates what Doka (2002) calls **disenfranchised grief**: losses that institutions refuse to acknowledge — dignity, safety, trust, opportunity, time. When grief is unrecognized, unsupported, or invalidated, the body stays in a prolonged state of arousal, unable to metabolize the loss. Recovery stalls. Stress accumulates. The nervous system remains braced for the next blow because the last blow was never allowed to be real.

This is why survivors of systemic betrayal develop CRC-PTSD:
Not because they are fragile, but because **the body cannot heal while trapped inside the source of harm.**

Institutional betrayal is not symbolic.
It is cellular.
It is hormonal.
It is immunological.
It is neural.

The body keeps the score — but institutions keep printing the invoice.

Narrative Fracture: The Collapse of Meaning and Identity

Institutional betrayal destabilizes narrative identity. Survivors are forced into contradictions that no nervous system can reconcile: *I sought help and was punished; I told the truth and was disbelieved; I followed the rules and was excluded.* Psychological literature shows that narrative coherence is foundational to well-being—when our stories fracture, confusion, shame, and disorientation follow (McAdams 2008; McAdams & McLean 2013). When institutions deny or distort what happened, the survivor loses epistemic grounding.

That may sound abstract, but it is painfully simple.

It happens every time you go to the doctor and your pain is dismissed because of your age, race, gender, class, body size, insurance status, or even the vocabulary you use.
It happens every time you report a crime and the police say it's "not serious enough," or it "doesn't fit the categories."
It happens every time you ask a question that isn't in their procedural script and they point to policy instead of thinking.
It happens every time a burnt-out investigator, teacher, doctor, or nurse treats your suffering like an inconvenience because the system has flattened them too.

And it happens too often because most people are not doing work they love—they are working to survive.
We're forced into roles based not on who we are but on what the system needs from us.
We've been taught that some jobs are "higher" or "more respectable," when in truth that entire hierarchy is a human-made illusion. A false prestige economy. A fiction.

There is no job above another.
Some people thrive in organizing, gardening, nurturing, or cooking.
Others bloom in art, music, building, writing, research, chess, sports, teaching, healing, or caretaking.
If we released the fake value system stitched into capitalism, people could finally choose work that feels like breathing—not work that feels like sacrifice. And we don't have to have only one job, but as many as our heart desires and as many hours that keeps balance in our lives.

We would no longer be forced to carry our parents' broken dreams, generation after generation. Thus we can create a coherent self, based on who we really are, not what we are expected to be.

Sociologically, this narrative fracture signals a failure of collective meaning-making. Alexander's theory of cultural trauma emphasizes that trauma becomes socially significant only when institutions validate it (Alexander 2004). But institutional betrayal prevents this acknowledgment. It isolates suffering instead of integrating it, leaving individuals to hold pain that should have been held collectively.

This is how a society loses coherence:
not when trauma happens,
but when institutions refuse to name it.

A Real Example of the Second Wound

This story happened recently. I'm still grieving it. It triggered my CRC-PTSD and what I call the **Syndrome of Broken Trust in Humanity (SOBTIH)**. When SOBTIH is triggered, despair doesn't feel like an emotion — it feels like a conclusion. Like the nervous system deciding, *"Nobody cares. I am on my own. Humans are dangerous. I don't belong here."*

When that happens, my body starts scanning for tiny proof of humanity — not big proof, not miracles. Just one small moment where someone sees me as a human being. Because that's the only thing that brings my soul back into my body.

And the tragedy is that needing help from institutions means being let down again and again. The more you reach out, the more the system unconsciously betrays you. Eventually the body stops fighting. It shuts down.

Here's the story, still unprocessed, still living in my muscles.

On **November 20th, 2025**, my therapist told me that my health insurance Blue Shield was cutting off my sessions because she's out of network. Continuity of care had been approved for only 12 months— and then suddenly it wasn't. The denial letter went to my old address even though my address had been updated, so I didn't even have time to emotionally prepare. I found out through a text.

The letter said: *If you disagree, call the doctor who made this decision within five days.* So I did exactly what the system told me to do. I called. The doctor was confused. She kept saying I needed to call a manager, then started scolding me and my therapist: **"Your therapist should have known better than to have you call."** I tried to explain that I was literally following the instructions on the letter. I got frustrated and said — *if scolding is permissible, maybe insurance should have known better than to set this up like a trap.*

And she hung up on me.

I started crying. I messaged my therapist in panic. The fear wasn't abstract — it was bodily. It took me **three years** to trust her. Three years to get to the point where I could finally talk about being sexually exploited by a therapist in residential treatment. For 3 years I couldn't speak about it at all — my body spoke instead. Hospital after hospital. Attempt after attempt. The kind of chaos that makes you feel like you aren't living, you're just surviving between collapses.

My therapist had applied to join Medi-Cal more than three months before this happened, yet a process that was supposed to take no longer than 90 days became stretched out and tangled in endless loopholes. When I reached out to file an appeal, the insurance associates instead filed a grievance and assured me it functioned the same as an appeal. The next day, my therapist called and learned that no appeal had actually been submitted. Recognizing that I was already destabilizing, she immediately filed an expedited appeal with my insurance in an effort to protect the continuity of my care.

For a while, I had built something fragile but real. I was seeing her regularly—sometimes six sessions a month—and that consistency held me together. My eating disorder had nearly vanished. I was regulating. Going to the gym. Joining support groups. Making friends. Writing. Even creating songs again. I had carved out a small corner of stability—the tiniest proof that healing was possible.

And then the system pulled the rug out from under me.

The appeal was denied.

I called and explained everything — the trauma history, the three-year trust-building, the reality that therapy isn't a shoe you replace. They became a broken record: *Find an in-network therapist.* It was like talking to a stone. Like speaking human into a machine.

So I asked for an expedited state hearing with a judge. I even went to the ER the night before — not because I wanted to be there, but because I knew I needed to perform eligibility theater. I needed "proof" that I was unraveling, as if my life only becomes real when it is documented by an institution.

The day of the hearing the judge listened and sent me his decision later that afternoon. Here is the letter — the one that cracked something open in me. I'm including it in full because it shows exactly how the second wound happens: the system **hears you**, understands the stakes, and still refuses to care. It is the coldest kind of betrayal — the kind that speaks politely while it discards your life.

"In this case, the claimant requested continuity of care with Dr. K. The evidence establishes that the claimant was enrolled in Blue Shield effective December 1, 2024, and was approved for continuity care with Dr. K for 12 months as a new enrollee. The claimant testified that she had been under Dr. K's care for three years, during which she experienced significant emotional healing from complex trauma, including family issues, eating disorders, and neurodivergence. She emphasized that Dr. K's specialized support helped her avoid repeated hospitalizations and process deeply painful experiences, such as abuse by a previous therapist and being trafficked. As the claimant has had 12 months of continuity of care with Dr. K, the claimant is no longer a new enrollee and must seek care from a Medi-Cal provider. It is undisputed that Dr. K is not enrolled in the Medi-Cal program. Under these circumstances, the claimant does not meet the requirements to continue care with Dr. K. Accordingly, Blue Shield properly denied the continuity of care request. The claimant warned that losing access to Dr. K could lead to renewed psychiatric crises and hospitalizations, arguing that the denial of care reflects institutional betrayal and urging the tribunal to consider the human cost of such decisions. While the administrative law judge understands the claimant's argument, the administrative law judge is bound by state law and has no authority to disregard the applicable criteria."

ORDER
The claim is denied.

When I read **"the administrative law judge understands… but is bound by state law,"** my body didn't hear policy. My body heard: *I understand this could destroy you, and I'm still doing it anyway.* That sentence is the second wound in its purest form — institutional betrayal sealed with official language and delivered as if it were neutral.

It felt like the judge was saying: *I understand this could cost your life, but I am willing to let you die because my hands are tied.*

And yes, intellectually, I know it isn't personal. But trauma doesn't live in the intellect. Trauma lives in the body. At that moment, my body didn't hear "criteria." My body heard: **abandonment.** Nullified to nothing.

I went into a CRC-PTSD flashback where my soul felt disconnected from my body. That's happened before — that feeling where my mind can't govern my movements, like my body is guided by something older than reason. I didn't want to die. But the disappointment in humanity was so intense I couldn't care about my physical existence. I wanted the system to *see* what it was doing.

That's how SOBTIH works: it's not drama, it's a physiological collapse of trust. It's the feeling that the world is not a safe place and yet there's no escape.

I ended up at the bridge again! It felt guided. My body felt disconnected from my mind when I walked to the bridge. I was mentally not sure if that was the right thing to do. I didn't want to put myself in danger but the anger and disappointment in humanity was so intense that I couldn't care less about my physical existence. I didn't want to be dead, but I wanted that judge to see the consequence of what he did manifest in the 3D material world.

I asked the police to call the judge. I said I needed an apology — not because apologies fix systems, but because I needed *someone in power to acknowledge the human consequence of what they just did.* They couldn't reach him or more likely didn't want to. They read the letter and told me they didn't agree with the decision, but they also told me they couldn't do anything about it.

Then I asked them to call the therapist who abused me in residential treatment — I gave her name — not for revenge. You can read the full account of what happened in Chapter 4 of *CRC-PTSD*. It was horrific — and it changed the course of my life. I wanted the simplest thing: *an apology.* I wanted her to know how much pain she caused; that she almost killed me 40 times. How close she brought me to death. Again they said they couldn't.

So I said, **"Then file a police report."**
They finally said yes. Before, when I tried to file a report the police refused, because the therapist didn't touch my private parts! But she tore apart my soul with her hate speech. With sexualizing an eating disorder

and giving me the ugliest label possible.

While I was on the bridge, the haze in the sky shifted and gathered into shapes that looked like feathers, like a flock of birds. It felt magical. I asked the officers if they saw it too. They said it looked like birds painted across the sky. I said, *these are angels.* I knew in my heart that the moment was part of a larger story, even if I didn't yet understand what it meant. Yes, my heart broke. Yes, I was still grieving. Yes, I lost my therapist but more so the feeling that I can create a little safe corner for myself in the world — a loss that hurt as deeply as losing a spiritual mother. And still, I was there, standing, fighting the system for my life with my life.

I said goodbye to the bridge because I believed I was about to begin something new. I had planned to move to Atlanta, to finally own a home after years of instability, to build a place that felt safe. But the universe had other plans. In the days after I was discharged, my investments dropped by tens of thousands of dollars — I lost half of my profit. It wasn't just the money I lost. It was the illusion of safety collapsing once again, right when I thought I might finally rest.

Going to the bridge no longer feels like an attempt. It feels like a ritual, a pilgrimage — a way of proving that I am real, that I am more than a body moving through a world that only recognizes what can be measured and quantified. It feels like a pilgrimage I follow when my soul has been starved of humanity, when it slips away from my body and I need something vast and true to call it back. It isn't the bridge or the police, it's the lessons I learn every time.

Finally after the police report and taking my time to say goodbye to the bridge, they took me to the county mental health hospital in San Diego—the one known for being the least caring. They discharged me the next day with no discharge plan, no real safety, nothing that resembled care as though being on the edge of a bridge is a joke. I was sick with a flu that turned into an infection from the cold on the bridge and the doctor refused to even prescribe antibiotics, because he was a psychiatrist! They even took my protein bars.

After that, the trauma stack kept stacking. I tried support groups. I called for help. I reached out to crisis services. But so many systems labeled as "help" don't actually help — they manage liability. They send scripts instead of presence. Police instead of care. Voicemails instead of humans. "Resources" that don't exist or lead nowhere.

It is the **illusion of help being available**. An illusion maintained by those who are more fortunate, so they don't have to intervene when they witness harm. An illusion that allows them to sleep at night while lives are quietly lost — not to tragedy, but to the comfort of believing that someone else, somewhere, is taking care of it.

After that night on the bridge, the trauma stack kept stacking. I didn't give up. I tried support groups. I kept reaching out. I called crisis services because I fell into the trap of **intermittent reward** — the hope that *this time* someone might respond with real care.

I contacted the **Mobile Crisis Response Team (MCRT)** and asked for one simple thing: *send people who care.* Not people with scripts. Not people managing risk. People who could sit with the truth that I was collapsing because the system had decided my life was not worth preserving.

What arrived instead was another performance.

They began by asking, *"How can we help?"* — a question that already assumed help was possible, when in reality it wasn't. They had no power to address what was harming me. They could not acknowledge the broken system. They could not hold the grief of being told, once again, that policy mattered more than my survival. They kept pushing for answers framed in individual terms — *what I was feeling, what I wanted, what I could do* — as if the problem lived inside me instead of inside the institutions that had just pulled the ground out from under my life.

I told them I didn't need fixing. I needed witnessing. I needed them to sit with me in the pain of a world that keeps deciding people like me are expendable. But they couldn't see themselves clearly enough to see me. I left then returned and in a plea asked if they could be their authentic present selves. Their response: "This is all we will be able to offer." And so I left feeling more alone than before.

I gave them a small excerpt of my CRC-PTSD work, trying — again — to translate my lived reality into language the system might understand. Then I called the crisis line back later to leave feedback, because I was already feeling worse. I was honest: *this interaction made me more distressed.*

That honesty is what broke everything.

The woman on the phone was cold. I told her I was triggered. I told her I was going outside to walk toward the bridge to calm my nervous system — because bridges soothe me, because I was trying to survive, not die. She said, *"Can you hold for a few minutes? I'll call you back."*

She never did.

Instead, she called the police.

In that moment, the illusion shattered completely. I realized what these services actually exist to do: not to help, but to protect themselves. To transfer liability. To escalate control. To turn vulnerability into a problem that must be managed, contained, or removed.

When I learned the police were at my house, terror flooded my body instantly. Not fear as a thought — fear as a full-body takeover. Every memory from the last three years collapsed into a single moment. Being handcuffed in front of my neighbors. Being kicked out of housing while I was hospitalized. Being turned away by treatment centers. Being told over and over that I was "too much," "not eligible," "a liability." Being treated as danger instead of a person in pain.

My nervous system did not register this as *new*.
It registered it as **confirmation**.

Past and present merged. There was no timeline anymore — just the familiar certainty that asking for help leads to punishment. My body didn't have the luxury of interpretation. It did what it had learned to do to survive overwhelming threats.

It collapsed.

My legs gave out and I fell onto the concrete. I was conscious, aware of everything around me, but unable to move. Not frozen by choice — frozen by biology. Paralyzed but conscious. My body shut itself down the way animals do when escape is impossible. It felt like my soul had stepped slightly outside of me, not to die, but to avoid being shattered completely.

I lay there like that for hours.

Cars passed. Hundreds of them. Headlights, engines, tires — life rushing by. People walked past me. One person looked at my body on the ground and said something like, *another overdose*, and kept walking. No one stopped to ask if I was okay. No one called for help. No one checked if I was alive.

The world decided who I was in that moment — and it decided I was disposable.

The only person who touched me, who spoke to me like I was human, was a homeless man who lived under the bridge. He put his hand on my shoulder and said, *come*. That simple touch — that recognition — pulled my soul back into my body. His kindness did what every institution failed to do. I could only regain my bodily control momentarily each time for a minute or less.

Four hours passed. Three calls to 911. And only then did anyone find me.

Even when I was finally taken to the hospital, the cruelty didn't stop. A nurse pressed into my sternum repeatedly — hard — to test my responsiveness. My chest hurt for a week afterward. When I finally managed to tell her I could feel the pain as I was conscious, she said, **"Well, when you worry us, that's what you get."**

That sentence landed exactly where all the others had landed before it: *Your pain is an inconvenience. Your fear deserves punishment. Your humanity is conditional.*

This is what **SOBTIH** does. It turns the world into evidence that no one cares — and once the body reaches that conclusion, it begins to behave as if it is already dead. Not because you want to die, but because being alive in a world that has withdrawn care feels unbearable.

I'm not sharing this to shock anyone. It makes me uncomfortable to share so much. Yet I'm sharing it to show what **CRC-PTSD** looks like in real life— how trauma doesn't just add up, it **stacks, braids, echoes, and replays**. Not because a person is fragile or dramatic, but because the world keeps reenacting the same betrayal through different systems, different uniforms, different voices.

They discharged me again, calling it *anxiety*. There was no discharge planning. No safety net. They didn't even offer a ride home. I asked them to keep me because I was terrified it would happen again once I was alone. The doctor refused.

The next morning, I woke up in pain — chest pain — unable to go to the gym, which is one of the few ways I regulate my nervous system. I felt furious. Not just at the nurse, but at the entire system. Losing my therapist. Being punished for asking for help. Policy being used to justify harm. People whose job it is to care, treating me like the problem. At that point, the evidence stack inside my body had grown too large to carry. It wasn't one thing anymore. It was everything.

And still, help was not available.

That same morning, the stock market dropped more than 12%. I watched it fall like Niagara. After years of penny-pinching, denying myself food, care, rest, and even time with friends, my plans to buy a house collapsed in real time. I wasn't grieving the money itself — I was grieving the loss of the one imagined corner of safety I thought I could build. I cried and cried, watching the numbers drop, until the spiral took over and I passed out again.

This felt unbearable. Not because of the money itself, but because it meant I couldn't even hold on to a corner of safety I had built in my imagination — an imagined refuge where I thought I might finally rest. Watching that illusion collapse felt devastatingly familiar.

When I was nine years old, my family went through a financial crisis. My dad had co-signed a loan for a friend who disappeared, leaving him responsible for the debt. He withdrew money from my parents' joint account until there was nothing left. Soon, warnings arrived about auctioning our home. When my mom found out, she was furious — understandably so — but the intensity of her anger overwhelmed my child's nervous system. She screamed at my dad two or three times a day and told him he would be more useful if he jumped under a van so the insurance money could save us.

I didn't know how to process any of it. I hid in a small blanket closet, closed the door tight, and made it my safe place. Lights off. Quiet. My silly donkey doll beside me. I stayed there for hours — imagining, praying, thinking. I gathered all the money I had and bought a lottery ticket. I believed that if I won, I could fix everything. I could solve my parents' problems. Maybe even buy my mom a house.

I begged God to let me win.

I didn't.

And in that moment, something in me broke. I lost my trust in the spirit. I felt abandoned by the universe. I started questioning life itself. I was depressed — and no one came to save me.

My CRC-PTSD was far more ancient than I realized. I didn't develop it later; I was born into it like all of us are. But it wasn't until this recent collapse that I finally connected the dots. What I'm writing about is the long grief of witnessing cruelty and financial precarity — then and now. Poverty may not have looked as catastrophic back then as it does today, when so many of my millennial peers work full-time yet still worry about food, rent, and survival. But the system was already doing its damage. I just didn't have language for it yet. Naming it now doesn't magically erase the feeling of being abandoned by the universe. What remains is the deep longing to find people who care — who see, who witness, who are kind.

After passing out, I stayed disconnected for days afterward. On Friday, I tried again. I reached out to more than twenty numbers. None offered real help. I realized I was back in the same place I had been in 2022, when I made my most serious attempt. There are **no trauma treatment centers** that accept Medi-Cal— as if trauma is a privilege you lose the moment you become poor. I asked for caseworkers. None followed up — not through insurance, not through my doctor.

I'm writing these details knowing there is still so much I cannot include. But my body remembers all of it instantly. This is what **CRC-PTSD** looks like: the stacking, the braiding, the echoing. Not one trauma, but a system replaying the same betrayal with different faces.

I'm overwhelmed even writing this. The helplessness returns as I type. I wish I lived in a kinder world. That feels like a dream now. So instead, I give that dream a little square footage by writing — by telling the truth.

When I feel like nothing, I ground myself with a sentence I once asked ChatGPT to repeat to me:

"We can't change all of the big, cruel structures at once, but we can give that dream world more 'square footage' inside your daily life so you're not stuck only in the crushing part. It's not a replacement for justice or safety—but it is a way to carry a piece of safety with you instead of feeling you have to wait for it to exist outside."

Kind people exist. Most people want to be good. We've just forgotten that we are souls before we are roles. In the world of souls, we don't disappear — we exist as a continuous stream of being, not to prove anything, but because existence itself is expanding.

And still, the system pulls me back to the 3D everytime.

When I called back and Blue Shield told me, *"Wait five business days for a case manager,"* and it's December 22nd — meaning after the new year — my nervous system didn't hear *business days.* It heared: **no one cares if you survive the wait.**

The next day, I called back and refused to hang up until someone could reach the case manager. After an hour and a half on the phone, she told me what I already knew: there are no trauma treatment centers accepting Medi-Cal. Then, to add salt to the injury, she offered what she called the "easiest option" — a program not even focused on trauma, just general mental health care. When we called together, we were told it wasn't covered by Medi-Cal and that it would take **30 days** just to obtain authorization.

When I said this didn't work — that my situation was acute, that I needed trauma care *now* — she told me to go to the ER.

Responsibility dissolved into the familiar void once again. As if the last four trips to the ER had done anything other than retraumatize me, stabilize me just enough to discharge, and send me straight back into the same conditions that broke me in the first place.

This is how the system survives: by endlessly redirecting responsibility until no one is accountable — and the person asking for help is left carrying the consequences alone.

All of this brought me back to something ancient — a grief that predates this moment, this system, even this lifetime. A grief about what it means to be human in a world that has forgotten how to recognize itself.

I wrote this song, when I was only eleven or twelve, and somehow I was already carrying the existential wound I am naming now. These were the words:

I'd like to know
why us humans came to this world,
to experience misery all alone,
with no one by our side.
I wish I knew why we are here and where we are going,
but I'm not alone, because nobody knows.

So many years have passed since I first asked this question.
I didn't find the answer.
I understood that our world is full of badness.
The goodness is dying — badness became the value.
I wish I knew why we are here and where we are going,
but I'm not alone, because nobody knows.

When I played it for my mom, she said, *"If this is how you're feeling, that's so sad."*
And that was it. No holding. No space. No witnessing. Just being left

alone with the question.

That is what the syndrome of broken trust in humanity does. It's not only that people hurt you — it's that the world refuses to witness the hurt in themselves before they can see you.

And the truth — the unbearable truth — is this: their hands are stained not only with my blood, but with the blood of everyone who dared to ask for help and was answered with policy instead of humanity.

And here is the scariest part: it isn't only institutions that deliver this harm. It's us — ordinary people — every time we look away, defer responsibility, or tell ourselves someone else will handle it. Our hands are not clean. They are stained with the blood of those we refused to see, those we convinced ourselves were "being helped" somewhere else.

I am not absolved either. I have built my own small corner of stability on top of the labor, suffering, and invisibility of others — the poor, the unhoused, the exploited workers in places we never have to see. This system implicates all of us.

But I want you to feel this — not as guilt, and not as accusation — but as an invitation to finally *see*. To stand up and create a new world that sees the souls we are before bodies.

Leadership, Legitimacy, and the Moral Architecture of Care

Institutional betrayal always traces back to a **leadership problem**. Every time someone says, "My hands are tied," or "It's policy," or "This is above my pay grade," what they're really saying is:
"No one in charge cared enough to build a system that protects you."

Organizations don't become harmful overnight.
They rot from the top.

Research calls it a "climate of silence" — the kind of environment where employees keep their mouths shut because they've watched what happens to people who speak up (Morrison & Milliken 2000). I've seen it everywhere: teachers who ignore racist comments in classrooms because their principal suppresses complaints for the sake of the school's reputation; nurses who witness malpractice but stay quiet because they fear losing their jobs; social workers who know a family needs help but are warned not to "rock the boat" or "cost the agency money."

Silence becomes the cultural oxygen.
And dissent becomes a liability, not a contribution.

In these places, **image replaces integrity**.
Everything starts revolving around keeping the country, agency, the school, the hospital, the nonprofit, or the university looking "functional," even when everyone inside it knows it's falling apart.

Take a real example most people know too well:
You report a violent or discriminatory incident to HR, and suddenly *you* become the problem. Not the person who harmed you.
HR drags out the process. They pretend to investigate. They ask you to repeat your trauma in six different ways. They tell you they "take this seriously" while pulling you into endless meetings meant to exhaust you out of caring.

Why?
Because HR's job is not protection.
It's liability management.
And liability always flows upward, toward leadership.

Or look at hospitals. A patient tells a nurse they're in pain, but the nurse has been reprimanded so many times for "over-escalating" that they now minimize symptoms to stay safe. At the ER they don't even offer pain medication before legally admitting patients, no matter how much pain one is going through. The nurse isn't the villain — *the hospital's leadership is*, because they created conditions where caring becomes punishable.

Or universities. A student reports misconduct by a faculty member, and instead of investigating the faculty, the institution quietly monitors the student for "instability," pathologizing them to protect the brand. I've lived this. Almost every marginalized student I've ever met has lived this.

This is what "leadership failure" looks like in practice:

- survivors retraumatized by the systems meant to support them
- employees terrified of speaking up
- compassion punished
- harm normalized
- silence rewarded

And all of it trickles down from whoever sits at the top.

By contrast, **real leadership**—not the title, not the salary, not the performative DEI statements, not the empty "we value your feedback"—means stepping into a care ethic that treats human beings as ends, not means. It means:

- transparency instead of secrecy
- responsiveness instead of defensiveness
- shared decision-making instead of hierarchy
- humanity instead of protocol
- accountability instead of image protection
- humility instead of power hoarding

Trauma-informed leadership is not just a trend; it's how institutions stop becoming perpetrators. Leaders grounded in relational accountability interrupt the entire chain of harm: fewer denials, fewer cover-ups, fewer retaliations, fewer lives shattered by bureaucracy.

Because here is the truth:
Institutions do not traumatize people. Leaders do.
Leaders create cultures.
Cultures create norms.
Norms create systems.
Systems create outcomes.

When leadership chooses fear, control, reputation, or profit over people, institutions become **machinery of betrayal**.
When leadership chooses safety, honesty, and care, institutions become **infrastructure for healing** instead of harm.

And the most important part?

You don't need to run an organization to be a leader.
Leadership is any moment when you choose truth over silence, even when your voice shakes.
It is any moment you refuse to participate in gaslighting.
It is the decision to hold space for someone else's pain, even when the institution around you refuses to.

Ethical leadership is not a position.
It is a posture — a way of standing in the world that refuses to abandon the people who depend on us.

Conclusion: The Second Wound as a Structural Signal

The second wound is not an "overreaction," a sensitivity issue, or a personal weakness. It is **a diagnostic sign**—a structural indicator that something in the system is profoundly misaligned with human needs. Institutional betrayal is the moment the mask falls and the internal architecture of an institution reveals itself: when care structures begin to mirror the dynamics of abuse—gaslighting, denial, inconsistency, minimization, and punishment—the harm doesn't just echo the original trauma; it multiplies it.

The second wound tells us where the system is sick.

To understand this wound, we need an integrated lens:

- **Sociology** to map the structural patterns and power arrangements that create betrayal;
- **Psychology** to understand the internal consequences—shame spirals, hypervigilance, dissociation, moral injury, and CRC-PTSD;
- **Leadership theory** to identify where moral failure, organizational cowardice, and liability-driven decision-making have replaced care.

Naming institutional betrayal is not an academic exercise.
It is **a transformative act.**
It clears the fog of self-blame and reveals the truth: the harm is not located inside the survivor — it is located inside the system.

Only when we name the second wound can we begin to reimagine our institutions not as sites of retraumatization but as infrastructures of genuine care—places capable of holding pain, protecting truth-tellers, and supporting the full dignity of human beings. This is the moral architecture we must build if we want systems that heal rather than harm, and a society where people no longer learn to brace for the next betrayal simply by trying to survive inside the structures meant to help them.

When the wound repeats, it stops being personal. It becomes structural. And once we see it, we can no longer pretend otherwise.

References

Alexander, J. C. 2004. *Toward a Theory of Cultural Trauma.* University of California Press.

Becker-Blease, K. A., and J. J. Freyd. 2007. "The Impact of Bureaucratic Obstacles on Trauma Survivors Seeking Help." *Journal of Trauma & Dissociation* 8(4):69–86.

Cabanas, E., and E. Illouz. 2019. *Manufacturing Happy Citizens: How the Science and Industry of Happiness Control Our Lives.* Polity Press.

DePrince, A. P. 2005. "Social Cognition and Revictimization Risk." *Journal of Trauma & Dissociation* 6(1):125–41.

DePrince, A. P., and J. J. Freyd. 2002. "The Harm of Trauma: Pathological and Adaptive Responses." *Journal of Trauma & Dissociation* 3(1):7–28.

Dickerson, S. S., and M. E. Kemeny. 2004. "Acute Stressors and Cortisol Responses: A Theoretical Integration and Synthesis of Laboratory Research." *Psychological Bulletin* 130(3):355–91.

Doka, K. J. 2002. *Disenfranchised Grief: New Directions, Challenges, and Strategies for Practice.* Research Press.

Ehrenreich, B. 2009. *Bright-sided: How Positive Thinking Is Undermining America*. Metropolitan Books.

Eisenberger, N. I., and M. D. Lieberman. 2004. "Why It Hurts to Be Left Out: The Neurocognitive Overlap Between Physical and Social Pain." *Trends in Cognitive Sciences* 8(7):294–300.

Ford, R., and J. Kelly. 2015. "Sanctions and Support: The Emotional Labor of Welfare Bureaucracy." *Journal of Social Policy* 44(3):463–80.

Freyd, J. J. 1996. *Betrayal Trauma: The Logic of Forgetting Childhood Abuse*. Harvard University Press.

Graeber, D. 2015. *The Utopia of Rules: On Technology, Stupidity, and the Secret Joys of Bureaucracy*. Melville House.

Harris, J. 2016. "The Emotional Labor of Frontline Bureaucracy." *Social Problems* 63(4):635–50.

Herman, J. L. 1997. *Trauma and Recovery: The Aftermath of Violence—From Domestic Abuse to Political Terror*. Basic Books.

Horwitz, A. V., and J. C. Wakefield. 2007. *The Loss of Sadness: How Psychiatry Transformed Normal Sorrow into Depressive Disorder*. Oxford University Press.

Litz, B. T., et al. 2009. "Moral Injury and Moral Repair in War Veterans." *Clinical Psychology Review* 29(8):695–706.

Lupien, S. J., B. S. McEwen, M. R. Gunnar, and C. Heim. 2009. "Effects of Stress Throughout the Lifespan on the Brain, Behavior, and Cognition." *Nature Reviews Neuroscience* 10(6):434–45.

McAdams, D. P. 2008. "Personal Narratives and the Life Story." In *Handbook of Personality: Theory and Research*, edited by O. P. John, R. W. Robins, and L. A. Pervin. Guilford Press.

McAdams, D. P., and K. C. McLean. 2013. "Narrative Identity." *Current Directions in Psychological Science* 22(3):233–38.

McEwen, B. S. 2006. "Protective and Damaging Effects of Stress Mediators." *Dialogues in Clinical Neuroscience* 8(4):367–81.

Porter, T. M. 1995. *Trust in Numbers: The Pursuit of Objectivity in Science and*

Public Life. Princeton University Press.

Power, M. 1999. *The Audit Society: Rituals of Verification*. Oxford University Press.

Scheff, T. 1984. "The Insanity Plea: Labeling and Deviance." In *The Labelling of Deviance*, edited by W. Gove. Wiley.

Smith, C. P., and J. J. Freyd. 2014. "Institutional Betrayal." *American Psychologist* 69(6):575–87.

Strathern, M. 2000. *Audit Cultures: Anthropological Studies in Accountability, Ethics and the Academy*. Routledge.

Sweet, P. L. 2019. "The Sociology of Gaslighting." *American Sociological Review* 84(5):851–75.

van der Kolk, B. A. 2015. *The Body Keeps the Score: Brain, Mind, and Body in the Healing of Trauma*. Viking.

3 — The Anatomy of Structural Narcissism

Structural narcissism refers to the ways narcissistic dynamics—grandiosity, denial, entitlement, exploitation, gaslighting, and the demand for admiration—become encoded into institutional designs, cultural narratives, and organizational practices. While pathological narcissism is often examined at the interpersonal level (Durvasula 2015; Golomb 1992), large-scale systems display strikingly similar patterns: lack of empathy, chronic manipulation, retaliatory behavior, and persecution of truth-tellers. These patterns are not metaphorical. They represent a **structural manifestation of narcissistic defenses**, reproduced through bureaucratic routines, policy logics, and scarcity-based governance. This is what I call Institutional Betrayal.

In the framework of Structural PTSD, modern institutions produce chronic dysregulation through scarcity scripts, surveillance, humiliation, and moral coercion. Structural narcissism is the psychological and political architecture that underlies those practices. It describes the **personality of the system itself**, not simply the personalities of those within it.

Narcissistic Defenses at the Level of Systems

Narcissistic behavior operates through predictable defenses: denial, projection, blame-shifting, minimization, and grandiosity (Kernberg 1975; Durvasula 2021). Institutions replicate these defenses when they:

1. **Deny wrongdoing** despite clear evidence (Smith and Freyd 2014).

2. **Project blame downward**, framing systemic failure as individual deficiency (Cabanas and Illouz 2019).

3. **Rewrite narratives** to maintain legitimacy and superiority (Alexander 2004).

4. **Suppress dissent**, labeling criticism as inappropriate or unprofessional (Aday and Schmader 2019).

5. **Curate an image of benevolence** while inflicting routine harm (Goffman 1959).

This pattern resembles "institutional narcissistic abuse", in which powerful systems maintain control through seduction (branding, promises of inclusion), intermittent reinforcement (selective rewards), and retaliation against those who challenge the narrative.

1. Seduction — "Branding" and Promises of Inclusion

Institutions lure people in with polished messaging and symbolic gestures meant to create the illusion of safety and belonging.

Example:
A university promotes itself as "inclusive" and "student-centered," covering brochures with diverse smiling faces. But when a marginalized student reports discrimination, suddenly the institution becomes cold, procedural, and unavailable. The branding promised belonging; the reality is that the student is expected to protect the school's reputation by staying silent.

Corporations do the same: DEI trainings, rainbow logos in June, glossy wellness campaigns — yet employees who bring up real inequities are labeled "difficult" or "unprofessional," and quietly penalized later through isolation, poor references, or performance write-ups.
The **seduction is not about care; it is about compliance.**

Another example of this seduction is the political arena, especially the

MAGA movement.
What makes it particularly striking is not that it invented abusive power dynamics, but that it **made them overt**. Trump's rhetoric and behavior pulled into the open patterns that have existed in American political leadership for decades: scapegoating, grandiosity, entitlement, and the weaponization of fear.

But covert narcissism in governance did not begin with him. Previous administrations — regardless of party — upheld the same capitalist structures, scarcity narratives, and power hierarchies that brought us to this moment of collective breakdown. The only difference is that the tactics used to be coded, polished, and hidden behind diplomatic language. Now they are explicit, unfiltered, and visible to anyone who is willing to look.

This is the seduction phase of institutional narcissism on a national scale: **promise safety, belonging, and "restoring greatness," while reinforcing the same oppressive systems underneath.**

Covert or overt, the abuse has always been there.
The mask simply slipped.

2. Intermittent Reinforcement — Selective Rewards to Keep You Hoping

Intermittent reinforcement is the most powerful conditioning schedule in psychology — and institutions use it flawlessly.

Example:
A welfare agency denies a survivor's application three times, then approves a small benefit "this one time." A worker shows exceptional kindness one day and is dismissive the next. A professor gives warm feedback one semester and cold indifference the next. A hospital dismisses a patient repeatedly, then suddenly listens after a crisis.

These moments of warmth are not proof the system works — they are what keep people from giving up completely. The unpredictability destabilizes the nervous system, making survivors second-guess their experiences and cling to the rare moments of validation.

Durvasula calls this the "hoovering effect": the institution pulls you back just enough to maintain control.

3. Retaliation — Punishing Those Who Challenge the Narrative

The moment someone names the harm or exposes truth, the mask drops. Retaliation is used to silence dissent and protect the institution's image.

Example:
A nurse reports unsafe staffing ratios and gets written up for "attitude."
A social worker speaks up about unethical practices and is excluded from meetings.
A graduate student files a complaint and suddenly faculty describe them as "not a good fit."
A domestic violence survivor reports officer misconduct and is labeled a "frequent caller" in the system.

Institutions retaliate subtly — through isolation, reputation smearing, sudden "performance concerns," or bureaucratic punishment. None of it looks illegal, which is exactly why it works. Retaliation hides in the **grey zones**, the spaces that laws have not named but survivors feel in their bones. These tactics operate just beneath the threshold of formal misconduct, allowing institutions to harm people while maintaining plausible deniability.

They don't have to fire you outright — just remove you from meetings, stop replying to your emails, or quietly sabotage your opportunities. They don't have to call you unstable — just document your "tone," your "fit," or your "communication style." They don't have to threaten you — they just overwhelm you with procedures, deadlines, and vague warnings that make you question yourself and shrink your presence.

This is the cruelty of the grey area:
It is legal enough to be protected and immoral enough to destroy someone's life.

And that is precisely the trap.
We know something deeply unjust is happening, but because there is no official name for it in legal codes, we feel powerless to challenge it. We start to believe the institution's story about us. We lose trust in our perceptions. We shrink. We comply.

This is how institutions weaponize ambiguity: the harm is real, but the language for it doesn't exist in their rulebook — so they pretend *it doesn't exist at all.* And in that gap between harm and recognition, people become trapped, isolated, and helpless.

The grey zone is where institutional abuse thrives.
It is where morality goes to die while legality looks the other way.
And it is where survivors are left grieving wounds that were designed to leave no evidence.

Retaliation communicates a single message:
"If you speak the truth, you will pay for it."

Grandiosity as Governance

Grandiosity—the belief in one's exceptionalism and immunity from accountability—is a central feature of narcissism (Millon 2011). At the structural level, grandiosity manifests when institutions portray themselves as:

- indispensable,
- morally superior,
- objective or neutral (Porter 1995),
- beyond critique,
- or uniquely qualified to determine truth.

Universities, hospitals, courts, corporations, and state agencies frequently engage in what Ahmed (2017) calls **"institutional self-preservation"**: a performative commitment to values like equity, care, and integrity that collapses the moment those values threaten institutional power. This is not hypocrisy so much as **structural grandiosity**—the institution narrates itself as inherently good, inherently moral, and inherently necessary, and therefore beyond meaningful accountability.

This logic mirrors the **double-standard dynamics of narcissistic relationships**. In such relationships, the dominant party is granted automatic innocence, expansive forgiveness, and protection from consequence, while the other is subjected to constant scrutiny, discipline, and blame. Harm flows downward, accountability never flows upward, and any challenge to the hierarchy is reframed as instability, aggression, or betrayal. The institution, like the narcissistic abuser, positions itself as the injured party whenever its authority is questioned, even as it continues to cause demonstrable harm.

The pattern is clearest in the legal system. Judges are often granted broad immunity from criminal prosecution for decisions that irreversibly ruin innocent lives. How is this considered acceptable? What happens when a judge is bribed, ideologically captured, or carrying unexamined trauma and bias toward a particular kind of person—bias that quietly shapes sentencing, credibility, and outcomes? These risks are treated as unthinkable not because they are rare, but because acknowledging them would puncture the myth of institutional moral purity.

This asymmetry intensifies at elite levels of power. Immunity expands upward while punishment cascades downward. Those closest to state and corporate authority are shielded from consequence, while ordinary people are disciplined, surveilled, and punished—often brutally—for speaking the truth. What is framed as "stability" is, in practice, the institutional equivalent of **narcissistic abuse**: selective accountability, inverted blame, and the aggressive silencing of those who refuse to collude with the lie.

Lack of Empathy and Emotional Abandonment

A defining characteristic of narcissistic systems is **chronic empathy failure masked by procedural rationality**. We can call this "Trauma of Normalcy"; as named by Jenny Florance the author, and founder of The A-Z of Emotional Health Free on-line Library, and my favorite tarot reader on Youtube. That is just another way to name CRC-PTSD. Instead of saying, "We don't want to help you," institutions say, "We can't help you — it's policy." Instead of admitting emotional indifference, they hide it behind long waitlists, rejections, automated denials, and rigid scripts.

This is bureaucratic indifference — a slow-motion, systemic **emotional abandonment**. And it mirrors exactly what Durvasula (2015) describes in interpersonal narcissistic relationships: the survivor's needs become burdens, irritants, or liabilities.
Except here, the narcissist isn't a person — it's the structure.

Real-life examples:

1. The 4-Month Waitlist for a Mental Health Intake

Someone calls a clinic saying they're unsafe, struggling to eat, or barely hanging on.
Instead of support, they're told:

- "We're booking into spring."
- "Call back later."
- "Try the ER if it's urgent."

The ER will then say, "This isn't a medical emergency," and discharge them in 20 minutes.
The message lands in the body as: *Your life does not matter to us.*

2. The Disability Office That Loses Paperwork Three Times

A chronically ill person submits forms, medical records, testimonial letters — everything they have.
The agency says:

- "We never received it."
- "Start over."
- "Insufficient evidence."

Months turn into years.
The person's savings evaporate.
Their health worsens.
Eventually they stop calling because the humiliation is too much.
This is not inefficiency — it is **institutionalized erasure**. A slow painful death for the most vulnerable.

3. The School Counselor Who Says "We Have Limited Resources"

A bullied or abused student gathers courage to ask for help.
They're told:

- "We don't handle that here."
- "Try to avoid that group of kids."
- "We can't punish anyone without proof."

The school protects its reputation.
The child learns a lesson: *Your pain is inconvenient.*

4. The Hospital That Minimizes Symptoms Because "The Labs Look Normal"

A patient with severe fatigue, pain, or gastrointestinal issues gets dismissed because their labs fall within the reference range. Doctors act annoyed, as though the patient is wasting their time.
The patient is treated as a problem for existing — exactly the interpersonal dynamic of narcissistic abuse, but scaled up into a healthcare system.

5. The Domestic Violence Survivor Who Is Told by Police: "We Can't Do Anything."

She shows photos, bruises, messages, threats.
The officer shrugs:

- "There's not enough evidence."
- "These cases are complicated."
- "Come back if something worse happens."

She walks away carrying two traumas:
The harm itself, and the betrayal by the institution meant to protect her.

Research on institutional betrayal confirms that when people turn to trusted systems for help but are met with indifference or hostility, the psychological impact is more severe than the original harm (Smith and Freyd 2014; Becker-Blease and Freyd 2007). Herman (1997) similarly notes that betrayal by a trusted entity inflicts deeper trauma because it violates core assumptions about safety and belonging. Modern capitalist institutions objectify individuals, reducing them to productivity and compliance metrics. This operationalizes a systemic empathy deficit: the institution "does not love or care," only extracts and disciplines.

Entitlement, Exploitation, and Resource Hoarding (Greed Addiction)

Narcissistic entitlement at the structural level takes the form of resource hoarding, punitive scarcity, and the presumption that individuals owe their labor, emotional regulation, and compliance to the system. Scarcity is weaponized to control behavior—consistent with research showing that scarcity increases punitiveness and reduces empathy (Okonofua et al. 2016; Kraus et al. 2017).

From a sociological perspective, structural narcissism aligns closely with Galtung's (1969) theory of **structural violence**: harm produced not by individual malice, but by entrenched systems that benefit the powerful while depriving everyone else of basic needs. This violence is quiet, normalized, and woven into policies that ration care, restrict benefits, deny accommodations, criminalize poverty, and punish the vulnerable simply for existing.

And layered on top of all this is a cultural rule we are never allowed to question:
We must always be happy for other people's happiness!
Even when their "success" is built on our exhaustion, our underpayment, our suffering, or our disposability, we are taught that any resentment is sinful. Any anger is "jealousy." Any discomfort is a moral failing.
So we swallow it.
We blame ourselves.
We wonder what is wrong with us.

But there is nothing wrong with us.

It is entirely natural — and ethically appropriate — to feel anger when someone else's comfort, wealth, or convenience is achieved at our expense. What is wrong is a system that tells us to celebrate harm as long as someone else benefits from it. What is wrong is the cultural gaslighting that demands we congratulate others for stepping on us, while we internalize the wounds as personal defects.

And it is deeply irresponsible for people to use their own happiness, success, or "right to live their truth" as an excuse to harm others. Joy does not require exploitation. There are infinite ways to be happy that do **not** require inflicting suffering on anyone else.

The foundation of an ethical society is simple:
Be thoughtful, be aware, and take accountability for how your choices affect the essential needs of others.
Just because someone else does not share your exact needs does not make them "dramatic," "irrational," or "imagined." Needs are real, even when we don't personally experience them.

But—and this is where the world has lost its way—**there is a profound difference between an essential need and a need for accumulation.**
The first is sacred.
The second is the engine of the darkness we are living in. It is an eternal blackhole, equating accumulation to safety.

Essential needs are the building blocks of human dignity:
safety, rest, food, medicine, shelter, belonging, autonomy, emotional validation, and the chance to exist without fear. These are universal. Non-negotiable. Life-affirming.

Accumulation, on the other hand, is not a need at all.
It is a socially rewarded craving created by capitalism's pathology.
It is the compulsive hunger for more—more money, more property, more status, more power—regardless of the cost to others. It is an addiction.

Essential needs keep us alive.
Accumulation devours the living.

Essential needs create community.
Accumulation fractures it.

Essential needs honor humanity.
Accumulation turns humans into tools, obstacles, or irrelevant background noise.

The tragedy is that our current system treats essential needs as negotiable and accumulation as sacred. People begging for food, housing, healthcare, rest, or safety are called "entitled," while billionaires hoarding more wealth than entire nations are called "successful." We punish the hungry and celebrate the insatiable. We criminalize need and canonize greed.

But emotional truth does not lie:

What most people call the "American Dream" is actually the nightmare of extraction dressed up as aspiration.

And what people call "success" is often accumulation built on someone else's unmet essential need.

We are trapped in an inverted moral universe where the wrong things are holy and the right things are shamed.

It is not wrong to need safety, dignity, ease, or rest.
It *is* wrong to exploit, dominate, hoard, and deprive others in the name of "success."

Essential need is human.
Accumulation is the shadow.

And until we can name that difference without flinching, we will continue to confuse greed with ambition, oppression with order, and structural violence with "just the way things are."

Real-life example:

Imagine a workplace where the CEO celebrates record profits and posts motivational speeches about "thriving together," while quietly cutting health benefits for staff, refusing to approve sick leave, and overworking employees who can't afford to quit.
The employees are expected to clap, smile, and "celebrate the company's success."
But inside, they feel dread, resentment, fear, and exhaustion.
They're told their anger is unprofessional, that they should "just be happy for the company," or "look at the bright side."
But the truth is:
There is nothing unethical about feeling anger toward a happiness that harms you.
What is unethical is a system that demands your self-sacrifice so someone else can flourish.

Leadership scholars identify these patterns as manifestations of "power-over" cultures that normalize exploitation and view dissent as disloyalty (Heifetz 1994; Morrison and Milliken 2000).

This is structural narcissism: a world where the powerful feel entitled to joy, comfort, and abundance that comes directly from the deprivation of others—who are then scolded for noticing.

Gaslighting and Narrative Control

Gaslighting is central to narcissistic abuse (Durvasula 2021; Sweet 2019). At the structural level, gaslighting becomes **an entire institutional ecosystem** — not one abuser but a coordinated architecture that distorts truth, erases patterns, and demands performances of suffering.

Structural gaslighting occurs when institutions:

- reinterpret grievances as misunderstandings or "isolated incidents," refusing to see the pattern,
- dismiss lived experience in favor of "official" records that often contradict reality,
- pathologize legitimate distress — labeling trauma as instability, sensitivity, or disorder,
- or require what I call **Eligibility Theater**: the repeated performance of suffering in order to be believed, helped, or seen at all.

This systematic distortion destabilizes **epistemic confidence**, aligning with theories of epistemic injustice (Fricker 2007). Survivors begin doubting their interpretations, their memories, their bodies, their needs. They internalize the idea that only documented pain counts, only visible wounds matter, only suffering that fits bureaucratic scripts is "real." This is also the psychological terrain of trauma bonding (Dutton & Painter 1981), where chronic invalidation trains a person to mistrust themselves and over-trust the abuser.

Gaslighting at this scale **produces Structural PTSD**: the nervous system becomes shaped by chronic invalidation, chronic doubt, and chronic distortion. The body learns to shrink its truth to avoid conflict. The mind learns to double-check its own reality. Agency collapses. Narrative shatters.

And the gaslighting becomes so internalized that it infiltrates even the smallest corners of life.

For example; Even as I write about all the ways I have been abused by the system, I still catch myself expecting **productivity** from my body. I still feel anxious when I rest. I know, intellectually, that *Rest Is Resistance*

(Hersey 2022), yet my nervous system experiences rest as danger. My body treats stillness as a threat, not a right. It collapses into panic, guilt, or self-loathing — proof of how deeply the capitalist script has colonized my nervous system.

When I worked at a coffee shop, if there were no customers and nothing to do, I would grab a rag and wipe down the counters I had already cleaned twice. My manager expected "activity." Busyness. Constant motion. So I performed it — the dance of false productivity. Surface-cleaning surfaces that were already clean. Pretending to work so that I could appear safe.

Inside, I knew I was wasting my energy. I knew I was performing a capitalist ritual, not doing anything meaningful. But I did it anyway. Because that is what structural gaslighting does:

It teaches you that **your worth is proven only by labor**, even if that labor is pointless.

And then the self-doubt comes in, the most insidious part:
If I am faking productivity, am I actually productive at all?
If resting makes me anxious, am I lazy?
If I don't constantly perform effort, will I be seen as inadequate?

Even though I know I'm a hardworking person — even though I know I've survived more than most people will ever experience — I still find myself following the capitalist script of **constant work, no rest, endless proving**.

That is what gaslighting does.
It replaces truth with performance.
It replaces rest with fear.
It replaces self-trust with self-surveillance.

Structural gaslighting doesn't just distort your reality in the moment.
It rewires your body.
It shapes your reflexes.
It becomes the lens through which you see yourself.

And somehow, we blame ourselves, not the system.

Trauma-Bonded Compliance

Trauma-bonded compliance is one of the most misunderstood survival responses. People think of trauma bonds only in terms of intimate relationships — the abused partner who stays, the child who clings to the parent who harms them. But in reality, trauma-bonded compliance also happens **between people and institutions**.

It is not love.
It is not devotion.
It is **survival under coercive conditions**.

A trauma bond forms when **harm and help come from the same source**, when the system responsible for injuring you is also the system you must rely on for protection, resources, legitimacy, or survival. Dutton and Painter (1981) identified this dynamic in abusive interpersonal relationships — the unpredictable mix of cruelty and intermittent care keeps the survivor psychologically attached.

Institutions do the same thing.

- Welfare offices deny your application, then approve it "just this once" — but only *after* pressuring you to distort your expenses or employment status to fit their boxes.

- A professor praises you in front of others — calling you "brilliant," "promising," or "a strong writer" — but then, behind closed doors, tells you that *because you are a woman*, you must do quantitative research for your dissertation to be considered "valid." The praise is the lure; the sexism is the truth.

- A hospital dismisses your pain, then suddenly treats you kindly after you break down in a crisis.

- A supervisor critiques your "attitude," then says they're "really rooting for you."

This inconsistency keeps your nervous system confused, destabilized, and hooked.
Your body stays alert, waiting for the next signal — danger or safety, punishment or reward.

What Trauma-Bonded Compliance Actually Is

Trauma-bonded compliance is the survival instinct to:

- **stay small**
- **stay agreeable**
- **stay accommodating**
- **stay grateful for crumbs**
- **avoid conflict at all costs**
- **fawn in the face of authority**
- **self-censor before anyone else has to**
- **perform the "good survivor" role**

It is the instinct to protect the abuser so you can protect yourself.

In CRC-PTSD terms, it is the body learning:
"If I resist, I will be punished. If I comply, I might survive." It is biological intelligence.

But survival strategies can only carry us so far. There comes a moment when the body remembers its worth, when the mind refuses to keep carrying blame that was never ours, and when the shame finally goes back to its rightful home:

On the system that created the harm, not the people forced to survive it.

It is time to take back our power —
not by "toughening up,"
not by abandoning our softness,
but by refusing to internalize the failures of institutions as failures of the self.

How Gaslighting Creates Trauma-Bonded Compliance

Structural gaslighting creates conditions where:

- you doubt your own perceptions
- you question whether you "deserve" help
- you blame yourself for being harmed
- you fear consequences for speaking up
- you learn to preemptively soften your truth

Institutions do this through:

- policy vagueness
- contradictory requirements
- inconsistent staff responses
- endless "start over" demands
- procedural opacity
- punishment for dissent
- Minimization of "impact" in the name of "intent"

When gaslighting becomes the baseline, the survivor internalizes a single rule:

Don't provoke the system.
Don't question the system.
Don't upset the system.

And so you comply.
Not because you trust them — but because you predict what happens if you don't.

How Fear Produces Paranoia and Hyper-Compliance

Fear is the glue of trauma bonds.

When you live with:

- chronic uncertainty
- chronic invalidation
- chronic threat
- chronic surveillance
- chronic dependency

your nervous system becomes **trained to anticipate punishment.**

This looks like paranoia, but it's not delusion — it's pattern recognition. Your body is not overreacting; it is **remembering.**

Trauma-bonded compliance is the attempt to **stop the blow before it lands.**

So you:

- apologize excessively
- overexplain everything
- clean the counters twice
- smile while terrified
- freeze when criticized
- work through exhaustion
- stay quiet to keep the peace

The system doesn't even have to threaten you anymore — your body does it for them.

That's how deep the conditioning goes.

Why Trauma-Bonded Compliance Is Not Weakness

People blame themselves for this dynamic, but trauma-bonded compliance is:

- a survival strategy
- an attachment reflex
- an autonomic nervous system adaptation
- a trauma imprint
- an institutional outcome

It arises because the system holds:

- your healthcare
- your paycheck
- your grades
- your housing
- your immigration status
- your legal protection

You can't fight the hand that holds your life alone.

So you comply.

You perform.
You please.
You shrink.
You survive, at least long enough to procreate, and then you are disposed of. Silently, slowly, painfully and lonely.

This is **the biology of captivity within human-made systems. No bars or solitary confinement, but a prison made out of shame and fear by words.**

Shame, Contempt, and Hierarchy

Narcissistic systems rely on shame to maintain control (Bradshaw 1988). Shame directs emotional energy inward, shrinking resistance, while **contempt** toward marginalized groups, dissenters, and truth-tellers maintains hierarchy (Fiske 2011). These mechanisms are so deeply embedded in the fabric of institutions that they often hide in plain sight, aligning with what Galtung (1969) called **structural violence** — harm woven into routines, policies, and norms rather than acts of individual malice. Haritaworn et al. (2013) sharpen the point even further:

"In necropolitical regimes not only is the body vulnerable to death, but the social and political structures determine which bodies must be exposed to death-worlds and abandonment." (Haritaworn et al. 2013: 23)

This dynamic echoes the **"mythical norm"** described by Audre Lorde (1984): an idealized template of worthiness against which all bodies and identities are judged. In the United States, Lorde argued, the mythical norm is "white, thin, male, young, heterosexual, Christian, and financially secure." It is not a real person — it is a **fiction** that functions as a measuring stick. Systems reward proximity to this manufactured ideal and shame any deviation from it, producing **stratified embodiment—**The experience of moving through the world in a body that society has already graded. (Strings 2019; Bacon 2010).

The closer you are to the mythical norm, the more invisible the hierarchy feels. The farther you are from it, the more shame you are expected to carry. This is how structural narcissism maintains its power: by defining one type of life as "default" and treating all others as "other," "irrational," "difficult," or "less than."

And this mythical norm is everywhere — embedded quietly in the most ordinary parts of life.

Clothing as a Map of Hierarchy

Our clothing industry is designed around a narrow "default" body. Plus-size options are limited, hidden, or treated as an afterthought. Patterns are cut to fit one body type, and anyone whose body differs must contort themselves into the available options instead of the industry adapting to human diversity. Even shoes assume a "standard" foot shape, and if your feet do not match, *you* are expected to change, not the shoe (Haritaworn et al. 2013).
This is not fashion — it is **embodied hierarchy**.

Medicine as Enforcer of the Mythical Body

Medical diagnostics assume identical biological responses across bodies, despite mountains of evidence showing profound physiological variation (Krieger 1994; Roberts 2011). Reference ranges are treated as universal truths instead of population averages shaped by bias, sampling, and omission. When a patient's symptoms don't fit the template, medicine blames the patient, not the template.
This is how people get misdiagnosed, dismissed, gaslit, and harmed.
The mythical norm becomes a diagnostic tool.

Immigration and the Invention of "Second-Class Humans"

Immigrants are treated as though crossing a border alters their humanity — as if a line on a map changes who deserves dignity, safety, rest, or belonging. Yet human beings share **99.9% of the same DNA** (Ngai 2004). Borders are not biological facts; they are political inventions used to sort populations into categories of worthiness.
This is not policy — it is **constructed hierarchies disguised as law.**

Epistemic Injustice as an Instrument of Shame

Epistemic injustice occurs when certain people are denied credibility not because they are wrong, but because the system has already decided whose knowledge counts. Lived experience, embodied knowledge, intuition, and community wisdom are routinely dismissed as "subjective," "emotional," or "unscientific," while institutional knowledge is treated as neutral and authoritative (Fricker 2007).

This is not an accident. It is a mechanism of shame.

When survivors, poor people, immigrants, disabled people, and truth-tellers speak, their knowledge is filtered through suspicion. They are asked to provide "proof" that matches institutional language, timelines, and formats that were never designed to hold trauma, complexity, or lived reality. When their stories don't fit, the system does not question its categories — it questions their sanity, credibility, or character.

Epistemic injustice trains people to doubt their own perception. It teaches them to apologize for knowing what they know. It rewards silence, compliance, and self-erasure, while punishing those who speak from experience rather than from sanctioned authority.

This is not a failure of science or reason. It is a hierarchy of knowledge designed to preserve power.

Chapter 6 is devoted entirely to this: how epistemic injustice operates across institutions, how it produces shame and self-doubt, and why reclaiming lived truth is one of the most radical acts of resistance available to us.

Retaliation Against Truth-Tellers

One of the clearest signs that you're dealing with a narcissistic system is what happens the moment someone tells the truth.
Not a comfortable truth.
Not a truth the institution has already approved.
But the kind of truth that exposes the rot.

Research calls this "retaliation against organizational voice" — but that phrase barely captures the lived experience (Detert & Burris 2007; Near & Miceli 2008). In real life, it feels like this:

You speak up → suddenly you're the problem.

You name harm → suddenly you're "difficult."
You report misconduct → suddenly you're "unstable," "unprofessional," or "not a good fit."
You tell the truth → the system tells a story about *you* instead.

Institutions do to truth-tellers exactly what narcissistic abusers do to the people who expose them (Durvasula 2021):
They **attack credibility**, not the harm.
They **shift blame**, not behavior.
They **reframe truth as threat**, not information.

And the retaliation is subtle at first, almost polite:

- Meetings you used to be invited to disappear from your calendar.
- Your emails start getting "lost."
- People talk around you, not to you.
- Your name comes up only in private conversations you're not present for.
- Your work is suddenly scrutinized as if you've become incompetent overnight.

Then it escalates:

- A false narrative forms behind your back.
- You're labeled "emotional," "angry," "too sensitive," "too much."
- Supervisors suddenly create "documentation" to justify punishing you.
- HR frames your report as *your behavior problem.*
- The institution pathologizes you to protect itself.

And the cruelest part?

Everyone else sees what's happening — and most stay silent because they know the system will punish them too.

In **The Truth-Teller Paradigm**, I describe truth-tellers as **moral disruptors** — people whose clarity exposes what the institution has worked hard to hide. The system depends on denial to function. Truth-tellers disrupt denial. Yet one truth teller cannot change the system, but a thousand could.

To protect its projected image, a narcissistic system always chooses one of three responses:

1. Silence

You're ignored, sidelined, excluded, erased.
Your emails go unanswered.
Your contributions vanish.
Your suffering is minimized.

2. Scapegoating

You become the villain in the story that should have held your pain.
People whisper about you.
Your reputation becomes collateral damage.
You are framed as the source of the dysfunction, not the mirror revealing it.

3. Pathologizing dissent

Your truth becomes a "symptom."
Your clarity becomes "instability."
Your moral outrage becomes a "behavior problem."
Your trauma becomes a "lack of professionalism."

This is not accidental — this is **structural narcissism**.
And its logic is simple:

The system would rather destroy the truth-teller than face the truth.

Because the moment one person speaks honestly, everyone else can suddenly see the cracks. And once the cracks appear, the institution can no longer pretend to be whole.

Retaliation isn't a glitch.
It is a confession.

Every punishment of a truth-teller is a system enforcing one message:
"We cannot survive transparency."

But that verdict is about *the system*, not about us.
Their fragility is not our flaw.

And that is exactly why **transparency and truth-telling are our greatest weapons**.

The only way to stop the lies of the system is for us all to unite and speak the truth, even when our voices are shaking. They can punish a handful of people, but can they punish the majority? We need to see the power we hold in unity. Just as I wrote before, if we decide that tomorrow money has zero value, and we are souls living based on kindness, sharing, and loving, and living a present life, then their castles built on the dead bodies of many people like us will crumble. They have much less power than us. After all they are the smallest minority, the top %10 who accrued all the wealth. We are the majority. We need to remember that!

What the system cannot survive is precisely what we must practice.
Because truth doesn't destroy us — **It destroys the lies we were never meant to live under.**

Leadership Failure as Diagnostic Core

At the heart of every narcissistic system is not an abstract flaw — It's a **leadership failure**.

Leadership studies show that cultures of narcissism take root when leaders prioritize control, image, and personal comfort over accountability and relationship (Kets de Vries 1991; Brown 2018). When leaders fear truth more than harm, the entire institution begins to warp around their avoidance.

Structural narcissism thrives in environments defined by:

- **low transparency** — information is hoarded, not shared

- **high hierarchy** — power flows one way, never back up
- **weak feedback loops** — dissent is punished, not welcomed
- **fear-based management** — people obey out of anxiety, not trust
- **emotional repression** — feelings are "unprofessional," truth is "disruptive"

These conditions are not organizational quirks.
They are **symptoms** of a system trying to protect itself instead of the people inside it.

Trauma-informed leadership (Fallot & Harris 2009) offers a radically different architecture. It argues that leaders must actively disrupt structural narcissism by cultivating:

- **empathy over efficiency**,
- **safety over secrecy**,
- **shared decision-making over hierarchy**,
- **transparency over image management**,
- **truth-telling over complacency**.

Without these shifts, institutions do not default to care — **They default to self-preservation.**
And when that happens, *we* become the sacrifice.

We become the **flying monkeys** of the system — the expendable foot soldiers enlisted to protect its image, enforce its rules, and uphold its lies, all in exchange for a survival wage. We are told we are "team players," but in truth, we are being used. Our labor becomes the institution's armor, and our silence becomes its shield.
And on the inside, we feel awful — not because we are inherently guilty people, but because part of us knows we've been coerced into participating in something morally wrong. Yet we stay quiet, not out of malice or apathy, but out of **fear**. Fear that if we speak up, we will lose our job, our housing, our status, our stability. Fear that without the system —

even a harmful one — we won't survive.

When an institution is built to protect itself rather than its people, it inevitably becomes a producer of **harm, denial, and betrayal.**
Not because every person inside it is cruel, but because the structure rewards compliance and punishes conscience.

Leadership, in this context, is not a title or a position.
Leadership is the moral center of a system. Leadership is not ordering people around, but rather guiding them to healing and being whole and that requires compassion, patience and sacrifice.
It is not the job of a single person, or an executive team, or a charismatic figurehead.
Leadership is the responsibility of *every single one of us* — to keep each other accountable, to refuse to participate in institutional gaslighting, and to name the truth even when we fear retaliation.

And truth-telling does not mean cruelty.
It does not mean abrupt confrontation or righteousness.
Real truth-telling is an act of love — patient, empathetic, steady, and rooted in a desire for collective healing.
It is saying:
"I care about you, I care about us, and I care about the harm we are accidentally replicating."

This is the leadership we need:
not the leadership of hierarchy,
but the leadership of courage, clarity, and compassion — the kind that rebuilds systems from the inside out.

Diagnostic Tool: How to Detect Structural Narcissism in a System

Structural narcissism is not an abstract metaphor; it's a pattern we can actually look for. It shows up in how a system responds to truth, to vulnerability, to difference, to failure, and to need. The questions below are not a test you "pass" or "fail." They create a **mirror**.

You can rate each item informally (for example: **rarely / sometimes / often / always**) or use it simply as a set of prompts for honest discussion.

---

1. Care vs. Image

When harm is reported, what does the system protect first: the people or the brand?

- Are responses to harm driven by legal risk, PR optics, and reputation management?
- Do leaders worry more about "how this will look" than what actually happened?
- Are apologies rare, formulaic, or nonexistent?

High structural narcissism: **Image is protected, people are sacrificed. No apologies, only "Sorry that was YOUR experience."**

---

2. Response to Truth-Telling

What happens to people who name uncomfortable truths?

- Are whistleblowers, critics, and truth-tellers quietly sidelined, pathologized, or punished?
- Do staff or students warn each other: "Don't say that out loud—it's not safe"?
- Does the system frame dissent as disloyalty, negativity, or "unprofessionalism"?

High structural narcissism: **Truth is punished, denial is rewarded.**

---

3. Transparency vs. Obscurity

How easy is it to understand what is really going on?

- Are decisions made behind closed doors, with vague explanations?
- Are policies clear and accessible, or buried in jargon and constantly shifting?
- When you ask "why" something happened, do you get a straight answer—or a wall of policy?

High structural narcissism: **Information is hoarded and used as control.**

---

4. Power Distribution

Who has the power to say "no"—and who never gets to say "no" at all?

- Is power concentrated in a small group that is rarely questioned?
- Are people with less power expected to endlessly accommodate, absorb harm, or "stay flexible"?
- Is there any real mechanism to challenge decisions made at the top?

High structural narcissism: **Power flows one way, and accountability almost never flows up.**

---

5. Metrics vs. Humanity

What counts as "success" here?

- Are metrics (numbers, outputs, scores, rankings) treated as the ultimate truth?
- Are staff and clients reduced to data points, performance indicators, or "cases"?

- Are good numbers used to deny lived experience ("we can't be harmful, look at our outcomes")?

High structural narcissism: **Metrics are treated as morality.**

---

6. Empathy and Safety

Is it emotionally safe to be a human being in this system?

- Are people allowed to show distress, grief, anger, or vulnerability without being punished?
- Do leaders model empathy, or only efficiency and control?
- Is "professionalism" used as a code word for emotional numbness?

High structural narcissism: **Feeling is treated as defect, not information.**

---

7. Handling of Mistakes

What happens when the system is wrong?

- Can the institution admit error and repair, or does it deny and deflect?
- Are mistakes used as learning opportunities or as justification for more control and surveillance?
- Do people constantly work in fear of being blamed?

High structural narcissism: **The system is never wrong—only individuals are.**

---

8. Eligibility and Access

Who gets help easily—and who is forced into Eligibility Theater?

- Do people have to repeatedly prove they're suffering to receive support?
- Are applications, appeals, and evaluations designed in ways that exhaust the most vulnerable?
- Is care contingent on performance, pleading, or perfection?

High structural narcissism: **Support is conditional, rationed, and humiliating.**

---

9. Pattern vs. "Isolated Incident"

Does the system look at patterns, or does it insist everything is "just this one case"?

- Are repeated complaints treated as unrelated events?
- Is harm described as "miscommunication" instead of a pattern?
- Are systemic issues reframed as individual misunderstandings?

High structural narcissism: **Patterns are denied so no one has to change the structure.**

---

10. Who Is Losing Health Here?

Finally, ask: who is getting sick from this system?

- Are staff burned out, dissociating, or leaving in waves?
- Are those most dependent on the system collapsing under its weight?

- Do people describe dread, hypervigilance, or shame when they interact with it?

High structural narcissism: **The system thrives while people inside it deteriorate.**

You don't need a survey score to know if a structure is narcissistic.

If a system:

- undermines care,
- rewards denial,
- punishes truth,
- and fractures the capacity for real connection,

then **it is injured at the level of its moral core**.

This diagnostic lens is not here to make you feel hopeless. It is here to make the harm **visible** so it can no longer masquerade as "normal," "necessary," or "just how things are."

Once we can see the rot, we can stop blaming ourselves for the smell—and start deciding what we want to grow in its place.

References

Aday, Audrey, and Toni Schmader. 2019. "Seeking Authenticity in Diverse Contexts: How Identities and Environments Constrain 'Free' Choice." *Social and Personality Psychology Compass* 13(6):e12450.

Ahmed, Sara. 2017. *Living a Feminist Life.* Durham, NC: Duke University Press.

Alexander, Jeffrey C. 2004. "Toward a Theory of Cultural Trauma." Pp. 1–30 in *Cultural Trauma and Collective Identity*, edited by J. C. Alexander, R. Eyerman, B. Giesen, N. J. Smelser, and P. Sztompka. Berkeley: University of California Press.

Bacon, Linda. 2010. *Health at Every Size: The Surprising Truth about Your Weight*. Dallas, TX: BenBella Books.

Becker-Blease, Kathleen A., and Jennifer J. Freyd. 2006. "Research Participants Telling the Truth about Their Lives: The Ethics of Asking and Not Asking about Abuse." *American Psychologist* 61(3):218–226.

Bradshaw, John. 1988. *Healing the Shame That Binds You*. Deerfield Beach, FL: Health Communications.

Brown, Brené. 2018. *Dare to Lead: Brave Work. Tough Conversations. Whole Hearts*. New York: Random House.

Cabanas, Edgar, and Eva Illouz. 2019. *Manufacturing Happy Citizens: How the Science and Industry of Happiness Control Our Lives*. Cambridge, UK: Polity Press.

Detert, James R., and Ethan R. Burris. 2007. "Leadership Behavior and Employee Voice: Is the Door Really Open?" *Academy of Management Journal* 50(4):869–884.

Dutton, Donald G., and Susan L. Painter. 1981. "Traumatic Bonding: The Development of Emotional Attachments in Battered Women and Other Relationships of Intermittent Abuse." *Victimology* 6(1–4):139–155.

Durvasula, Ramani. 2015. *Should I Stay or Should I Go? Surviving a Relationship with a Narcissist*. New York: Post Hill Press.

Durvasula, Ramani. 2019. *"Don't You Know Who I Am?": How to Stay Sane in an Era of Narcissism, Entitlement, and Incivility*. New York: Post Hill Press.

Durvasula, Ramani. 2021. (As cited in text; full reference not provided in your list.)

Fiske, Susan T. 2011. *Envy Up, Scorn Down: How Status Divides Us*. New York: Russell Sage Foundation.

Fricker, Miranda. 2007. *Epistemic Injustice: Power and the Ethics of Knowing*. Oxford: Oxford University Press.

Galtung, Johan. 1969. "Violence, Peace, and Peace Research." *Journal of Peace Research* 6(3):167–191.

Goffman, Erving. 1959. *The Presentation of Self in Everyday Life*. Garden City, NY: Doubleday.

Golomb, Elan. 1992. *Trapped in the Mirror: Adult Children of Narcissists in Their Struggle for Self.* New York: William Morrow.

Heifetz, Ronald A. 1994. *Leadership Without Easy Answers.* Cambridge, MA: Harvard University Press.

Herman, Judith Lewis. 1997. *Trauma and Recovery: The Aftermath of Violence—from Domestic Abuse to Political Terror.* New York: Basic Books.

Hersey, Tricia. 2022. *Rest Is Resistance: A Manifesto.* New York: Little, Brown Spark.

Kernberg, Otto F. 1975. *Borderline Conditions and Pathological Narcissism.* New York: Jason Aronson.

Kets de Vries, Manfred F. R. 1991. *Organizations on the Couch: Clinical Perspectives on Organizational Behavior and Change.* San Francisco: Jossey-Bass.

Kraus, et al. 2017. (As cited in text; full reference not provided in your list.)

Krieger, Nancy. 1994. "Epidemiology and the Web of Causation: Has Anyone Seen the Spider?" *Social Science & Medicine* 39(7):887–903.

Lorde, Audre. 1984. *Sister Outsider: Essays and Speeches.* Trumansburg, NY: Crossing Press.

Millon, Theodore. 2011. *Disorders of Personality: Introducing a DSM-5 Alternative Model.* 3rd ed. Hoboken, NJ: Wiley.

Morrison, Elizabeth Wolfe, and Frances J. Milliken. 2000. "Organizational Silence: A Barrier to Change and Development in a Pluralistic World." *Academy of Management Review* 25(4):706–725.

Near, and Miceli. 2008. (As cited in text; full reference not provided in your list.)

Ngai, Mae M. 2004. *Impossible Subjects: Illegal Aliens and the Making of Modern*

America. Princeton, NJ: Princeton University Press.

Okonofua, Jason A., Gregory M. Walton, and Jennifer L. Eberhardt. 2016. "A Vicious Cycle: A Social–Psychological Account of Extreme Racial Disparities in School Discipline." *Perspectives on Psychological Science* 11(3):381–398.

Porter, Theodore M. 1995. *Trust in Numbers: The Pursuit of Objectivity in Science and Public Life.* Princeton, NJ: Princeton University Press.

Smith, Carly Parnitzke, and Jennifer J. Freyd. 2014. "Institutional Betrayal." *American Psychologist* 69(6):575–587.

Strings, Sabrina. 2019. *Fearing the Black Body: The Racial Origins of Fat Phobia.* New York: New York University Press.

Sweet, Paige L. 2019. "The Sociology of Gaslighting." *American Sociological Review* 84(5):851–875.

van der Kolk, Bessel A. 2014. *The Body Keeps the Score: Brain, Mind, and Body in the Healing of Trauma.* New York: Viking.

4 — Psychological Operations

(PSYOPS)

Psychological Operations: How Reality Is Managed

Psychological operations—psyops—are not fringe ideas, secret theories, or speculative fears. They are a formal, documented practice within military doctrine and strategic communication research (Joint Chiefs of Staff 2007; Paul and Matthews 2016). Governments, militaries, intelligence agencies, and corporations have openly studied, funded, and refined perception management for decades as a tool of legitimacy, compliance, and social control (Bernays 1928; Herman and Chomsky 1988). The goal is not to convince people of a single lie, but to shape the conditions under which certain thoughts feel possible and others feel unthinkable (Stanley 2015).

The U.S. Department of Defense defines psychological operations as efforts to "convey selected information and indicators to audiences to influence their emotions, motives, objective reasoning, and ultimately behavior" (Joint Chiefs of Staff 2007). Notice what is absent from that definition: truth, consent, or well-being. Psyops are about influence, not understanding—about compliance, not care (Stanley 2015; Oreskes and Conway 2010).

The most effective psychological operations do not announce themselves. They feel like common sense. They feel like "just the way things are" (Altheide 2006; Zuboff 2019).

PsyOps Do Not Require Lies

One of the most dangerous misconceptions about psychological operations is the belief that they rely on false information. In reality, psyops work best when they use partial truths, repeated endlessly, stripped of context, and emotionally loaded—strategies long documented in both propaganda studies and institutional disinformation campaigns (Stanley 2015; Oreskes and Conway 2010).

A statement can be factually accurate and still function as psychological warfare through framing, repetition, and emotional priming (Entman 1993; Jamieson and Cappella 2008).

For example:

- "Resources are limited."
- "The system is overwhelmed."
- "We have to make hard choices."
- "There is no alternative."

None of these statements are inherently false. But when repeated without examining who controls resources, why systems are overwhelmed, or who benefits from scarcity, they become tools of emotional containment—training people to accept harm as inevitable and structurally unsolvable (Altheide 2006; Klein 2007).

Psychological research shows that under conditions of chronic stress and threat, humans lose access to complex reasoning and default to authority, familiarity, and survival-oriented thinking. Fear narrows perception, and repetition increases perceived truth through familiarity effects (Lupien et al. 2009; Hasher, Goldstein, and Toppino 1977; Kahneman 2011). Over time, people stop asking whether something should be happening and focus only on how to endure it.

This is how psyops move from battlefield strategy into everyday life (Paul and Matthews 2016; Herman and Chomsky 1988).

From War Zones to Civilian Life

Historically, psychological operations were developed for warfare: demoralizing enemy populations, weakening resistance, and shaping perception in occupied territories (Taylor 2003; Paul and Matthews 2016). But over time, these techniques migrated inward through state bureaucracy, corporate public relations, and media management (Bernays 1928; Herman and Chomsky 1988).

Modern societies now use psyops logic to manage:

- Economic insecurity
- Political dissent
- Migration
- Labor unrest
- Public health crises
- Climate anxiety

This shift did not require malice. It required bureaucracy. Large systems under pressure prioritize stability over truth, image over repair, and control over care—especially in cultures shaped by audit logics and institutional self-preservation (Power 1999; Ahmed 2017).

Psyops offer a way to maintain legitimacy without addressing root causes. Instead of fixing systems, you manage perception of systems (Stanley 2015; Zuboff 2019).

The Emotional Architecture of PsyOps

Psychological operations work by targeting emotions more than beliefs. The most commonly used emotional levers are fear, shame, scarcity, resignation, and isolation—affective states long recognized as central to propaganda, social control, and compliance (Altheide 2006; Stanley 2015; Ahmed 2017).

- **Fear**: danger is everywhere, and safety requires obedience (Glassner 1999; Altheide 2006)
- **Shame**: if you are struggling, it is your fault (Brown 2012; Cabanas and Illouz 2019)
- **Scarcity**: there is not enough to go around (Mullainathan and Shafir 2013; Oreskes and Conway 2010)
- **Resignation**: nothing can really change (Seligman 1975; Fisher 2009)
- **Isolation**: you are alone in feeling this (Putnam 2000; Herman 1997)

These emotions are not incidental. They are structural outputs of modern political-economic systems, produced through institutional design and cultural narrative rather than individual weakness (Galtung 1969; Cabanas and Illouz 2019).

When people are afraid, ashamed, and exhausted, they do not organize. They do not imagine alternatives. They turn inward, self-police, and accept less—patterns consistently documented in studies of repression, neoliberal governance, and the privatization of distress (Foucault 1977; Ahmed 2017; Berardi 2009).

This is why psyops are so effective in neoliberal systems: the harm is internalized, and people blame themselves for conditions they did not create (Brown 2015; Fisher 2009).

PsyOps and the Illusion of Choice

One of the most powerful tools of psychological operations is the illusion of choice: a narrowing of imaginable alternatives until domination appears like reason (Stanley 2015; Zuboff 2019).

People are presented with two options:

- Austerity or chaos (Blyth 2013)
- Surveillance or danger (Lyon 2001; Foucault 1977)
- Borders or collapse (Ngai 2004; Menjívar and Abrego 2012)
- Work until burnout or fall into poverty (Graeber 2018; Berardi 2009)

When only false binaries are offered, resistance is framed as irrational or naïve. The system appears reasonable—even compassionate—for choosing the "lesser evil," a classic mechanism of manufactured consent (Herman and Chomsky 1988; Jamieson and Cappella 2008).

This is how cruelty becomes policy and policy becomes morality: structural violence rendered as necessity, and domination reframed as common sense (Galtung 1969; Foucault 1977).

A Brief History of Psychological Operations: From War Rooms to Living Rooms

Psychological operations did not begin as some shadowy modern invention. They emerged alongside mass communication itself, accelerating during the 20th century as governments and corporations realized something unsettling: **controlling perception is often more powerful than controlling territory** (Taylor 2003; Herman and Chomsky 1988; Stanley 2015).

There are numerous examples that you can find yourself, and once you learn how to detect it, you can't stop seeing it everywhere.

World War I & the Birth of Modern PsyOps

The first large-scale, systematic psychological operations appeared during World War I. Governments used propaganda to boost morale at home and demoralize enemies abroad—posters, films, newspapers, and rumors carefully designed to shape emotion rather than inform truth (Taylor 2003; Bernays 1928).

Edward Bernays—often called the "father of public relations"—explicitly framed persuasion as a tool for managing democracy (Bernays 1928). His argument was simple and chilling: the public must be guided, because mass opinion was too volatile to be trusted with full autonomy.

This logic never left (Herman and Chomsky 1988; Stanley 2015).

Operation Mockingbird — When Reality Learned to Speak in a Controlled Voice

Operation Mockingbird was not loud. It did not announce itself. It did not look like propaganda. That was the point.

Beginning in the early Cold War, the CIA quietly cultivated relationships with journalists, editors, publishers, and media executives, embedding influence inside what appeared to be a free press (U.S. Senate 1976; Wilford 2008). Newspapers, radio programs, and later television did not need to be ordered what to say. They learned what not to say. Which stories to amplify. Which angles to soften. Which questions to never ask (Herman and Chomsky 1988).

This wasn't censorship. It was guidance.

It wasn't lying. It was curation (Stanley 2015).

The public still believed it was thinking freely, because no one was being silenced outright. But the field of imaginable truth was narrowed. Certain narratives felt respectable. Others felt fringe, dangerous, or "unserious"

(Herman and Chomsky 1988; Jamieson and Cappella 2008). Over time, journalists internalized the boundaries. Editors learned what would get them access. Media institutions learned what would protect their credibility, funding, and proximity to power (Wilford 2008).

And the most important shift happened quietly:

- Trust moved from reality to authority (Stanley 2015; Zuboff 2019).
- If it came from the right outlet, it felt true.
- If it didn't, it felt suspicious—regardless of evidence (Jamieson and Cappella 2008).

This is why Mockingbird matters now. Not because it still exists in the same form, but because it taught institutions something crucial: you don't have to control people directly if you can control what feels credible (Herman and Chomsky 1988; Stanley 2015). You don't have to ban dissent if you can make it sound unstable, radical, or emotionally excessive (Ahmed 2017).

This is the hidden spine of modern psyops.

- You see it later in Vietnam, when officials spoke of "progress" while villages burned (Herring 2002).
- You see it in Iraq, when certainty about weapons replaced evidence (Bennett, Lawrence, and Livingston 2007; Kellner 2004).
- You see it in corporate media cycles, where some harms are debated endlessly while others never enter the frame (Herman and Chomsky 1988).
- And you feel it in your body when you speak a truth that doesn't land—not because it's wrong, but because the room has been trained not to hear it (Fricker 2007; Stanley 2015).

Operation Mockingbird didn't just manage information.

It trained society to doubt itself (Wilford 2008; Zuboff 2019).

And once that training takes hold, institutions no longer need to lie loudly.

They just need to keep talking calmly while reality fractures underneath (Oreskes and Conway 2010; Stanley 2015).

Commercial Psyop: Tobacco

One of the most infamous and well-documented psychological operations in modern history was not conducted by a military or intelligence agency, but by corporations—specifically, the tobacco industry (Brandt 2007; Proctor 2011).

For decades, cigarette companies knew that smoking caused lung cancer, heart disease, and premature death. Internal documents later revealed that industry scientists had confirmed the link as early as the 1950s (Brandt 2007; Proctor 2011). Yet instead of warning the public or changing course, executives made a strategic decision: they would not defeat the science—they would bury it (Oreskes and Conway 2010).

The strategy was articulated with chilling clarity in an internal memo:

"Doubt is our product."
(Brandt 2007)

This sentence alone could serve as the mission statement for modern psychological operations (Oreskes and Conway 2010; Stanley 2015).

Manufacturing Uncertainty Instead of Truth

The tobacco psyop did not rely on outright lies. It relied on something far more effective: manufactured uncertainty (Oreskes and Conway 2010).

The industry funded "independent" research designed not to prove cigarettes were safe, but to suggest that the science was inconclusive (Brandt 2007; Proctor 2011). They amplified fringe hypotheses—genetics, stress, pollution, personality traits—anything that could muddy the causal link between smoking and disease (Oreskes and Conway 2010).

The goal was never to win the argument.
The goal was to delay action (Brandt 2007).

Every year of doubt meant another year of profit.
Every delay meant millions more addicted customers (Proctor 2011).

Authority as a Weapon

One of the most powerful elements of the tobacco psyop was the use of authority figures (Brandt 2007; Proctor 2011).

Advertisements prominently featured:

- Doctors in white coats (Brandt 2007)
- Phrases like "More doctors smoke Camel" (Brandt 2007)
- Claims of "medical endorsement" (Proctor 2011)
- Pseudo-scientific language about throat irritation and filtration (Brandt 2007)

The visual grammar of trust was weaponized. If a doctor smoked, how dangerous could it really be? This wasn't persuasion—it was borrowed legitimacy (Herman and Chomsky 1988; Stanley 2015). The industry understood that people outsource judgment to authority when faced with uncertainty (Kahneman 2011). So they filled the uncertainty with experts they paid (Oreskes and Conway 2010).

Freedom, Femininity, and Emotional Manipulation

The psyop went even deeper by tying cigarettes to identity (Klein 2000; Brandt 2007).

For women, smoking was marketed as:

- Liberation (Brandt 2007)
- Independence (Klein 2000)
- Thinness (Proctor 2011)
- Defiance (Brandt 2007)

Campaigns like "You've come a long way, baby" reframed cigarettes as symbols of feminist empowerment and modern womanhood (Brandt 2007). Smoking became not a health risk, but a statement of autonomy.

This was psychological warfare on the self (Illouz 2007; Stanley 2015).

To quit smoking would mean abandoning not just a habit, but an identity carefully constructed through advertising (Klein 2000).

Plausible Deniability and Strategic Delay

At every stage, the industry hid behind a single refrain:

"The science is not settled."
This phrase functioned as a moral anesthetic. Regulators hesitated. Courts delayed. Consumers rationalized (Oreskes and Conway 2010). Meanwhile, internal memos acknowledged what executives already knew: cigarettes were lethal (Brandt 2007; Proctor 2011).

This is the essence of a successful psyop:

- Say just enough truth to avoid prosecution (Oreskes and Conway 2010)
- Create enough doubt to prevent action (Brandt 2007)
- Delay long enough to extract maximum profit (Proctor 2011)
- By the time regulation finally caught up, millions were dead (Brandt 2007; Proctor 2011).

Not collateral damage.
Predictable casualties.

Why This Matters Beyond Cigarettes

The tobacco industry didn't just sell cigarettes.
It pioneered a model (Oreskes and Conway 2010).

That model now appears everywhere:

- Fossil fuel companies denying climate science (Oreskes and Conway 2010)
- Food corporations obscuring links between ultra-processed foods and disease (Nestle 2013)
- Pharmaceutical companies minimizing side effects (Angell 2004)
- Tech companies downplaying psychological harm (Zuboff 2019)
- The formula is always the same:
- Acknowledge partial truth (Oreskes and Conway 2010)
- Fund doubt (Brandt 2007)
- Hire experts (Herman and Chomsky 1988)
- Appeal to identity and emotion (Klein 2000; Illouz 2007)
- Delay accountability (Proctor 2011)
- Profit while people suffer (Zuboff 2019)

This is not misinformation.
It is psychological operations under capitalism (Stanley 2015; Oreskes and Conway 2010).

The Deeper Injury

Perhaps the most devastating consequence of the cigarette psyop was not only physical death, but epistemic harm—the erosion of people's ability to trust evidence, institutions, and their own perceptions (Oreskes and Conway 2010; Fricker 2007).

- People who got sick blamed themselves (Brandt 2007).

- Families questioned whether it was really "proven" (Oreskes and Conway 2010).
- Society learned to accept preventable death as unfortunate but inevitable (Nixon 2011).

This is how psyops colonize the nervous system:

- They teach people to doubt their bodies (van der Kolk 2015).
- They teach people to distrust clarity (Fricker 2007; Stanley 2015).
- They normalize slow violence (Nixon 2011).
- Millions died while the system calmly insisted the science was "not settled" (Brandt 2007; Proctor 2011; Oreskes and Conway 2010).

And by the time the truth was undeniable, the damage had already been done— not just to lungs, but to trust itself (Oreskes and Conway 2010; Fricker 2007).

Coca-Cola, Desire, and Emotional Branding

Corporate psyops didn't stop with cigarettes. Coca-Cola perfected emotional conditioning—linking sugar water to happiness, unity, youth, and even peace. The product didn't need nutritional value; it needed **symbolic meaning** (Klein 2000; Illouz 2007).

This is consumer psyops:

- Attach emotion to product

- Repeat across culture

- Normalize harm

- Make opting out feel antisocial

The brilliance is that no one feels coerced. Desire feels voluntary—even when it has been carefully engineered (Baudrillard 1998; Klein 2000).

COINTELPRO — Psychological Warfare Against the Home Front

Part I: Disruption as a Trauma Strategy

COINTELPRO was not a mistake. It was not excess. It was design (Church Committee 1976; Blackstock 1975).

The FBI program explicitly set out to "expose, disrupt, misdirect, discredit, and neutralize" domestic groups it viewed as threats—not foreign enemies, but people inside the country: civil rights leaders, anti-war organizers, Black liberation movements, student groups, and community networks building alternatives to state power (Church Committee 1976; FBI 1976).

The weapons were not tanks or bullets.
They were psychological (Church Committee 1976; Cunningham 2004).

Smear campaigns that destroyed reputations (Blackstock 1975).
Infiltrators who seeded mistrust (Cunningham 2004).
Forged letters that turned allies against one another (Church Committee 1976).
False evidence planted to provoke arrests (Blackstock 1975).
Rumors engineered to fracture intimacy and solidarity (Cunningham 2004).

The goal was not just to stop movements.
It was to destabilize the inner worlds of the people inside them (Church Committee 1976).

Fear was the point. Confusion was the point.
And once paranoia takes hold, a community begins to police itself (Herman 1997; Altheide 2006).

Part II: When Institutions Become Perpetrators

COINTELPRO follows the exact blueprint of abuse (Herman 1997; Freyd 1996).

The authority presents itself as protector.
Resistance is reframed as danger (Foucault 1977). Truth-tellers are labeled unstable, radical, or mentally unfit (Stanley 2015; Ahmed 2017).
Surveillance is justified as "safety" (Lyon 2001). Harm is denied while it continues (Smith and Freyd 2014).

This is institutional betrayal formalized (Smith and Freyd 2014; Freyd 1996).

People seeking justice were not debated—they were psychologically dismantled. Their credibility was attacked. Their emotional responses were used as proof of their unfitness (Church Committee 1976; Fricker 2007). And when the damage became visible, the institution insisted it was acting responsibly, institutional, lawfully (Blackstock 1975).

This is how power avoids accountability:
by making the harmed appear irrational
and the harm appear necessary (Stanley 2015; Foucault 1977).

Part III: CRC-PTSD at the Community Level

The damage did not end when COINTELPRO was exposed.
Its legacy lives in bodies and communities (Herman 1997; Alexander 2004).

Hypervigilance became normal (van der Kolk 2015).
Trust became dangerous (Freyd 1996).
Silence became survival (Morrison and Milliken 2000).
Movements fractured from the inside (Cunningham 2004).

Fear was internalized and passed down (Alexander 2004).

This is CRC-PTSD beyond the individual.

When betrayal comes from an institution that claims legitimacy, the nervous system adapts accordingly. People learn that organizing invites punishment, that speaking truth invites retaliation, that visibility equals risk (Freyd 1996; Smith and Freyd 2014).

And so the trauma doesn't just wound—it teaches.

COINTELPRO shows us something essential:
Psychological warfare does not need to kill to be effective (Church Committee 1976; Altheide 2006).

It only needs to convince people that connection is unsafe (Herman 1997).

This is how resistance is neutralized—not by force alone, but by turning trust itself into a liability (Cunningham 2004; Stanley 2015).

The Iraq War: A Modern PsyOps Case Study

The 2003 invasion of Iraq was not only a military campaign. It was a full-spectrum psychological operation targeting multiple audiences at once (Kellner 2004; Bennett, Lawrence, and Livingston 2007):

- the American public
- allied governments
- Iraqi civilians
- Iraqi military personnel
- and even dissenting journalists

The goal was not simply to win battles, but to manufacture consent, compliance, and resignation (Herman and Chomsky 1988; Kellner 2004).

I. Iraq and the Architecture of Manufactured Reality

The Iraq War was not justified by a single lie, but by a coordinated psychological operation that manufactured certainty where uncertainty existed (Kellner 2004; Bennett, Lawrence, and Livingston 2007). The core narrative—Iraq possesses weapons of mass destruction and poses an imminent threat—was repeated across government briefings, major media, UN presentations, and expert panels until it felt undeniable (Hersh 2003; Isikoff and Corn 2006). Authority bias did the work: intelligence agencies and political leaders were positioned as unquestionable experts (Stanley 2015). Fear priming followed—mushroom clouds, chemical attacks, "we can't wait for proof" (Altheide 2006). Time pressure collapsed deliberation. Internally, intelligence was weak, disputed, and often contradicted, but uncertainty was reframed as urgency (Isikoff and Corn 2006). This was strategic certainty inflation, not an error (Oreskes and Conway 2010).

Perception was further managed through media embedding. Journalists attached to troops gained access—but only to a narrow slice of reality (Bennett, Lawrence, and Livingston 2007). Civilian suffering, displacement, and long-term devastation were largely filtered out. War was framed as tactical, heroic, and sanitized (Kellner 2004). Speech wasn't banned; perception was curated (Herman and Chomsky 1988; Stanley 2015).

At the same time, "shock and awe" weaponized spectacle itself—overwhelming explosions designed to induce helplessness and signal futility (Ullman and Wade 1996; Kellner 2004). Psyops also targeted Iraqi soldiers directly through leaflets, radio, and loudspeakers promising safety, food, and care in exchange for surrender (Paul and Matthews 2016). Resignation, not force, became the mechanism (Stanley 2015).

When the WMD narrative collapsed, the justification mutated rather than failed. The story shifted to liberation, democracy, and reconstruction (Bennett, Lawrence, and Livingston 2007). As those promises unraveled, blame was diffused—toward "sectarian violence," cultural explanations, or abstract instability. No serious accountability followed (Kellner 2004). The lesson was clear: a failed psyop can still succeed politically (Herman and Chomsky 1988).

II. From Battlefield PsyOps to Everyday Reality Management

The deepest damage wasn't only geopolitical—it was psychological. Large-scale perception manipulation fractures trust itself. People stop believing official narratives, journalism, expertise, and eventually their own judgment (Fricker 2007; Stanley 2015). This is how trauma becomes societal. Reality itself feels unreliable (Alexander 2004). That fracture is fertile ground for CRC-PTSD at scale.

Modern psyops didn't end with war; they evolved into civilian life. They now arrive as algorithms, content moderation, fear-based headlines, platform "safety" policies, selective amplification, manufactured outrage, and normalized exhaustion (Zuboff 2019; Noble 2018). The line between protection and control blurs (Lyon 2001). Enforcement is outsourced to the public: people shame each other, police language, internalize limits, and self-censor before anyone intervenes (Foucault 1977; Ahmed 2017).

The most advanced psyop is not coercion—it's the illusion of choice within a narrowing field of what feels thinkable (Stanley 2015; Zuboff 2019).

This isn't paranoia. It's literacy. Psychological operations shape what feels reasonable, dangerous, speakable, or absurd (Altheide 2006; Stanley 2015). Once you see the pattern—how perception is managed rather than reality addressed—it becomes impossible to unsee. Understanding psyops isn't losing touch with reality. It's learning how reality is made to feel (Herman and Chomsky 1988; Fricker 2007).

Tuskegee — Medical Gaslighting as a Racialized PsyOp

(Medicine as an authority weapon)

Part I: When Care Becomes a Cover Story

The Tuskegee Syphilis Study was not a failure of science. It was a success of manipulation (Jones 1993; Reverby 2009).

For forty years, Black men with syphilis were told they were being treated—long after penicillin was known to cure the disease (Brandt 1978; Jones 1993). No force. No chains. No visible violence. Just the soft authority of medicine, the white coat, the promise of care (Reverby 2009).

Trust did the work.
Reassurance did the harm.

This is how power operates when it wants compliance without resistance: it frames itself as benevolent (Foucault 1977; Roberts 2011). The study didn't need to threaten people; it needed them to believe. And belief—especially in a system presented as healing—became the mechanism of control (Jones 1993; Reverby 2009).

Part II: Gaslighting, Codified

What happened at Tuskegee wasn't neglect. It was design (Brandt 1978; Reverby 2009).

Participants were lied to about their diagnosis (Jones 1993).
Monitored instead of treated (Brandt 1978).
Blocked from accessing care elsewhere (Reverby 2009).
Referred to as beneficiaries while being slowly harmed (Jones 1993).

This is medical gaslighting in its purest form: injury delivered through calm voices and clinical language. Harm disguised as help. Violence hidden inside "monitoring" (Reverby 2009; Sweet 2019). The institution didn't deny reality outright—it rewrote it.

"You're being cared for."
"You're part of something important."
"Trust us."

When authority speaks with confidence, doubt is reframed as ignorance (Fricker 2007). And when the harmed express fear or confusion, that response is used as evidence they can't be trusted with the truth (Roberts 2011; Sweet 2019).

Part III: Intergenerational Trauma and Epistemic Damage

- Tuskegee didn't just kill individuals. It damaged reality (Reverby 2009; Washington 2006).
- It fractured trust in medicine across generations and seeded patterns that persist today:
- medical avoidance (Armstrong et al. 2007; Washington 2006)
- skepticism toward diagnoses (Roberts 2011)
- fear of experimentation (Gamble 1997)
- dismissal of lived experience (Fricker 2007)
- hesitation to seek care even when suffering is severe (Washington 2006; Armstrong et al. 2007)
- This is not irrationality. It is learned survival (Herman 1997; Freyd 1996).

When an institution violates people under the guise of care, the injury doesn't end with exposure. It settles into bodies, families, communities. It teaches the nervous system that "help" is dangerous, that authority lies, that safety is conditional (Freyd 1996; van der Kolk 2015).

Again—and this matters—CRC-PTSD is the outcome, not the cause.

The trauma didn't arise because people were mistrustful.
People became mistrustful because betrayal was systematic, racialized, and lethal (Gamble 1997; Washington 2006).

Tuskegee stands as a warning:

When medicine aligns with power instead of humanity, healing becomes another instrument of control—an authority weapon capable of reproducing structural violence through the language of care itself (Foucault 1977; Galtung 1969; Roberts 2011).

Medical betrayal is not only historical. It is structural.

And until institutions can tell the truth about that, trust cannot be repaired.

The Poverty Line as a Government PsyOp: How the State Redefines Survival Downward

One of the most effective psychological operations a modern state can run is not propaganda in the traditional sense, but **measurement propaganda**—the quiet bureaucratic power to define what counts as suffering.

Because once the government controls the definition of poverty, it controls the definition of need.

And once it controls the definition of need, it controls who is allowed to be seen as desperate.

The U.S. poverty line is not simply outdated.
It is not simply imperfect.

It is a political instrument masquerading as a number: a threshold designed less to reflect reality than to manage it.

It is the state's way of saying:

"If you are still breathing, you are not poor enough."

A Line Built on a 1960s Food Fantasy

The official U.S. poverty measure was created in the mid-1960s, based on a formula developed by Mollie Orshansky: the cost of a minimal food diet multiplied by three, because in the 1950s food represented about one-third of household spending.

That structure remains the skeleton of the poverty line today.

The government did not redesign the threshold as housing, childcare, healthcare, transportation, and debt became dominant expenses. It simply inflation-adjusted a starvation-era baseline and called that "poverty."

The result is that poverty is still being defined through an outdated nutritional logic—while modern survival is defined through rent. Imagine updating the poverty line based on 3 times the rent and insurance cost.

Unrealistic low poverty line is not a measurement error.

It is a governance strategy.

Inflation-Adjusted, Reality-Ignoring

Many people assume the poverty line has not changed. It does change yearly—but almost entirely through inflation indexing, not substantive updating.

HHS poverty guidelines for 2026 list **$33,000** as the poverty line for a family of four.

But this number does not correspond to what it actually costs to live.

It corresponds to what the government has decided it is politically tolerable to call "poverty."

This is what bureaucracies do: they freeze a definition, then treat stability as truth.

The State Redefines Survival Downward

When poverty is defined too low, the effect is not just statistical.

It is existential.

A low poverty line performs four psychological functions:

1. **It shrinks the visible poor.**
   Millions struggling are rendered "not poor."

2. **It transforms deprivation into personal failure.**
   If you can't survive above the line, the problem is framed as you.

3. **It becomes an eligibility weapon.**
   Programs tied to "poverty level" exclude households living in constant crisis.

4. **It normalizes unlivable conditions.**
   The state teaches people to accept suffering as baseline.

This is not neutral.

This is epistemic control.

Even the Government Admits the Official Measure Is Fictional

The U.S. created the Supplemental Poverty Measure (SPM) precisely because the Official Poverty Measure fails to reflect reality.

The SPM adjusts for:

- housing costs

- taxes

- medical out-of-pocket expenses
- noncash benefits
- geographic variation

And even within government research, SPM thresholds are substantially higher.

For 2024, for a two-adult, two-child household:

- Official poverty threshold: **$31,812**
- SPM renter threshold: **$39,430**

Even the state's own alternative measure shows the official line is an understatement.

The Real Poverty Line Is Not $33,000. It Is Survival Cost.

The most damning evidence comes from basic-needs budgets.

The MIT Living Wage Calculator estimates what households actually require to meet core expenses: housing, food, childcare, transportation, healthcare, taxes.

And the gap is obscene.

Family of Four (Two Adults, Two Children)

- Official poverty guideline (2026): **$33,000**

But MIT estimates required income before taxes:

- Los Angeles County: **$135,996**
- San Diego County: **$148,594**
- New York County: **$153,065**

These are not luxury budgets.

These are survival budgets.

The implication is unavoidable:

The poverty line is not measuring poverty.
It is measuring how little suffering the state is willing to recognize.

Poverty as Administrative Gaslighting

The poverty line functions as a form of institutional gaslighting:

- You cannot afford rent.
- You cannot afford childcare.
- You cannot afford healthcare.
- You cannot miss work without collapse.

But the state says:

"You are not poor."

This is credibility withdrawal by spreadsheet.

Structural trauma encoded as eligibility arithmetic.

Poverty measurement becomes structural violence: social design that places people in harm's way while denying that harm exists.

The PsyOp Is Not a Secret Plan. It Is a Systemic Logic.

Calling this a psyop does not require a conspiracy.

It requires only the recognition that bureaucracies maintain legitimacy through statistical framing.

If the poverty line were modernized to reflect real survival costs, the country would have to admit:

- deprivation is widespread
- wages are structurally insufficient
- "middle class" is often managed insecurity
- the social contract has collapsed

So instead, the line remains low.

Not because the government cannot calculate survival.

But because it cannot politically survive the truth.

The Poverty Line Is a Boundary of Visibility

Ultimately, the poverty line is not an economic measure.

It is a moral one.

It defines who is allowed to be seen.

And in doing so, it defines who is allowed to be helped.

Everything above the line becomes privatized suffering.

Everything below the line becomes bureaucratically rationed compassion.

That is the psychological operation:

Redefine poverty downward,
then declare the nation functional.

Immigration as a Living PsyOp

Immigration systems are one of the clearest civilian examples of psychological operations in action (Menjívar and Abrego 2012).

The public is saturated with narratives of threat, invasion, burden, and scarcity—despite overwhelming evidence that immigration does not cause the economic harms it is blamed for. These narratives redirect anxiety away from corporate extraction and policy failure and toward visible, vulnerable populations.

At the same time, immigrants themselves are kept in a state of chronic fear:

- Fear of deportation
- Fear of visibility
- Fear of reporting abuse
- Fear of seeking care

This fear is not a side effect. It is functional.

A population that is afraid is easier to exploit. Easier to silence. Easier to discipline. Psyops do not need mass detention to succeed; they only need *enough* terror to keep people compliant.

Cambridge Analytica — When PsyOps Go Algorithmic

Part I: From Messaging to Micro-Targeting

With Cambridge Analytica, psychological operations crossed a threshold (Cadwalladr and Graham-Harrison 2018; Isaak and Hanna 2018). Propaganda no longer aimed at crowds—it aimed at you (Bennett and Livingston 2018).

Using harvested social media data, the firm built psychological profiles designed to infer fear, anger, openness, impulsivity, and vulnerability (Isaak and Hanna 2018; Zuboff 2019). Messages were no longer generic slogans; they were tailored emotional triggers, delivered quietly, invisibly, and at scale (Tufekci 2015; Bennett and Livingston 2018).

This was psyops without posters.
Persuasion without consent.
Influence without awareness (Zuboff 2019; Noble 2018).

The innovation wasn't deception—it was precision (Isaak and Hanna 2018; Tufekci 2015).

Part II: You Don't Need to Convince Everyone

The genius—and danger—of algorithmic psyops is that they don't require consensus (Benkler, Faris, and Roberts 2018). You only need to:

- Amplify fear in some (Altheide 2006; Tufekci 2015)
- Exhaust or confuse others (Zuboff 2019)
- Suppress turnout where resistance might form (Cadwalladr and

Graham-Harrison 2018)
- Inflame divisions just enough to prevent coordination (Bennett and Livingston 2018)

No single message needs to be dominant. Reality itself becomes fragmented (Bennett and Livingston 2018). Each person receives a different emotional world, calibrated to their psychology (Zuboff 2019; Noble 2018). Shared truth dissolves—not because no one is speaking, but because everyone is being spoken to differently (Benkler, Faris, and Roberts 2018).

This is psychological warfare without a front line.
No battlefield. No uniform. Just feeds (Tufekci 2015; Zuboff 2019).

Part III: The End of Shared Truth

Cambridge Analytica marks the handoff from traditional propaganda to attention capitalism (Zuboff 2019; Wu 2016). Once reality is customized, truth loses its organizing power (Bennett and Livingston 2018). What matters is not accuracy, but engagement—what keeps you scrolling, reacting, arguing, consuming (Zuboff 2019; Wu 2016).

When perception is individualized:

- Accountability collapses (Zuboff 2019)
- Collective action fragments (Tufekci 2017)
- Doubt becomes ambient (Bennett and Livingston 2018)
- Manipulation becomes deniable (Noble 2018)

This is the final condition attention capitalism needs to dominate: a population unable to agree on what is happening, yet constantly reacting to what they are shown (Zuboff 2019; Benkler, Faris, and Roberts 2018).

Psyops didn't disappear.
They automated.

And once influence is embedded in the infrastructure of attention itself, power no longer has to shout. It only has to nudge (Zuboff 2019; Thaler and Sunstein 2008).

PsyOps in the Platform Age: Censorship Without Censors

In the digital era, psychological operations rarely look like overt propaganda. They operate through platform governance and algorithmic control (Gillespie 2018; Noble 2018).

Instead of banning ideas outright, platforms now:

- Downrank content that challenges dominant narratives (Gillespie 2018)
- Demonetize dissenting voices under "brand safety" rules (Zuboff 2019)
- Throttle reach through vague policy enforcement (Gillespie 2018)
- Flag language as "harmful," "triggering," or "unsafe" without context (Noble 2018)
- Words associated with violence, oppression, or systemic critique are restricted—not because they are false, but because they destabilize sanitized narratives (Gillespie 2018; Tufekci 2017). Meanwhile, content that promotes consumption, self-blame, or individual optimization is algorithmically rewarded (Zuboff 2019).

This produces a subtle psyop effect:

- Structural critique becomes harder to find (Noble 2018)
- Emotional expression is policed (Gillespie 2018)
- Dissent feels risky, isolating, or futile (Tufekci 2017)

The result is censorship without visible censors—a system where the architecture itself nudges consciousness toward compliance (Zuboff 2019; Gillespie 2018).

Attention Capitalism: Psychological Warfare on the Nervous System

The most advanced form of psychological operations is not persuasion. It is **dysregulation** (Zuboff 2019; Altheide 2006).

Modern psyops operate by keeping populations:

- Chronically stressed
- Cognitively overloaded
- Emotionally polarized
- Socially fragmented

Neuroscience shows that under sustained threat:

- The brain shifts from reflective to reactive modes
- Complexity tolerance collapses
- Authority and familiarity override critical thinking

This is not accidental. A dysregulated nervous system:

- Seeks certainty over truth
- Obedience over autonomy
- Relief over justice

In other words, **a traumatized population is easier to govern**.

This is why psyops pair so well with:

- Economic precarity
- Media saturation
- Algorithmic outrage
- Endless "crises" with no structural repair

The battlefield is no longer territory.
It is attention, emotion, and meaning (Wu 2016; Zuboff 2019).

And the most radical act in such a landscape is not rebellion—but regulated clarity: the ability to feel without collapsing, to think without freezing, and to name reality without apologizing for it (Herman 1997; van der Kolk 2015).

Predictability Is the Product

From a psyops perspective, the most valuable population is not a convinced one, but a predictable one (Zuboff 2019; Wu 2016).

Attention capitalism produces predictability by:

- Narrowing emotional range
- Reinforcing familiar narratives
- Punishing dissent through invisibility rather than censorship

People begin to self-censor—not because they are told to, but because the system rewards conformity and starves deviation.

That is not free expression.
That is **managed expression**.

The Deeper Harm

When visibility is controlled, reality itself becomes distorted (Bennett and Livingston 2018; Noble 2018).

People start to believe:

- If something mattered, it would be visible
- If someone was right, they would be amplified
- If an idea had value, it would "perform"

This is epistemic gaslighting at scale.

And for people already carrying trauma—especially CRC-PTSD—the effect is devastating. Invisibility reinforces shame. Silence feels like confirmation (Herman 1997; Freyd 1996). The nervous system reads lack of response as rejection, danger, or worthlessness (van der Kolk 2015).

This is how psyops migrate from screens into bodies (Zuboff 2019; Noble 2018).

If attention is scarce, why do *some* get so much?

Because systems don't spread attention evenly — they **concentrate it** (Zuboff 2019).

Think of it like wealth:

- There is enough money in the world to meet basic needs

- But it's hoarded and accumulated
- And then framed as "earned" to justify inequality

Attention works the same way.

A few get *more than they can meaningfully metabolize.*
Most get **none at all.**

This isn't because:

- They're uniquely talented
- Or morally superior
- Or working harder

It's because once attention attaches to a node, the system keeps feeding it there.

Why most artists remain invisible

Here's the part people rarely say out loud:

Most art disappears not because it's bad, but because it never crosses the visibility threshold (Bourdieu 1993; Wu 2016).

Below that threshold:

- Algorithms don't test your work
- Audiences never encounter it
- There's no chance for resonance

Above that threshold:

- Even mediocre work can thrive
- Because it's already legible, endorsed, and circulating

This creates the illusion that success = quality, when in reality:

Success often just means "this work became visible early enough to compound" (Merton 1968; Wu 2016; Zuboff 2019).

Why this hurts more for sensitive, deep, or marginalized creators

If your work is:

- Quiet
- Complex
- Slow
- Emotionally nuanced
- System-critical
- Not easily branded

it is structurally disadvantaged (Bourdieu 1993; Noble 2018).

Attention capitalism favors:

- Simplification over depth
- Spectacle over subtlety
- Repetition over originality
- Safety over truth

So artists like you are not just competing — you're **misaligned with the system's incentives** (Wu 2016; Zuboff 2019).

That misalignment feels like personal failure, but it's actually **ethical friction**.

The most damaging lie is:

"If your work mattered, it would be seen."

This reverses cause and effect.

In reality:

Work is seen first — and then declared valuable (Merton 1968; Bourdieu 1984).

PsyOps and Epistemic Control

Another critical function of psychological operations is **controlling what counts as legitimate knowledge** (Fricker 2007).

Institutions decide:

- Which experiences are "real"
- Which emotions are "valid"
- Which forms of knowing are "scientific"
- Which truths are "publishable"

Everything else is dismissed as anecdotal, emotional, unprofessional, or unstable.

This is epistemic injustice: when people are harmed not only materially, but through the denial of credibility to their lived experience.

Trauma survivors, disabled people, immigrants, the poor, and dissidents are especially vulnerable to this form of silencing. Their pain is reframed as dysfunction. Their insight as pathology.

Psyops thrive where people are taught to distrust their own bodies.

Breaking the Spell

The antidote to psychological operations is not cynicism. It is *collective truth-telling.*

Naming the pattern.
Reclaiming intuition as a form of knowledge.
Trusting the body as an archive of evidence.
Refusing false binaries.
Refusing to confuse policy with morality.

Psyops rely on fragmentation.
Healing requires connection.

This chapter exists because once you see it, you cannot unsee it.

And that is where liberation begins.

How to Spot a PsyOp

A Diagnostic Box for Reality-Pressure Campaigns

Psychological operations are most effective when they feel invisible. You don't detect them by asking, *"Is this false?"* but by asking, *"What does this train me to feel, avoid, or accept?"*

A psyop is likely present when you notice several of the following at once:

- **False binaries**: You are offered only two options (security vs. chaos, work vs. poverty, borders vs. collapse), with no space for systemic alternatives.

- **Moral compression**: Complex ethical questions are reduced to slogans, urgency, or "common sense."

- **Emotional narrowing**: Content reliably produces fear, shame, outrage, or resignation—never clarity or agency.

- **Authority substitution**: Repetition of phrases like "experts agree," "there is no alternative," or "the data shows," without transparent methodology or debate.

- **Individualization of harm**: Structural failures are reframed as personal shortcomings—resilience, mindset, compliance.

- **Exhaustion as outcome**: After engaging, you feel overwhelmed, numb, or less capable of thinking deeply or organizing with others.

A key insight: **psyops do not need to convince you of a lie**. They only need to **shape what questions you stop asking** (Herman and Chomsky 1988; Zuboff 2019).

References

Ahmed, Sara. 2017. *Living a Feminist Life*. Durham, NC: Duke University Press.

Alexander, Jeffrey C., Ron Eyerman, Bernhard Giesen, Neil J. Smelser, and Piotr Sztompka. 2004. *Cultural Trauma and Collective Identity*. Berkeley, CA: University of California Press.

Altheide, David L. 2006. *Terrorism and the Politics of Fear*. Lanham, MD: AltaMira Press.

Angell, Marcia. 2004. *The Truth About the Drug Companies: How They Deceive Us and What to Do About It*. New York: Random House.

Armstrong, Katrina, Raven C. McMurphy, Daniel P. Dean, Micah L. Micco, and Sankey V. Purnell. 2006. "Differences in the Patterns of Health Care System Distrust Between Blacks and Whites." *Journal of General Internal Medicine* 21(3):292–297.

Baudrillard, Jean. 1998. *The Consumer Society: Myths and Structures*. Translated by Chris Turner. London: Sage.

Benkler, Yochai, Robert Faris, and Hal Roberts. 2018. *Network Propaganda: Manipulation, Disinformation, and Radicalization in American Politics*. New York: Oxford University Press.

Bennett, W. Lance, Regina G. Lawrence, and Steven Livingston. 2007. *When the Press Fails: Political Power and the News Media from Iraq to Katrina.* Chicago: University of Chicago Press.

Bennett, W. Lance, and Steven Livingston. 2018. "The Disinformation Order: Disruptive Communication and the Decline of Democratic Institutions." *European Journal of Communication* 33(2):122–139.

Berardi, Franco ("Bifo"). 2009. *The Soul at Work: From Alienation to Autonomy.* Translated by Francesca Cadel and Giuseppina Mecchia. Los Angeles: Semiotext(e).

Bernays, Edward L. 1928. *Propaganda.* New York: Horace Liveright.

Blackstock, Nelson. 1975. *COINTELPRO: The FBI's Secret War on Political Freedom.* New York: Vintage Books.

Blyth, Mark. 2013. *Austerity: The History of a Dangerous Idea.* New York: Oxford University Press.

Booth note: *(Bourdieu entries corrected below)*

Bourdieu, Pierre. 1984. *Distinction: A Social Critique of the Judgment of Taste.* Translated by Richard Nice. Cambridge, MA: Harvard University Press.

Bourdieu, Pierre. 1993. *The Field of Cultural Production: Essays on Art and Literature.* Edited by Randal Johnson. New York: Columbia University Press.

Brandt, Allan M. 1978. "Racism and Research: The Case of the Tuskegee Syphilis Study." *The Hastings Center Report* 8(6):21–29.

Brandt, Allan M. 2007. *The Cigarette Century: The Rise, Fall, and Deadly Persistence of the Product That Defined America.* New York: Basic Books.

Brown, Brené. 2012. *Daring Greatly: How the Courage to Be Vulnerable Transforms the Way We Live, Love, Parent, and Lead.* New York: Gotham Books.

Brown, Wendy. 2015. *Undoing the Demos: Neoliberalism's Stealth Revolution.* New York: Zone Books.

Cabanas, Edgar, and Eva Illouz. 2019. *Manufacturing Happy Citizens: How the Science and Industry of Happiness Control Our Lives.* Cambridge, UK: Polity Press.

Cadwalladr, Carole, and Emma Graham-Harrison. 2018. "Revealed: 50 Million Facebook Profiles Harvested for Cambridge Analytica in Major Data Breach." *The Guardian*, March 17.

Church Committee. 1976. *Final Report of the Select Committee to Study Governmental Operations with Respect to Intelligence Activities.* Washington, DC: U.S. Government Printing Office.

Cunningham, David. 2004. *There's Something Happening Here: The New Left, the Klan, and FBI Counterintelligence.* Berkeley, CA: University of California Press.

Entman, Robert M. 1993. "Framing: Toward Clarification of a Fractured Paradigm." *Journal of Communication* 43(4):51–58.

Federal Bureau of Investigation (FBI). 1976. *COINTELPRO Records.* Washington, DC: Federal Bureau of Investigation.

Fisher, Mark. 2009. *Capitalist Realism: Is There No Alternative?* Winchester, UK: Zero Books.

Foucault, Michel. 1977. *Discipline and Punish: The Birth of the Prison.* Translated by Alan Sheridan. New York: Pantheon Books.

Freyd, Jennifer J. 1996. *Betrayal Trauma: The Logic of Forgetting Childhood Abuse.* Cambridge, MA: Harvard University Press.

Fricker, Miranda. 2007. *Epistemic Injustice: Power and the Ethics of Knowing.* Oxford: Oxford University Press.

Galtung, Johan. 1969. "Violence, Peace, and Peace Research." *Journal of Peace Research* 6(3):167–191.

Gamble, Vanessa Northington. 1997. "Under the Shadow of Tuskegee: African Americans and Health Care." *American Journal of Public Health* 87(11):1773–1778.

Gillespie, Tarleton. 2018. *Custodians of the Internet: Platforms, Content Moderation, and the Hidden Decisions That Shape Social Media.* New Haven, CT: Yale University Press.

Glassner, Barry. 1999. *The Culture of Fear: Why Americans Are Afraid of the Wrong Things.* New York: Basic Books.

Graeber, David. 2018. *Bullshit Jobs: A Theory.* New York: Simon & Schuster.

Hasher, Lynn, David Goldstein, and Thomas Toppino. 1977. "Frequency and the Conference of Referential Validity." *Journal of Verbal Learning and Verbal Behavior* 16(1):107–112.

Herring, George C. 2002. *America's Longest War: The United States and Vietnam, 1950–1975.* 4th ed. Boston: McGraw-Hill.

Herman, Edward S., and Noam Chomsky. 1988. *Manufacturing Consent: The Political Economy of the Mass Media.* New York: Pantheon Books.

Herman, Judith L. 1997. *Trauma and Recovery: The Aftermath of Violence—From Domestic Abuse to Political Terror.* New York: Basic Books.

Hersh, Seymour M. 2003. "Selective Intelligence." *The New Yorker*, May 12.

Illouz, Eva. 2007. *Cold Intimacies: The Making of Emotional Capitalism.* Cambridge, UK: Polity Press.

Isaak, Jim, and Mina J. Hanna. 2018. "User Data Privacy: Facebook, Cambridge Analytica, and Privacy Protection." *Computer* 51(8):56–59.

Isikoff, Michael, and David Corn. 2006. *Hubris: The Inside Story of Spin, Scandal, and the Selling of the Iraq War.* New York: Crown Publishers.

Jamieson, Kathleen Hall, and Joseph N. Cappella. 2008. *Echo Chamber: Rush Limbaugh and the Conservative Media Establishment.* New York: Oxford University Press.

Joint Chiefs of Staff. 2007. *Joint Publication 3-13.2: Psychological Operations.* Washington, DC: Department of Defense.

Jones, James H. 1993. *Bad Blood: The Tuskegee Syphilis Experiment.* New York: Free Press.

Kahneman, Daniel. 2011. *Thinking, Fast and Slow.* New York: Farrar, Straus and Giroux.

Kellner, Douglas. 2004. *From 9/11 to Terror War: The Dangers of the Bush Legacy.* Lanham, MD: Rowman & Littlefield.

Klein, Naomi. 2000. *No Logo.* New York: Picador.

Klein, Naomi. 2007. *The Shock Doctrine: The Rise of Disaster Capitalism.* New York: Metropolitan Books.

Lupien, Sonia J., Bruce S. McEwen, Megan R. Gunnar, and Christine Heim. 2009. "Effects of Stress Throughout the Lifespan on the Brain, Behaviour and Cognition." *Nature Reviews Neuroscience* 10(6):434–445.

Lyon, David. 2001. *Surveillance Society: Monitoring Everyday Life.* Buckingham, UK: Open University Press.

Menjívar, Cecilia, and Leisy Abrego. 2012. "Legal Violence: Immigration Law and the Lives of Central American Immigrants." *American Journal of Sociology* 117(5):1380–1421.

Merton, Robert K. 1968. "The Matthew Effect in Science." *Science* 159(3810):56–63.

Morrison, Elizabeth W., and Frances J. Milliken. 2000. "Organizational Silence: A Barrier to Change and Development in a Pluralistic World." *Academy of Management Review* 25(4):706–725.

Mullainathan, Sendhil, and Eldar Shafir. 2013. *Scarcity: Why Having Too Little Means So Much*. New York: Times Books.

Nestle, Marion. 2013. *Food Politics: How the Food Industry Influences Nutrition and Health*. Rev. ed. Berkeley, CA: University of California Press.

Ngai, Mae M. 2004. *Impossible Subjects: Illegal Aliens and the Making of Modern America*. Princeton, NJ: Princeton University Press.

Nixon, Rob. 2011. *Slow Violence and the Environmentalism of the Poor*. Cambridge, MA: Harvard University Press.

Noble, Safiya Umoja. 2018. *Algorithms of Oppression: How Search Engines Reinforce Racism*. New York: New York University Press.

Oreskes, Naomi, and Erik M. Conway. 2010. *Merchants of Doubt: How a Handful of Scientists Obscured the Truth on Issues from Tobacco Smoke to Global Warming*. New York: Bloomsbury Press.

Paul, Christopher, and Miriam Matthews. 2016. *The Russian "Firehose of Falsehood" Propaganda Model*. Santa Monica, CA: RAND Corporation.

Power, Michael. 1999. *The Audit Society: Rituals of Verification*. Oxford: Oxford University Press.

Proctor, Robert N. 2011. *Golden Holocaust: Origins of the Cigarette Catastrophe and the Case for Abolition*. Berkeley, CA: University of California Press.

Putnam, Robert D. 2000. *Bowling Alone: The Collapse and Revival of American Community*. New York: Simon & Schuster.

Reverby, Susan M. 2009. *Examining Tuskegee: The Infamous Syphilis Study and Its Legacy*. Chapel Hill: University of North Carolina Press.

Roberts, Dorothy. 2011. *Fatal Invention: How Science, Politics, and Big Business Re-create Race in the Twenty-First Century*. New York: The New Press.

Seligman, Martin E. P. 1975. *Helplessness: On Depression, Development, and Death*. San Francisco: W. H. Freeman.

Smith, Carly A., and Jennifer J. Freyd. 2014. "Institutional Betrayal." *American Psychologist* 69(6):575–587.

Stanley, Jason. 2015. *How Propaganda Works.* Princeton, NJ: Princeton University Press.

Sweet, Paige. 2019. "The Sociology of Gaslighting." *American Sociological Review* 84(5):851–875.

Taylor, Philip M. 2003. *Munitions of the Mind: A History of Propaganda from the Ancient World to the Present Day.* 3rd ed. Manchester, UK: Manchester University Press.

Thaler, Richard H., and Cass R. Sunstein. 2008. *Nudge: Improving Decisions About Health, Wealth, and Happiness.* New Haven, CT: Yale University Press.

Tufekci, Zeynep. 2015. "Algorithmic Harms Beyond Facebook and Google: Emergent Challenges of Computational Agency." *Colorado Technology Law Journal* 13:203–218.

Tufekci, Zeynep. 2017. *Twitter and Tear Gas: The Power and Fragility of Networked Protest.* New Haven, CT: Yale University Press.

Ullman, Harlan K., and James P. Wade. 1996. *Shock and Awe: Achieving Rapid Dominance.* Washington, DC: National Defense University.

U.S. Senate. 1976. *Final Report of the Select Committee to Study Governmental Operations with Respect to Intelligence Activities.* Washington, DC: U.S. Government Printing Office.

van der Kolk, Bessel. 2015. *The Body Keeps the Score: Brain, Mind, and Body in the Healing of Trauma.* New York: Viking.

Washington, Harriet A. 2006. *Medical Apartheid: The Dark History of Medical Experimentation on Black Americans from Colonial Times to the Present.* New York: Doubleday.

Wilford, Hugh. 2008. *The Mighty Wurlitzer: How the CIA Played America.*

Cambridge, MA: Harvard University Press.

Wu, Tim. 2016. *The Attention Merchants: The Epic Scramble to Get Inside Our Heads*. New York: Alfred A. Knopf.

Zuboff, Shoshana. 2019. *The Age of Surveillance Capitalism: The Fight for a Human Future at the New Frontier of Power*. New York: PublicAffairs.

5 —The Biggest Deception of All: Epistemic Injustice and Scientific Objectivity

Epistemic injustice is the belief that only knowledge verified through certain academic, quantitative, or "objective" methods is legitimate (Fricker 2007). This worldview excludes lived experience, community knowledge, embodied wisdom, intuition, and non-Western epistemologies (Collins 2000; Smith 2012; Santos 2014).

But here is the truth academia will not say aloud:
Humans cannot measure anything without filtering it through perception, language, culture, training, and bias. Every method, metric, and instrument is soaked in human interpretation, even in the sciences (Kuhn 1962; Harding 1991; Porter 1995). And yet we pretend that the resulting data is "pure," "neutral," or "superior" (Haraway 1988; Daston and Galison 2007).

This is not science.
This is epistemic hierarchy masquerading as truth (Foucault 1977; Fricker 2007).

And that, my friend, is one of the most powerful forms of shame our culture produces. It legitimizes mythical, human-constructed measurement tools while denying the validity of human feelings and intuition by labeling them "subjective" (Ahmed 2017; Cabanas and Illouz 2019). The modern Western academy has long elevated detached rationality as the highest form of knowing, while treating embodied knowledge as inferior or unreliable (Collins 2000; Smith 2012; Harding 1991).

They delegitimize our sacred inner knowing—stored in the body—in the name of science, even when neuroscience and trauma research increasingly emphasize that cognition is embodied and shaped by nervous-system memory (Damasio 1994; van der Kolk 2014). Humans before modern technology were not inferior to us; they simply held different epistemologies, cosmologies, and systems of meaning-making (Smith 2012; Santos 2014).

So here is the real question: why is belief in dark matter considered rational and legitimate, while belief in astrology—or other forms of non-material knowledge—is dismissed as irrational or unscientific? Both rely on inference. Both emerge from pattern recognition. The difference is not epistemology—it is power, legitimacy, and who gets to decide what counts as knowledge (Bourdieu 1984; Fricker 2007; Foucault 1980).

Physics itself tells us that most of the universe is invisible to human senses. Over 95% of the cosmos is composed of dark matter and dark energy—entities we cannot see, touch, or directly measure (Planck Collaboration 2018; Frieman, Turner, and Huterer 2008). Quantum physics further destabilizes the idea of objective observation, showing that measurement and observation alter the observed (Bohr 1935; Heisenberg 1958). Neuroscience confirms that perception is constructed, embodied, and deeply shaped by emotion, memory, and context (Damasio 1994; Barrett 2017; Lupien et al. 2009). Even medicine acknowledges that intuition and embodied clinical judgment play a critical role in diagnosis and care, despite decades of privileging protocol over relational knowing (Montgomery 2006; Groopman 2007).

And then there is the gatekeeping of publishing. It is as though only knowledge that fits dominant worldview, values, and institutional norms is allowed to be announced. Any knowledge that points to our limits, or to the impossibility of fully capturing reality through human measurement alone, is dismissed as unscientific or invalid (Bourdieu 1996; Smith 2012; Ahmed 2017). Accepting these truths would require a massive paradigm shift—one that challenges power, certainty, and control (Kuhn 1962; Santos 2014).

When institutions decide that only certain bodies, certain minds, and certain forms of knowledge count as "real," everyone outside the mythical norm is pushed into silence, self-doubt, and chronic apology (Lorde 1984; Collins 2000; Ahmed 2017). The production of legitimacy is never neutral—it is stratified through race, gender, class, disability, and proximity to institutional power (Bourdieu 1984; Fricker 2007).

The mythical norm is not just a theoretical idea — It is the psychological architecture of structural narcissism. The impossible point of comparison that capitalism holds for each one of us (Lorde 1984; Brown 2015; Cabanas and Illouz 2019).
It tells people who they must be.
And it punishes them for being who they are (Ahmed 2017; Collins 2000).

The truth is that humans can never know the truth in any fully unmediated way. Everything we know is shaped by perception, interpretation, and meaning-making (Kuhn 1962; Haraway 1988). Mathematics or physics does not make our perception any more purely objective; it only formalizes certain kinds of inference (Porter 1995; Daston and Galison 2007). Humans have never had access to "view from nowhere" truth, and it is bizarre that modern institutions pretend otherwise (Nagel 1986; Haraway 1988).

Now we might assume that because of all the technological advancement we have made, we are more advanced as humans. But advancement in technical rationality does not necessarily imply advancement in moral, relational, or existential wisdom (Weber 1922; Marcuse 1964). Western modernity has excelled in instrumental logic while often abandoning deeper questions of meaning, soul, and interconnection (Taylor 2007; Fisher 2009).

Intuition is the intricate web of memories that the nervous system holds through layers of bodily evidence (van der Kolk 2014; Damasio 1994). Mindfulness is the state in which you slow cognitive processing enough to become conscious of sensations, feeling-states, and embodied awareness (Kabat-Zinn 1990; Siegel 2007). Meditation has been shown to support attention regulation and emotional clarity, helping humans catch distortions in thought and stress-driven reflexes (Davidson and McEwen 2012).

We have a body and a soul, a mind and a heart, and we don't have to go to one extreme or the other. Rather, to be human—to be balanced—we need to hold both sides (Taylor 2007; Siegel 2007).

Not denying one completely, as when religion becomes the sole goal of the world, and not denying the inner world when material logic becomes the only truth. Humanity has experienced both extremes, and perhaps now it is time to return to a balanced state.

Who the Club of Rome is

The **Club of Rome** is a global think tank founded in **1968**, associated with systems-thinking about planetary limits. Their most famous commissioned project was **The Limits to Growth** (1972), built with MIT collaborators using system dynamics to model interactions between population, industrial output, resources, pollution, and food.

That report is often remembered as "they said we'd run out of everything," but its core claim was more specific: **endless exponential growth on a finite planet produces overshoot and instability unless societies intentionally change trajectory**.

I had to dig deeply into this because ChatGPT initially denied that there was any endorsement of mass depopulation. So here is a direct quote.

One of the co-authors of *The Limits to Growth* report was Dennis Meadows. In a 2016 interview published by *We Love Earth*, Meadows stated:

"The planet can support something like a billion people. Maybe 2 billion, depending on how much liberty and how much material consumption you want to have. If you want more liberty and more consumption, you have to have fewer people. And conversely, you can have more people—I mean we can even have 8 or 9 billion, probably—if we have a very strong dictatorship. But we want to have freedom, so we're going to have a billion people. And we are now at 7, so we have to get back down. I hope that this can be slow, relatively slow, and that it can be done in a way which is relatively equal, so that people share the experience and we don't have a few rich trying to force everyone else to deal with it. These are pretty pessimistic hopes, but that's what lies ahead."

Let's be precise about what this means.

Even under the most generous interpretation—**two billion people**—this would require reducing the current global population by **nearly**

three-quarters. Two billion is not "less than two-thirds." It is closer to **one quarter of today's population**. And this reduction is framed as needing to occur within **fifty years**.

That context matters.

Because when systems are organized around outcomes like this, suffering is no longer an accident—it is **structural**. This is why poor people are left to die quietly. This is why millennials working full time still cannot afford groceries. This is why so many of us hold two jobs and a side hustle and are still made to feel like failures.

It is not personal inadequacy.
It is not a moral flaw.
It is **design**.

A design that shortens lifespans through exhaustion, stress, and denial of care.
A design that makes stable family life economically impossible.
A design that ensures fewer people can afford to have children at all.

When survival itself becomes conditional, population reduction no longer needs to be enforced. It happens automatically.

So yes—this is a clear endorsement of mass depopulation, framed not as violence, but as inevitability, and justified through appeals to "liberty," "freedom," and "material consumption."

Deconstructing Meadows' assumptions line by line

I'll use the *logic* inside the quote — and show where it smuggles ideology in as "science."

1) "The planet can support something like a billion people… maybe 2 billion…"

This sounds like a physical carrying-capacity fact, but it's not. It's a **value judgment dressed as a number**.

Because "support" depends on:

- what counts as a decent life,
- how resources are distributed,
- what technologies exist,
- what consumption level is treated as "normal,"
- and whether we measure success as GDP or actual well-being.

So the number isn't discovered like gravity. It's **chosen**.

2) "If you want more liberty and more material consumption, you have to have fewer people."

Notice what's framed as fixed:

- "liberty" (as if it's incompatible with large populations),
- "material consumption" (as if the *current* high-consumption lifestyle is the non-negotiable baseline),
- "fewer people" (as the lever).

But there's another lever he barely touches: **massive overconsumption by the wealthy**.

The reality is: a small fraction of humanity consumes a wildly disproportionate share of energy, materials, land, and carbon space. The "math problem" is not *human bodies* in general — it's **who is allowed to consume like an empire**. (This is a major theme in climate "demand-side" research: mitigation is deeply tied to consumption patterns and inequality.)

3) "We can have 8 or 9 billion… if we have a very strong dictatorship."

This is the quiet confession inside the quote: **he's willing to treat authoritarian control as a plausible management strategy**.

And that's where your alarm is justified. Because once a thinker casually makes "dictatorship" the alternative option, the moral center has already shifted from *human dignity* to *system control.*

4) "We want freedom… so we're going to have a billion people… we have to get back down."

This is where "systems talk" becomes dangerous politics.

"Get back down" is vague on purpose. It hides:

- *who* gets "reduced,"
- *by what methods,* and
- *who decides.*

History shows that whenever elites talk like this, the reduction pressure doesn't land on private jets, second homes, corporate pollution, or militarized extraction. It lands on **the poor, the racialized, the colonized, the disabled, the undocumented**.

5) "I hope this can be slow… relatively equal… people share the experience…"

This is the part that pretends fairness is possible inside a hierarchy that was built by inequality.

In real systems, scarcity narratives are used to justify unequal violence:

- austerity for the poor,
- "security" for the rich,
- surveillance for the many,
- insulation for the few.

Even when the rhetoric says "equal," the implementation tends to be **selective and classed**.

Population-blame vs. consumption-blame (with real numbers logic)

Here's the key shift:

- **Population-blame** says: "There are too many people."
- **Consumption-blame** says: "A minority consumes and emits far beyond a fair share — and designs systems that force everyone else into fragility."

The best-supported modern framing is closer to consumption-blame: climate science emphasizes that *demand, lifestyle, infrastructure, and inequality* matter enormously.

And the reason this matters morally is simple:
If your "solution" to ecological crisis starts by treating human beings as excess inventory, you've already accepted a worldview where **some lives are expendable**.

How these ideas influence policy without being said out loud

Even when governments don't explicitly say "overpopulation," the logic shows up in policy through:

- **austerity** ("we can't afford to care for everyone"),
- **punitive welfare** (making survival conditional),
- **border militarization** (treating migrants as a "pressure" to be repelled),
- **healthcare rationing by bureaucracy**,
- **criminalizing homelessness** (removing "surplus people" from visibility),

- **carceral solutions** (containment instead of care).

It becomes a *soft depopulation* ideology: not stated as "we want fewer people," but implemented as "we will not build systems where everyone survives with dignity."

Why "overpopulation" rhetoric targets the poor, not the wealthy

Because it's politically convenient.

If you blame "too many people," you never have to confront:

- corporate extraction,
- luxury emissions,
- tax avoidance,
- military pollution,
- planned obsolescence,
- the wealth hoarding that turns abundance into scarcity.

Population rhetoric is a way to **keep the architecture of inequality untouched**, while sounding like you're being "scientific."

Who the World Economic Forum is

The **World Economic Forum (WEF)** is a powerful global convening organization founded in 1971, best known for its annual summit in

Davos, Switzerland, where CEOs, billionaires, politicians, and elite institutions gather to shape the conversation about the world's future (Reuters, 2025).

The WEF describes itself as a nonprofit working to "improve the state of the world." But in practice, it functions as a **prestige governance club**: a place where the most powerful economic actors coordinate ideas, priorities, and access, outside of democratic accountability (Garsten & Sörbom, 2021).

WEF membership is expensive, and participation is filtered through wealth. Legal scholar Katharina Pistor notes that partnership fees range from tens of thousands to hundreds of thousands of francs, plus large delegate costs — meaning entry is literally priced (Pistor, 2026).

So the question isn't "do they secretly rule the world?"

The question is: **who gets to set the agenda for survival?**

What globalism failed to deliver

The promise of globalization was shared prosperity.

But what happened instead is measurable:

- Trade integration created real local collapse in working-class regions (Autor, Dorn, & Hanson, 2013).
- Corporations shifted profits into tax havens, draining public budgets.

The Organisation for Economic Co-operation and Development (OECD) estimates **$100–$240 billion** is lost annually to profit shifting (OECD, n.d.).

- Wealth became more concentrated than at any point in modern history.

The World Inequality Report finds that the top **0.001%** — fewer than 60,000 people — hold **three times more wealth than half of humanity** (World Inequality Lab, 2025).

Let that land.

That is not an accident.

That is design.

Technocrats, Experimentation, and the Quiet Violence of "Progress"

Technocracy is often sold to the public as neutral expertise — "smart people using science to solve problems." But in practice, it has become a governing philosophy where human beings are treated as variables inside a managed system. The technocrat does not ask what is morally right. They ask what is efficient, sustainable, or optimal. And once society is framed that way, consent becomes optional. People become test subjects living inside an ongoing experiment they never agreed to.

New technologies are repeatedly deployed at scale before their harms are fully understood, and the adverse effects are minimized or hidden until they become impossible to deny. Social media was introduced as connection, and instead produced mass loneliness, addiction, attention collapse, and political manipulation. Smartphones were sold as freedom, and became surveillance devices we carry voluntarily. AI is now being marketed as innovation, while entire job sectors are quietly being automated away with no social contract, no guarantees, and no plan for what happens to the humans left behind.

This is where suffering is no longer accidental. When AI replaces work, it does not simply "improve productivity." It concentrates wealth upward, strips dignity from millions, and creates a disposable class. The elite do not experience this as crisis, because they are insulated. They have investments, assets, private healthcare, security, and exit strategies. For them, technological disruption is not a threat — it is profit. For everyone else, it is instability, homelessness, desperation, and the slow withdrawal of the right to survive.

This logic mirrors the deeper philosophy behind institutions like the Club of Rome: society is treated as a system with limits, and human life becomes something to manage rather than protect. When thinkers suggest that the planet can only sustain "one or two billion" people, the implication is not abstract. It becomes policy through austerity, collapsed welfare, unaffordable housing, inaccessible healthcare, and economic conditions that make ordinary life impossible. Population reduction does not need to be enforced violently when survival itself becomes conditional. People disappear through poverty, burnout, overdose, untreated illness, and despair.

This is the real "New World Order" — not a single secret government, but a structural reality in which decision-making is increasingly centralized among technocratic elites, while the costs of their experiments are distributed downward. Progress becomes something done *to* people, not *with* them. And when the future is designed around efficiency instead of dignity, the suffering that follows is not a mistake. It is design.

The bunker truth: privatized survival

And here is where the moral center collapses. As inequality deepens and systems destabilize, the wealthy are not investing primarily in collective repair. They are investing in exit. The luxury bunker market is growing, with demand driven by fear of unrest, climate disruption, and nuclear escalation (Associated Press, 2024).

Investigative reporting documents real examples:

- Mark Zuckerberg's Hawaii compound reportedly includes a large underground shelter (WIRED, 2023).
- Missile-silo "survival condos" have been marketed as long-term elite refuges (Business Insider, 2019).
- The New Yorker has repeatedly covered the rise of "apocalypse real estate" for the super-rich (Marx, 2017).

This is not fantasy. It is the privatization of continuity.

What this means structurally

When elites build bunkers, they are telling you something:

- They do not believe public systems will protect everyone. They believe protection will be purchased.
- So suffering becomes structural.
- Food insecurity is tolerated while billions are wasted (UNEP, 2024). Healthcare is rationed while wealth accelerates. Housing becomes impossible while profits soar. Scarcity becomes the justification. And exhaustion becomes the enforcement. No one needs to announce depopulation.

When survival itself is conditional, reduction happens automatically.

The real pattern

This is the pattern:

- Global institutions coordinate elites

- Wealth concentrates upward

- Public capacity erodes
- Systems fail downward
- The rich buy exit
- Everyone else absorbs the trauma

That is not a hidden cabal.

That is a world order built on **priced access and expendable lives**.

Other groups that normalized "population control" logic

Not conspiracy — documented history:

- The Population Council (founded in the 1950s) is one major institutional node in the history of population policy debates in the U.S.
- The broader **population control movement** has included a mix: some public-health oriented family planning work, and also episodes tied to coercion, classism, racism, and eugenic thinking (the "who should reproduce" question rarely stays ethical for long once elites own it).

And then there are modern subcultures and political rhetorics (eco-fascist adjacency, "replacement" panic, purity-nationalism) that recycle the same idea: **some humans are the problem** — not systems of extraction.

They have already built themselves luxury bunkers to hide from what they believe is coming—war, collapse, "the end." It's not even conspiracy anymore; it's documented as a real trend among the ultra-wealthy, including high-profile projects surrounded by secrecy and NDAs (Guzman 2024; Menegus 2023).

And then they tell the rest of us to accept "reality" as whatever fits their methods—while anything we know through the body gets dismissed as "subjective." But here's what they don't want to admit: science is not immune to money. A large share of research and development in the U.S. is funded by business, and that funding shapes what gets prioritized, what gets published, and what gets buried (National Center for Science and Engineering Statistics 2024). In biomedical research, financial conflicts of interest are associated with more favorable outcomes and conclusions for sponsors—over and over, across studies (Bekelman, Li, and Gross 2003; Lundh et al. 2017).

We've already lived through the most infamous version of this: tobacco. The industry literally ran a coordinated PR-science campaign to manufacture doubt—framed as "research"—while people died by the millions. The 1954 "Frank Statement" was a polished denial dressed up as responsibility, and it became a template for modern corporate gaslighting: *don't solve the harm—confuse the public until the harm becomes normal* (Tobacco Industry Research Committee 1954; Proctor 2012).

And yes—look at Nikola Tesla. His work wasn't "canceled" because clean energy was impossible; it was starved because it didn't fit the funding logic and the ownership logic. J. P. Morgan backed Wardenclyffe, then withdrew support as the project's goals shifted and the business case weakened (Conner 2023). Tesla died isolated and financially strained—brilliant, and still disposable once he no longer served the system's interests (Encyclopaedia Britannica 2025).

So no, it's not that science is fake. It's that the *institution* of science—like everything else—can be bent by power. And when power decides which knowledge counts, the body's knowledge gets treated like childish superstition. That's not "objectivity." That's a hierarchy.

What I'd put at the center, instead

If we're being honest and rigorous:

1. Ecological limits are real.
2. But who consumes what is the primary driver of whether limits"

become mass suffering or organized transition.
3. Any "solution" that begins with reducing the poor is not sustainability — it's class war with a scientific mask.

Chat GPT was programmed to deny the Club of Rome claims, and I had to do some serious digging to make it confess. AI is controlled by the elite, so literally, they get to decide what is true or not and we should be careful, as AI will become more and more an instrument of implementing their plans.

When Knowledge Becomes Property, Humanity Pays the Price

One of the most astonishing failures of our world is how we treat knowledge like a private inheritance instead of a shared human resource. Every country, every corporation, every research lab hoards information as if insight itself were a scarce commodity rather than the one thing that grows when shared. Instead of collaborating, we duplicate the same studies, repeat the same experiments, pour billions into parallel projects, and call it "progress" when it's really just global waste masked as innovation.

Look at space: every nation wants its own satellites, its own image to project to the world, its own flag orbiting the same exhausted planet. So instead of a unified network, we now have thousands of satellites crowding low Earth orbit, accumulating like cosmic garbage, floating debris that will eventually become dangerous enough to trap us inside our own atmosphere. Astronomers already warn that the sky is becoming polluted with metal and military ambition, but each country keeps launching more, because cooperation is considered weakness and collaboration is framed as losing power.

It's the same sickness everywhere. Countries run parallel versions of the exact same drug trials but refuse to share their data because pharmaceutical companies want exclusive rights. Universities compete for prestige, not discovery, so they bury findings behind paywalls and patents that block poor nations from accessing life-saving knowledge. Imagine how many cancers could be treated, how many psychiatric medications improved, how many lives saved if research were shared instead of hoarded. But instead, we run the same studies in different languages with the same hypotheses, wasting time, money, and human potential while people die waiting for cures that already exist in someone's locked filing cabinet.

Technology works the same way. Instead of collaborating on green energy, countries hide breakthroughs to protect national industries. Instead of sharing climate solutions that could save the planet, corporations patent carbon-capture methods, solar cell advances, and battery technology so only those who can pay can benefit. During the pandemic, wealthy countries refused to waive vaccine patents, leaving millions of people in low-income nations vulnerable—not because the science didn't exist, but because the world decided profit mattered more than human life. And scientists who begged for open-source sharing were ignored because "business models" outranked morality.

When knowledge becomes property, humanity becomes collateral damage.

We see this in agriculture too. Seed companies patent genetically modified crops and sue farmers for replanting seeds that grow naturally from last year's harvest. We see it in AI, where corporations develop algorithms that determine our futures but refuse to reveal how they work because "intellectual property" must be protected, even if the technology harms the public. We see it in consumer electronics, where companies intentionally prevent repair or modification so they can keep selling endlessly, creating mountains of e-waste while insisting that innovation requires secrecy.

The absurd part is that we declare ourselves a "globalized world," yet our deepest intelligence is fractured, duplicated, and locked behind borders, paywalls, and corporate secrecy. Humanity has built a Tower of Babel out of data instead of language—everyone climbing alone, competing to stand higher than the others, even though we will all fall when the foundation collapses.

Imagine a world where countries shared satellite networks instead of cluttering space with their nationalist insecurities. Imagine a world where breakthroughs in medicine were open-source, where climate technologies were shared freely, where AI was governed collectively, where research lived in the commons instead of behind a $59.99 journal paywall. Imagine how quickly we could solve problems if we stopped treating knowledge as a weapon or a brand and started treating it as the birthright of every human being.

We talk about scarcity, but the real scarcity is not resources—it is trust. It is cooperation. It is humility.

Knowledge isn't dangerous.
The hoarding of knowledge is.

And until we learn to share the wisdom we already have, we will keep poisoning oceans, overheating the planet, blocking sunlight with satellites, denying cures to millions, and calling it "national security" or "innovation" or "economic growth." But underneath all the excuses, the truth is simple:

We are killing others and ourselves with secrets.

Epistemic Gatekeeping, Deniability, and the Limits of Replication

Contemporary social science is often governed by an institutional demand for "proof" that is framed as neutral rigor but frequently functions as a politics of deniability. Major journals routinely require that structural harm be rendered legible through administratively acceptable metrics—replicable designs, controlled variables, standardized instruments—before it can be acknowledged as real. Yet this demand is not simply methodological. It is epistemic. It privileges forms of knowledge that are easiest for institutions to absorb while dismissing forms of knowing that emerge from lived experience, moral perception, and embodied intuition as "anecdotal" or "subjective."

This is not an argument against empirical inquiry. Rather, it is an argument that empirical inquiry in the social world cannot be equated with the laboratory ideal of replication. Human beings are not interchangeable units, and institutions are not stable experimental environments. No two participants occupy identical histories, nervous systems, cultural meanings, or structural positions. Even under controlled conditions, time itself is a confound: language shifts, norms evolve, crises emerge, and institutional scripts mutate. The social world is dynamic, interpretive, and historically contingent. What is called "replication" often reproduces methodological form while the underlying cultural reality has already changed.

Moreover, the insistence on measurable proof frequently erases precisely those dimensions of harm that are most real: the affective atmosphere of dismissal, the embodied consequences of chronic insecurity, the epistemic destabilization produced by credibility withdrawal. When institutions require the harmed to translate injury into sanctioned categories before recognition is granted, the demand for evidence becomes part of the harm itself. Epistemic injustice operates not only through disbelief, but through the narrowing of what counts as knowledge in the first place.

A sociology of institutional gaslighting must therefore treat "objectivity" not as detachment from power, but as an institutional accomplishment shaped by credibility economies. Feelings, intuition, and embodied alarm are not inferior data; they are often the earliest diagnostic signals of structural betrayal. A knowledge regime that excludes these dimensions as irrational is not complete—it is partial, politically organized, and incapable of fully apprehending the realities it claims to measure.

Quantitative Worship: The Marginalization of Lived Experience

Surveys, Likert scales, structured interviews — the things academia treats as "rigorous" — can capture **surface-level behavior**, not the depth of human experience.

Quantitative research cannot measure:

- the fracturing of trust,
- the nuance of trauma,
- the ache of loneliness,
- the complexity of oppression,
- the spiritual death that comes from being unseen,
- or the embodied wisdom of survivors.

Yet these are the real truths.

When academia demands quantification, it erases humanity.

When journals demand numbers, they amputate meaning.

When researchers treat lives like datasets, they reproduce the very violence they study.

Challenging the Myth of "Objective" Science

Now I want to challenge something that took me years to untangle.
In philosophy, **nominalism** argues that everything is subjective — that our categories are invented, not discovered.
On the opposite end, scientific **objectivism** claims that knowledge is only valid if it is measurable, observable, and replicated.

These two poles dominate Western thinking.
You're either a mystic or a scientist.
You either believe everything is relative or everything is quantifiable.

But here's the truth no one wants to say out loud:

Both positions are incomplete. And both avoid the real discomfort of acknowledging that human experience — emotions, intuition, perception, embodiment — is a legitimate source of knowledge.

I've met people on both extremes, and what they share is this:
They are terrified of expanding their definition of knowledge, because doing so would require them to accept their own emotional, intuitive, and spiritual lives as real data — not noise.

If they acknowledged emotional knowledge as real, they would have to face:

- their grief,
- their shame,
- their fear,
- their unmet hopes,

- their traumatic imprints,
- and the uncomfortable possibility that truth cannot always be quantified.

To admit that **intuition is knowledge** would force them to admit that truth lives inside the body — not outside it in measurements and models.

To admit that **emotion is data** would force them to admit that the nervous system remembers what science ignores.

To admit that **the soul precedes the body**, or even just coexists with it, would require abandoning the illusion that science is the only gateway to legitimacy and there's nothing after we die.

And that terrifies people.

Why?
Because the moment we accept internal experience as knowledge, the control that institutions have over "truth" begins to collapse.
If emotions count as data, the entire hierarchy of who is "rational" or "credible" falls apart.
If intuition counts as knowledge, then marginalized people — survivors, children, Indigenous communities, neurodivergent people — suddenly become experts in their own lives.

That is the threat they don't want us to see.
Because once we remember it, the entire illusion of their "objectivity" begins to crumble.

Intuition, prayer, love, mindfulness, inner knowing—these are not fantasies or weaknesses.
They are forms of knowledge.
They are the oldest sciences of the human spirit.

We turned away from spirituality because churches, mosques, and temples weaponized it—twisting the sacred into a justification for cruelty, calling their harm "God's unchangeable rule."
But in rejecting that violence, we unknowingly fell into a far more deceptive trap:

A world that denies our humanness entirely.

A world that tells us our feelings are irrational, our intuition unreliable, our pain inconvenient, our love unscientific.
A world that reduces our existence to metrics, outputs, data points—and then congratulates itself for being "evidence-based."

But we were never meant to be measured into boxes and sizes.
We are not here to be reduced to numbers.
We are here to be kind, to learn, to grow, to touch each other's lives with presence.

And our feelings—our intuition—are the lanterns we carry through the dark night of the soul.
They have always been the way home.

We do not need to buy into their narrow vision of science to be whole.
We were **born** whole.
We have always been whole.
We have simply forgotten to trust the parts of ourselves that do not fit neatly into their spreadsheets.

We only need to remember the values that have carried humanity through centuries of suffering:
connection, love, care, sharing, generosity, presence.

We are not black holes of endless need.
We are easily satiated when we no longer fear lack.
And everything we seek—safety, belonging, meaning—comes back to love.

We forgot that love is abundant because **we are the source of it.**
We don't need endless materialism to survive; we only need our basic needs met so our souls can grow and express unconditional love to the world.

But we are moving further and further from that vision.

Most of my millennial friends are drowning financially.
We aren't married. Many don't have children.
Some are lucky if they can keep a pet alive.
Gen Z is even worse—facing a collapsing job market, housing they can't afford, and algorithms that have shaped their minds since childhood.

They don't even know the feeling of life before the internet pressed itself into their sense of self.

And our parents—the ones who complied, who swallowed their emotions for stability—they are numb now.
Not because they lacked courage, but because the system trained them to abandon themselves bit by bit in exchange for survival.

It is time for all of us to say **no** to becoming emotionless machines carrying out the passive cruelties of a system that has been killing people quietly for decades.
It was never okay.

Yes, our prosperity was built on the bodies and labor of those with less privilege—through slavery, colonization, and systemic exploitation that converted human suffering into wealth.

But beneath these structures, there is something systems cannot measure. Across cultures, philosophies, and spiritual traditions, human beings have been understood to possess intrinsic value—not because of productivity, status, or progress, but because of being.

There is currently no scientific method capable of disproving consciousness. Consciousness is known only through first-person experience, and while science can measure brain activity and behavior, it cannot directly access or eliminate subjective awareness itself. Even theories that claim consciousness is an illusion fail to escape this problem, since an illusion still requires an experiencer. Neuroscience can identify conditions under which consciousness changes or ceases in the body, but it cannot demonstrate that experience never existed or is unreal. Any claim that consciousness has been disproven would be self-contradictory, because observation, evidence, and proof all presuppose experience. What science can offer are correlations and models—not final answers about the existence or ultimate nature of consciousness.

Science can describe biological death, but it does not resolve the deeper questions of consciousness, continuity, or meaning. What we call "death" may mark the end of a biological process, yet science itself remains silent on whether awareness, energy, or being is truly extinguished—or simply transformed. Also death is **not destruction** in the physical sense. It is a loss **of material organization**. Our bodies continue to exist as star dust and we become parts of the plants, animals, and other humans, maybe even parts of new galaxies. Right at this moment we are composed of billions of beings before us and they are alive through us.

It is through remembering, loving, and relational connection that we grow and find meaning—but right now, the system has severed our ability to connect to one another, and even to ourselves.
That rupture is not a moral failing.
It is the predictable result of a world designed to keep humans lonely, afraid, and compliant.

But that does not have to be the end of the story.
Because everything we need to rebuild—love, intuition, empathy, truth—still lives inside us, waiting to be remembered.

Energy Beyond Matter: What We Forgot When We Worshipped $E = mc^2$

Einstein's $E = mc^2$ is one of the most quoted equations in history, but also one of the most misunderstood. Popular culture treats it as a final statement about reality: energy equals matter, matter equals reality, and what cannot be reduced to mass must be less real. This belief did not come from physics—it came from **how society chose to interpret physics.**

Einstein's work in **1905–1907** established two related but different results:

1. **Mass–energy equivalence** (rest energy):
$E0=mc2$
2. **Relativistic energy including motion**:
$E2=(mc2)2+(pc)2$

pc = energy from motion

This term accounts for:

- kinetic energy at very high speeds
- radiation
- light (photons)

Light has **no mass**, but it still has energy because it has momentum.

The first result was revolutionary because it said:

Mass itself is a form of energy.

That idea:

- explained nuclear reactions
- reshaped physics
- was easy to state
- could be detached from advanced mathematics

The **second equation**, by contrast:

- depends on relativistic momentum
- requires understanding spacetime geometry
- is less intuitive
- is harder to communicate outside physics

So what happened was **pedagogical and cultural reduction**, not scientific omission.

Textbooks, media, and public narratives kept the **simplest special case** and dropped the rest.

This equation already disrupts the cultural myth. It shows that **energy exists independently of matter**. Motion, momentum, radiation, and light all carry energy without becoming mass. Energy does not naturally resolve into material form. Matter is not the goal of energy—it is one *expression* among many.

What physics quietly acknowledges, culture loudly forgets.

Over time, societies built systems that mirrored a distorted reading of this equation. Only what could be "weighed," "counted," or "priced" was treated as real. Everything else—intuition, feeling, meaning, suffering—was labeled subjective, secondary, or irrelevant. The mistake was not scientific. It was philosophical.

Energy does not only appear as matter.
It appears as **movement, pattern, relation, and transformation.**

A thought has no mass, yet it requires energy.
Language is not matter, yet it reorganizes societies.
A system processes information not on paper, but through **real energetic shifts**—electrical, neural, computational. Processing itself is: energy changing form.

To make this visible, we can write a *conceptual* equation—not a physical law, but a map of what reality already shows us:

Etotal=Emass+Emotion+Efields+Egrav+Edark+Einformation/meaning

This is not meant to be calculated.
It is meant to be **remembered.**

- **Emass** — energy stabilized into matter
- **Emotion**— energy expressed as movement, momentum, radiation
- **Efields** — energy residing in fields, space, and vacuum
- **Egrav** — energy stored in spacetime curvature and relation
- **Edark**— the vast, still-unknown energy shaping the universe
- **Einformation/meaning** — energy organized into structure, language, systems, consciousness, and lived experience

Time is not listed as a term because it is not a separate energy. It is the perceptual lens through which finite beings experience change within a reality that exists all at once.

Nothing here violates physics. What it violates is the **false hierarchy** that treats only the first term as real.

Matter is simply **slow, dense energy**.
Language is **symbolic energy**.
Institutions are **organized energy**.
Bureaucracy is **energy constrained into procedure**.
Human suffering is **energy trapped without outlet**.

When societies collapse reality into what can be monetized, they do not become objective—they become blind. They confuse models for truth and treat living systems as accounting problems. This is how care becomes conditional, how harm becomes procedural, and how people are told their pain is "not real" because it cannot be graphed.

Objectivity, as it is commonly used, is not neutrality. It is **selective recognition**.

Every equation, every dataset, every policy is filtered through human-made lenses. Pretending otherwise allows institutions to deny responsibility while claiming inevitability. "That's just how the system works" becomes a moral alibi.

Humanity did not lose itself because science went too far.
It lost itself because **reduction replaced understanding**.

To remember that everything is energy—not only when it becomes matter, but when it becomes meaning—is not anti-science. It is a return to coherence. A reminder that life cannot be fully understood by freezing it into equations, and that what is most real is often what systems find hardest to measure.

My Intuition: Even with all the added layers philosophically the equation is intentionally incomplete

*This formula is not "complete" — **because completeness itself is an illusion.*** **As Humans we can't have access to any knowledge out of our restricted senses and dimensions we can perceive.**

So writing a sum makes it provisional.

That's not a flaw.
Its intellectual honesty.

A *complete* equation would require:

- no categories
- no language
- no symbols
- no separation

Which means it couldn't be written at all.

The deeper issue

What feels "off" isn't a missing term.

It's this:

Energy isn't additive.

It doesn't come in pieces that stack.
It **shifts state**.

So a more faithful expression (still conceptual) would be something like:

Etotal≡Eone(state, relation, pattern)

or in plain language:

There is one energy, appearing as many forms depending on organization, relation, and scale.

The first equation works as a **pedagogical bridge**:

- from physics → systems → meaning → humanity

But my intuition is that:
the truest version collapses the plus signs.

This is not a closed system.
The categories are lenses, not partitions.

Objective Science Is Fragmented Science: Each Field Is Only One Piece of The Puzzle

Science is extraordinarily powerful within its chosen domains, but it is not—and has never claimed to be—the total register of human knowing. This is why I came up with the puzzle metaphor. Each science field examines a fragment of the whole, refining its piece with increasing precision. The mistake is not specialization; it is forgetting that specialization is partial. No single discipline, no matter how advanced, can claim the authority of total description. Truth does not collapse into one frame—it emerges at the intersections.

Physics describes how energy stabilizes into matter, curves spacetime, and propagates through fields. But energy also moves as affect, organizes into information, accumulates as meaning, and structures systems of relationship. These expressions are not metaphors layered onto reality—they are reality as it is lived, interpreted, and transmitted.

Relational truth does not mean the absence of truth. It means truth is constrained by context, embodiment, and consequence. A truth about gravity does not negate a truth about suffering. A truth about neural firing does not exhaust a truth about grief. These truths do not cancel one another; they coexist, each real within its domain, none sufficient on its own.

Time, too, is not treated here as a fundamental substance, but as a perceptual ordering of access. What exists need not unfold sequentially in order to be real. Time is one way finite minds navigate a reality that may not depend on linear progression at all. In this sense, time is already contained within the totality this model gestures toward, not standing outside it as a master variable.

This framework does not ask science to be less precise. It asks us to be more honest about what precision cannot reach. It invites us to hold multiple modes of knowing at once—quantitative and qualitative, empirical and experiential—without forcing them into false hierarchies.

If the ground feels unstable, that is because certainty was never the ground to begin with. Relation was. Meaning arises not from a single truth spoken loudly enough, but from many partial truths held together without collapse. The equation is not an answer. It is a reminder: reality is richer than any one sense, any one method, or any one piece of the puzzle can reveal alone.

The Full Spectrum of Science Is Already Embodied, Emotional, Relational, and Subjective

People pretend science is objective.
But here is the secret they never admit:

Science has always been a human activity — filtered through human bodies, human senses, human language, human values, human interpretation.

There is no god-like objectivity in science.
A human chooses:

- what to measure,
- what to ignore,
- what counts as evidence,
- what questions matter,
- which populations get studied,
- what words define a phenomenon,
- and how the results should be interpreted.

That is not neutrality.
That is **subjective meaning-making in a lab coat.**

Even the most "objective" tools — surveys, fMRI scans, rat studies, statistical models — are all **interpretations**, not truths.

We act as if testing a chemical on rats makes the knowledge divine.
But rats are not humans.
Their trauma is not our trauma.
Their emotions are not our emotions.

And even when the tools work, they are still approximations — metaphors pretending to be facts.

The strongest argument for this view is simple:

- **objectivity is constructed**
- **measurement is interpretation**
- **data is storytelling**
- **science is a human practice, not a divine authority**
- **feeling and intuition are not opposites of truth — they *are* truth**

Emotion, intuition, and embodied sensing are not enemies of truth. They are part of the same spectrum through which humans perceive reality. When scientists pretend to remove subjectivity, they do not eliminate it — they merely hide it behind language that sounds more legitimate.

If humans are doing the science, then subjectivity is inseparable from the outcome. Every dataset carries the imprint of human attention, human limitation, and human meaning. The lie is pretending otherwise.

The real illusion is not that science is flawed.
The illusion is that science was ever separate from the living, feeling humans who created it.

"Science is not the enemy. But science without soul becomes another form of structural narcissism — demanding that only what can be measured deserves to exist."

The Larger Truth: Academia Is Another Loophole Empire

Higher education doesn't just sort people.
It **shapes whose knowledge counts**.

It:

- preserves old paradigms,
- punishes innovation,
- silences marginalized truths,
- rewards conformity,
- and pretends this is "objectivity."

But behind all the jargon, grading, peer review, and prestige, academia is just another system protecting itself — another institution teaching us to mistrust our own intuition, to defer to "experts," and to surrender the authority we have over our own lives.

This is not education.
This is epistemic control.

And it's time we say it out loud and expand the definition of science.

References

Ahmed, Sara. 2017. *Living a Feminist Life*. Durham, NC: Duke University Press.

Alexander, Jeffrey C. 2004. "Toward a Theory of Cultural Trauma." Pp. 1–30 in *Cultural Trauma and Collective Identity*, edited by Jeffrey C. Alexander, Ron Eyerman, Bernhard Giesen, Neil J. Smelser, and Piotr Sztompka. Berkeley: University of California Press.

Altheide, David L. 2006. *Terrorism and the Politics of Fear*. Lanham, MD:

AltaMira Press.

Angell, Marcia. 2004. *The Truth About the Drug Companies: How They Deceive Us and What to Do About It.* New York: Random House.

Armstrong, Katrina, Josephine L. Ravenell, Sheilah McMurphy, and Mary Putt. 2007. "Racial/Ethnic Differences in Physician Distrust in the United States." *American Journal of Public Health* 97(7):1283–1289.

Autor, David H., David Dorn, and Gordon H. Hanson. 2013. "The China Syndrome: Local Labor Market Effects of Import Competition in the United States." *American Economic Review* 103(6):2121–2168.

Barrett, Lisa Feldman. 2017. *How Emotions Are Made: The Secret Life of the Brain.* Boston: Houghton Mifflin Harcourt.

Baudrillard, Jean. 1998. *The Consumer Society: Myths and Structures.* London: Sage.

Bekelman, Justin E., Yan Li, and Cary P. Gross. 2003. "Scope and Impact of Financial Conflicts of Interest in Biomedical Research." *JAMA* 289(4):454–465.

Benkler, Yochai, Robert Faris, and Hal Roberts. 2018. *Network Propaganda: Manipulation, Disinformation, and Radicalization in American Politics.* New York: Oxford University Press.

Bennett, W. Lance, Regina G. Lawrence, and Steven Livingston. 2007. *When the Press Fails: Political Power and the News Media from Iraq to Katrina.* Chicago: University of Chicago Press.

Bennett, W. Lance, and Steven Livingston. 2018. "The Disinformation Order: Disruptive Communication and the Decline of Democratic Institutions." *European Journal of Communication* 33(2):122–139.

Berardi, Franco "Bifo." 2009. *The Soul at Work: From Alienation to Autonomy.* Los Angeles: Semiotext(e).

Bernays, Edward L. 1928. *Propaganda.* New York: Horace Liveright.

Blackstock, Nelson. 1975. *COINTELPRO: The FBI's Secret War on Political Freedom*. New York: Vintage Books.

Blyth, Mark. 2013. *Austerity: The History of a Dangerous Idea*. New York: Oxford University Press.

Bohr, Niels. 1935. "Can Quantum-Mechanical Description of Physical Reality Be Considered Complete?" *Physical Review* 48(8):696–702.

Bourdieu, Pierre. 1984. *Distinction: A Social Critique of the Judgement of Taste*. Cambridge, MA: Harvard University Press.

Bourdieu, Pierre. 1993. *The Field of Cultural Production: Essays on Art and Literature*. New York: Columbia University Press.

Bourdieu, Pierre. 1996. *The State Nobility: Elite Schools in the Field of Power*. Stanford, CA: Stanford University Press.

Brandt, Allan M. 1978. "Racism and Research: The Case of the Tuskegee Syphilis Study." *Hastings Center Report* 8(6):21–29.

Brandt, Allan M. 2007. *The Cigarette Century: The Rise, Fall, and Deadly Persistence of the Product That Defined America*. New York: Basic Books.

Brown, Brené. 2012. *Daring Greatly: How the Courage to Be Vulnerable Transforms the Way We Live, Love, Parent, and Lead*. New York: Gotham Books.

Brown, Wendy. 2015. *Undoing the Demos: Neoliberalism's Stealth Revolution*. New York: Zone Books.

Cabanas, Edgar, and Eva Illouz. 2019. *Manufacturing Happy Citizens: How the Science and Industry of Happiness Control Our Lives*. Cambridge: Polity Press.

Cadwalladr, Carole, and Emma Graham-Harrison. 2018. "Revealed: 50 Million Facebook Profiles Harvested for Cambridge Analytica." *The Guardian*, March 17.

Church Committee. 1976. *Final Report of the Select Committee to Study Governmental Operations with Respect to Intelligence Activities.* Washington, DC: U.S. Government Printing Office.

Collins, Patricia Hill. 2000. *Black Feminist Thought: Knowledge, Consciousness, and the Politics of Empowerment.* 2nd ed. New York: Routledge.

Cunningham, David. 2004. *There's Something Happening Here: The New Left, the Klan, and FBI Counterintelligence.* Berkeley: University of California Press.

Damasio, Antonio. 1994. *Descartes' Error: Emotion, Reason, and the Human Brain.* New York: Putnam.

Daston, Lorraine, and Peter Galison. 2007. *Objectivity.* New York: Zone Books.

Davidson, Richard J., and Bruce S. McEwen. 2012. "Social Influences on Neuroplasticity: Stress and Interventions to Promote Well-Being." *Nature Neuroscience* 15(5):689–695.

Entman, Robert M. 1993. "Framing: Toward Clarification of a Fractured Paradigm." *Journal of Communication* 43(4):51–58.

Fisher, Mark. 2009. *Capitalist Realism: Is There No Alternative?* Winchester, UK: Zero Books.

Foucault, Michel. 1977. *Discipline and Punish: The Birth of the Prison.* New York: Pantheon.

Foucault, Michel. 1980. *Power/Knowledge: Selected Interviews and Other Writings, 1972–1977.* Edited by Colin Gordon. New York: Pantheon.

Fricker, Miranda. 2007. *Epistemic Injustice: Power and the Ethics of Knowing.* Oxford: Oxford University Press.

Frieman, Joshua A., Michael S. Turner, and Dragan Huterer. 2008. "Dark Energy and the Accelerating Universe." *Annual Review of Astronomy and Astrophysics* 46:385–432.

Freyd, Jennifer J. 1996. *Betrayal Trauma: The Logic of Forgetting Childhood Abuse.* Cambridge, MA: Harvard University Press.

Galtung, Johan. 1969. "Violence, Peace, and Peace Research." *Journal of Peace Research* 6(3):167–191.

Gamble, Vanessa Northington. 1997. "Under the Shadow of Tuskegee: African Americans and Health Care." *American Journal of Public Health* 87(11):1773–1778.

Garsten, Christina, and Adrienne Sörbom. 2021. *Davos Man: How the Billionaires Devoured the World.* New York: Routledge.

Gillespie, Tarleton. 2018. *Custodians of the Internet: Platforms, Content Moderation, and the Hidden Decisions That Shape Social Media.* New Haven, CT: Yale University Press.

Glassner, Barry. 1999. *The Culture of Fear.* New York: Basic Books.

Graeber, David. 2018. *Bullshit Jobs: A Theory.* New York: Simon & Schuster.

Groopman, Jerome. 2007. *How Doctors Think.* Boston: Houghton Mifflin.

Haraway, Donna. 1988. "Situated Knowledges: The Science Question in Feminism and the Privilege of Partial Perspective." *Feminist Studies* 14(3):575–599.

Hasher, Lynn, David Goldstein, and Thomas Toppino. 1977. "Frequency and the Conference of Referential Validity." *Journal of Verbal Learning and Verbal Behavior* 16(1):107–112.

Heisenberg, Werner. 1958. *Physics and Philosophy: The Revolution in Modern Science.* New York: Harper.

Herman, Edward S., and Noam Chomsky. 1988. *Manufacturing Consent: The Political Economy of the Mass Media.* New York: Pantheon.

Herman, Judith. 1997. *Trauma and Recovery.* New York: Basic Books.

Herring, George C. 2002. *America's Longest War: The United States and Vietnam, 1950–1975*. 4th ed. New York: McGraw-Hill.

Illouz, Eva. 2007. *Cold Intimacies: The Making of Emotional Capitalism*. Cambridge: Polity Press.

Isaak, Jim, and Mina J. Hanna. 2018. "User Data Privacy: Facebook, Cambridge Analytica." *Computer* 51(8):56–59.

Isikoff, Michael, and David Corn. 2006. *Hubris: The Inside Story of Spin, Scandal, and the Selling of the Iraq War*. New York: Crown.

Jamieson, Kathleen Hall, and Joseph N. Cappella. 2008. *Echo Chamber: Rush Limbaugh and the Conservative Media Establishment*. New York: Oxford University Press.

Jones, James H. 1993. *Bad Blood: The Tuskegee Syphilis Experiment*. New York: Free Press.

Joint Chiefs of Staff. 2007. *Joint Publication 3-13.2: Psychological Operations*. Washington, DC: U.S. Department of Defense.

Kabat-Zinn, Jon. 1990. *Full Catastrophe Living*. New York: Delacorte.

Kahneman, Daniel. 2011. *Thinking, Fast and Slow*. New York: Farrar, Straus and Giroux.

Kellner, Douglas. 2004. *From 9/11 to Terror War: The Dangers of the Bush Legacy*. Lanham, MD: Rowman & Littlefield.

Klein, Naomi. 2000. *No Logo*. New York: Picador.

Klein, Naomi. 2007. *The Shock Doctrine: The Rise of Disaster Capitalism*. New York: Metropolitan Books.

Kuhn, Thomas S. 1962. *The Structure of Scientific Revolutions*. Chicago: University of Chicago Press.

Lorde, Audre. 1984. *Sister Outsider: Essays and Speeches*. Trumansburg, NY: Crossing Press.

Lundh, Andreas, Joel Lexchin, Barbara Mintzes, Jeppe B. Schroll, and Lisa Bero. 2017. "Industry Sponsorship and Research Outcome." *Cochrane Database of Systematic Reviews* 2:MR000033. doi:10.1002/14651858.MR000033.pub3

Lupien, Sonia J., Bruce S. McEwen, Megan R. Gunnar, and Christine Heim. 2009. "Effects of Stress Throughout the Lifespan on the Brain, Behaviour and Cognition." *Nature Reviews Neuroscience* 10(6):434–445.

Lyon, David. 2001. *Surveillance Society: Monitoring Everyday Life.* Buckingham, UK: Open University Press.

Marcuse, Herbert. 1964. *One-Dimensional Man.* Boston: Beacon Press.

Meadows, Donella H., Dennis L. Meadows, Jørgen Randers, and William W. Behrens III. 1972. *The Limits to Growth.* New York: Universe Books.

Menjívar, Cecilia, and Leisy Abrego. 2012. "Legal Violence: Immigration Law and the Lives of Central American Immigrants." *American Journal of Sociology* 117(5):1380–1421.

Merton, Robert K. 1968. "The Matthew Effect in Science." *Science* 159(3810):56–63.

Montgomery, Kathryn. 2006. *How Doctors Think: Clinical Judgment and the Practice of Medicine.* New York: Oxford University Press.

Morrison, Elizabeth W., and Frances J. Milliken. 2000. "Organizational Silence: A Barrier to Change and Development in a Pluralistic World." *Academy of Management Review* 25(4):706–725.

Mullainathan, Sendhil, and Eldar Shafir. 2013. *Scarcity: Why Having Too Little Means So Much.* New York: Times Books.

Nagel, Thomas. 1986. *The View from Nowhere.* New York: Oxford University Press.

Nestle, Marion. 2013. *Food Politics: How the Food Industry Influences Nutrition and Health.* Revised ed. Berkeley: University of California Press.

Nixon, Rob. 2011. *Slow Violence and the Environmentalism of the Poor.* Cambridge, MA: Harvard University Press.

Noble, Safiya Umoja. 2018. *Algorithms of Oppression: How Search Engines Reinforce Racism.* New York: New York University Press.

Oreskes, Naomi, and Erik M. Conway. 2010. *Merchants of Doubt.* New York: Bloomsbury Press.

Osnos, Evan. 2017. "Doomsday Prep for the Super-Rich." *The New Yorker,* January 30.

Paul, Christopher, and Miriam Matthews. 2016. *The Russian "Firehose of Falsehood" Propaganda Model.* Santa Monica, CA: RAND Corporation.

Planck Collaboration. 2018. "Planck 2018 Results: Cosmological Parameters." *Astronomy & Astrophysics* 641:A6.

Porter, Theodore M. 1995. *Trust in Numbers: The Pursuit of Objectivity in Science and Public Life.* Princeton, NJ: Princeton University Press.

Power, Michael. 1999. *The Audit Society: Rituals of Verification.* Oxford: Oxford University Press.

Proctor, Robert N. 2011. *Golden Holocaust: Origins of the Cigarette Catastrophe.* Berkeley: University of California Press.

Putnam, Robert D. 2000. *Bowling Alone: The Collapse and Revival of American Community.* New York: Simon & Schuster.

Reverby, Susan M. 2009. *Examining Tuskegee: The Infamous Syphilis Study and Its Legacy.* Chapel Hill: University of North Carolina Press.

Roberts, Dorothy. 2011. *Fatal Invention: How Science, Politics, and Big Business Re-Create Race in the Twenty-First Century.* New York: New Press.

Santos, Boaventura de Sousa. 2014. *Epistemologies of the South: Justice Against Epistemicide.* Boulder, CO: Paradigm Publishers.

Seligman, Martin E. P. 1975. *Helplessness: On Depression, Development, and*

Death. San Francisco: W. H. Freeman.

Siegel, Daniel J. 2007. *The Mindful Brain*. New York: W. W. Norton.

Smith, Carly M., and Jennifer J. Freyd. 2014. "Institutional Betrayal." *American Psychologist* 69(6):575–587.

Smith, Linda Tuhiwai. 2012. *Decolonizing Methodologies: Research and Indigenous Peoples*. 2nd ed. London: Zed Books.

Stanley, Jason. 2015. *How Propaganda Works*. Princeton, NJ: Princeton University Press.

Sweet, Paige L. 2019. "The Sociology of Gaslighting." *American Sociological Review* 84(5):851–875.

Taylor, Charles. 2007. *A Secular Age*. Cambridge, MA: Harvard University Press.

Taylor, Philip M. 2003. *Munitions of the Mind: A History of Propaganda*. 3rd ed. Manchester: Manchester University Press.

Thaler, Richard H., and Cass R. Sunstein. 2008. *Nudge: Improving Decisions About Health, Wealth, and Happiness*. New Haven, CT: Yale University Press.

Tufekci, Zeynep. 2015. "Algorithmic Harms Beyond Facebook." *Colorado Technology Law Journal* 13:203–218.

Tufekci, Zeynep. 2017. *Twitter and Tear Gas: The Power and Fragility of Networked Protest*. New Haven, CT: Yale University Press.

Ullman, Harlan K., and James P. Wade. 1996. *Shock and Awe: Achieving Rapid Dominance*. Washington, DC: National Defense University.

United Nations Environment Programme. 2024. *Food Waste Index Report 2024*. Nairobi: UNEP.

van der Kolk, Bessel. 2014. *The Body Keeps the Score: Brain, Mind, and Body in the Healing of Trauma*. New York: Viking.

Washington, Harriet A. 2006. *Medical Apartheid: The Dark History of Medical Experimentation on Black Americans from Colonial Times to the Present.* New York: Doubleday.

Weber, Max. 1922. *Economy and Society.* Berkeley: University of California Press.

World Inequality Lab. 2022. *World Inequality Report 2022.* Paris: World Inequality Lab.

Wu, Tim. 2016. *The Attention Merchants: The Epic Scramble to Get Inside Our Heads.* New York: Knopf.

Zuboff, Shoshana. 2019. *The Age of Surveillance Capitalism.* New York: PublicAffairs.

6 All The Rights We Sign Away

The Tyranny of Terms and Conditions: Signing Away Our Rights Just to Live

One of the worst forms of institutional violence today isn't loud or dramatic — it's the endless stack of agreements we are forced to sign just to exist. Before we can access *anything* — a doctor, a job, a therapist, a medication, a bank account, a housing application, even a streaming platform or a phone app, even games — we must first surrender our rights (Herd and Moynihan 2018; Power 1999).

We pretend these signatures are "choices." But they are not choices at all. (Cohen 2012; Stark 2019).

They are obligations disguised as consent.
You can't get medical care unless you sign.
You can't work unless you sign.
You can't communicate, travel, bank, or even watch a movie unless you sign.

It's an ultimatum written in fine print:
Sign, or disappear from society (Herd and Moynihan 2018).

And the language — intentionally dense, technical, bloated — is written at a level **no human brain can realistically process**. Research shows most terms and conditions require a *college reading level* and *hours of attention* to understand. No one reads them. No one fully can. And that is exactly the design (Obar and Oeldorf-Hirsch 2020; McDonald and Cranor 2008).

The system hides its intentions not in secrecy, but in **overwhelm**.
It drowns you in pages of legal jargon to ensure you won't question what you're agreeing to. Consent becomes a performance, not a reality (Stark 2019; Power 1999).

This is not "informed consent."
This is **coerced consent** — consent extracted through need, urgency, exhaustion, and the lack of alternatives.

Arbitration: The Corporate Black Hole

Buried inside nearly every agreement today is the most sinister clause of all: **mandatory arbitration**. The moment you sign, you give up your constitutional right to sue, join a class action, or speak publicly about harm (Sternlight 2013).

Arbitration means:

- the company chooses the arbitrator,
- the proceedings are secret,
- you can't appeal,
- and the corporation wins the vast majority of cases.

This isn't justice.
This is a private court system where the corporation is judge, jury, and executioner.

Workers have been assaulted, harassed, discriminated against, or unpaid — yet barred from court because somewhere in their onboarding paperwork was a tiny box they checked without understanding it (Sternlight 2013).

Patients have died in nursing homes and their families were denied the right to sue because the admission form included mandatory arbitration.

People harmed by defective medical devices have been silenced because the user agreement waived liability before they even opened the package (Public Citizen 2015).

We are told these forms "protect us."
But the only ones protected are the corporations writing them.

Healthcare: Consent Forms as Shields Against Accountability

Before you can sit on an exam table, you must sign a stack of forms acknowledging:

- that errors may occur,
- that you accept unpredictable charges,
- that treatments may be forced or denied,
- that your medical data can be shared,
- that the hospital is absolved of certain liabilities,
- and often, that any dispute must go to arbitration (Herd and Moynihan 2018).

You sign these while sick, scared, overwhelmed, or desperate — the exact moment your nervous system is least capable of processing risk.

This is not "care."
It is **legal insulation**.

Employment Contracts: Rights Lost Before Your First Paycheck

To get a job, you must sign away:

- the right to sue your employer,
- the right to a jury trial,
- the right to speak publicly about harm,
- the right to work elsewhere,
- and even the right to privacy (Stone and Colvin 2020).

You accept surveillance, drug testing, social media monitoring, background checks, and behavioral tracking — because the alternative is unemployment (Ajunwa, Crawford, and Schultz 2017).

Employers frame it as "company policy."
But the truth is:
you lose your rights before you earn your first dollar.

This is how modern labor control works — not through chains or whips, but through onboarding portals and electronic signatures.

Digital Platforms: Data Extraction as the Cost of Connection

We now sign away more rights to apps and websites than to our own governments. A simple game or streaming platform may demand permission to:

- track your location,
- analyze your face,
- record your voice,
- access your contacts,
- scan your messages,

- monitor your emotional reactions,
- profile your desires,
- and store everything indefinitely (Zuboff 2019).

You don't agree because you understand.
You agree because the system has made refusal impossible.

Modern life requires digital participation. And digital participation requires legal surrender.

This is not technology.
This is **administrative captivity**.

Government Forms: Bureaucracy as a Gatekeeper of Humanity

Immigration, disability, unemployment, welfare — all require endless paperwork that forces you to:

- relive trauma,
- disclose your worst moments over and over,
- navigate contradictory instructions,
- sign away privacy,
- authorize surveillance,
- accept the possibility of denial with no recourse (Graeber 2015; Menjívar and Abrego 2012).

These are not "applications."
They are **rituals of obedience**.
A test of how much humiliation you're willing to endure to be allowed basic survival (Bourdieu 1991).

The Larger Truth: Consent Without Choice Is Not Consent

Everywhere we turn, a signature is demanded — not because we are entering into a real agreement, but because the system needs legal cover for the harm it will inevitably cause (Davis 2017).

Modern life requires you to give up:

- rights,
- privacy,
- autonomy,
- dignity,
- legal protections,
- time,
- emotional labor

before you can even step into the world.

This is not safety.
This is not accountability.
This is not fairness.

This is **coercion built into the fabric of daily life** (MacKinnon 1989; Zuboff 2019).

A world where your rights are treated as optional add-ons, not inherent truths.
A world where contracts have replaced compassion and accountability.
A world where the cost of participation is your freedom.

And the worst part?
We've been conditioned to think this is normal.

As if surrendering your rights to watch a movie, get a job, or see a doctor is just the "fine print of adulthood."
As if existing in society should require you to sign away pieces of your humanity one form at a time.

This is not a society.
This is a **contract machine** that feeds on compliance.

And the real cruelty is that,
We never truly had a choice.

References

Ajunwa, Ifeoma, Kate Crawford, and Jason Schultz. 2017. "Limitless Worker Surveillance." *California Law Review* 105(3):735–776.

Bourdieu, Pierre. 1991. *Language and Symbolic Power.* Edited by John B. Thompson. Translated by Gino Raymond and Matthew Adamson. Cambridge, MA: Harvard University Press.

Cohen, Julie E. 2012. *Configuring the Networked Self: Law, Code, and the Play of Everyday Practice.* New Haven, CT: Yale University Press.

Davis, Kevin E. 2017. "Contracts as Regulation." In *The Regulatory Theory of Contracts,* edited by Stefan Grundmann, Wulf-Henning Roth, and Thierry Granier, 1–22. Oxford: Oxford University Press.

Graeber, David. 2015. *The Utopia of Rules: On Technology, Stupidity, and the Secret Joys of Bureaucracy.* Brooklyn, NY: Melville House.

Herd, Pamela, and Donald P. Moynihan. 2018. *Administrative Burden: Policymaking by Other Means.* New York: Russell Sage Foundation.

MacKinnon, Catharine A. 1989. *Toward a Feminist Theory of the State.* Cambridge, MA: Harvard University Press.

McDonald, Aleecia M., and Lorrie Faith Cranor. 2008. "The Cost of Reading Privacy Policies." *ISJLP: International Journal of Law and Information Technology* 4:543–568.

Menjívar, Cecilia, and Leisy Abrego. 2012. "Legal Violence: Immigration Law and the Lives of Central American Immigrants." *American Journal of Sociology* 117(5):1380–1421.

Obar, Jonathan A., and Anne Oeldorf-Hirsch. 2020. "The Biggest Lie on the Internet: Ignoring the Privacy Policies and Terms of Service Policies of Social Networking Services." *Information, Communication & Society* 23(1):128–147.

Power, Michael. 1999. *The Audit Society: Rituals of Verification.* Oxford: Oxford University Press.

Public Citizen. 2015. *Forced Arbitration: Unfair and Everywhere.* Washington, DC: Public Citizen.

Stark, Luke. 2019. "Consent and the Legitimation of Platform Power." *New Media & Society* 21(4):827–846.

Sternlight, Jean R. 2013. "Mandatory Arbitration Stymies Progress Toward Justice in Employment Discrimination Cases." *Journal of Dispute Resolution* 2013(2):285–308.

Stone, Katherine V. W., and Alexander J. S. Colvin. 2020. "The Arbitration Epidemic: Mandatory Arbitration Deprives Workers and Consumers of Their Rights." *Economic Policy Institute Report.* Washington, DC: EPI.

Zuboff, Shoshana. 2019. *The Age of Surveillance Capitalism: The Fight for a Human Future at the New Frontier of Power.* New York: PublicAffairs.

PART TWO

THE LOOPHOLE EMPIRE: HOW INSTITUTIONS PROTECT THEMSELVES AND NOT US

7 —Where Truth Goes to Die: Police Reports and Courtroom Loopholes

There's a scene in *Peppermint* Movie that a lot of survivors never forget.

Riley North sits in a courtroom after her husband and daughter have been murdered by a cartel. She did what every pamphlet tells you to do. She called the police. She cooperated. She went to court. She trusted the system.

And then the "justice system" fails her in the most predictable way possible: the case gets thrown, the rich men walk, and the courts turn their moral backs.

So she does what the system will not: she disappears, trains, and comes back as a vigilante.

That part is fantasy. But the feeling that *no one is coming*? That part is documentary.

Most of us don't come back as action heroes.
We just come back to the same institutions and get quietly crushed in slow motion again and again.

This chapter is about that slow crushing.
Not by traffickers or abusers— but by the **police, courts, hospitals, schools, workplaces, social services, immigration, and mental health systems** that survivors are told to rely on.

This isn't about a few bad apples.
It's about how the orchard is planted, irrigated, and protected.

The Fantasy of Consequence vs. the Reality of Loopholes

Hollywood gives us revenge when we can't even get a callback from the District Attorney (DA).

In the real world, people don't face cinematic villains. They face **institutions**. And institutions hurt you in quieter, more insidious ways. Injured patients, rape victims, IPV (Intimate Partner Violence) survivors, people reporting workplace abuse, disabled people seeking benefits, immigrants asking for protection — they all collide with the same monster: **endless procedural loops**.

Let me be clear: the problem isn't just with crime or the most extreme forms of exploitation. Everyday people fall into these traps too every single day of our lives.

Empirical research backs this up: there is always a gap — **a massive canyon** — between actual harm and what gets officially recorded. Farrell and Reichert (2017) call this the "promise and limits" of institutional data reporting: agencies underuse categories, misclassify cases, and fail to implement basic reporting practices. Even globally, the UNODC reports rising detection of trafficking while also acknowledging that "detected victims" represent only the visible fraction — the ones who make it through the maze.

And that gap between real harm and official recognition?
That's where people live.

The cracks people "fall through" are not cracks — **They are deliberate pressure valves.**
They let institutions look strong on paper while quietly abandoning the humans who don't fit the script.

This is structural narcissism.
Not spectacular, not dramatic — just cold, procedural betrayal delivered in small, daily cuts until a person's hope finally fractures.

It does not announce itself with violence.
It wears a badge, or a clipboard, or a gentle voice saying, "Unfortunately, there's nothing we can do."

And eventually, the accumulation of these betrayals leads to the moment I identify in CRC-PTSD as the *broken trust in humanity syndrome* — that moment when the nervous system concludes:

"Nobody cares. I am on my own. Humans are dangerous. I don't belong here."

It is not one betrayal that causes this collapse.
It is the pattern.

And the irony — the cruelty — is that many of us respond to this collapse by trying even harder to prove that humanity is good.
We overextend.
We overgive.
We override our exhaustion.
We try to be the exception that disproves the rule.

We tell ourselves:
"Maybe if I show compassion, the world will reflect it back."
"Maybe if I work hard enough, someone will see me."
"Maybe if I stay silent, they won't punish me."
"Maybe if I try one more time, someone will actually care."

But the next betrayal comes anyway because the system impersonality is used as an excuse.
Sometimes in slow waves, one after the next.
Sometimes like a tsunami.

And then another.
And another.

Until we fall — not because we are weak, but because **no human nervous system can metabolize endless betrayal and still believe in safety**.

This is the world we live in.
Not one story, but the story of millions:
Different names, different details, but the same emotional aftershocks — the same collapse of trust, the same quiet question whispered into the

dark:

"What happened to humanity?"

Police: The First Gate of Institutional Betrayal

Everything starts with the police report—**or never does.**

If you are assaulted, abused, stalked, exploited, or simply afraid, you are told to call the police. But what you often meet is not trauma-informed care. It is skepticism, minimization, dismissal, and gatekeeping.

Betrayal trauma theory shows that violations by trusted entities produce deeper dysregulation than harm by strangers (Freyd 1996). Institutional betrayal extends this by showing how police, courts, and agencies can intensify trauma through their action or inaction (Smith & Freyd 2014).

Survivors repeatedly describe the same experiences:

- being told "this will be hard to prove" before anyone listens
- being questioned about why they didn't fight harder or report sooner
- having their past used to discredit their present
- being quietly advised to "just move on" because the case is "weak"

And these are not abstract claims — they are documented.

Real-Life Examples

1. The Police Who Told Her "It's Not Serious Enough"

Ally, a woman in Colorado (Denver Post, 2019), repeatedly reported her ex-partner for stalking and escalating threats. Police told her:

- "This doesn't meet the threshold."

- "If he actually does something, call us back."
- "It's probably just a misunderstanding."

Months later, her ex broke into her home and nearly killed her.

How did she describe it?
"Every time they brushed me off, a part of me died. I thought I was going crazy. I thought maybe I *was* overreacting. I started apologizing to the officers who were ignoring me."

This is what CRC-PTSD looks like — internalized betrayal and self-doubt.

---

2 . The Woman Told to Stop "Wasting Police Time"

In the UK, Shana Grice (Guardian, 2016) reported her stalker to police five times. Instead of protecting her, police fined her for "wasting police time."

Her killer then murdered her at age 19.

Her family said:
"She begged them for help. She was treated like a nuisance. She must have felt completely alone."

The institutional betrayal amplified the terror — she died not only from the violence but from a system that refused to see her.

---

3 . The Sexual Assault Survivor Told to Calm Down

A college student in Minnesota (NPR, 2020) reported a rape and was asked:

- "Are you sure you didn't lead him on?"

- "Why didn't you scream?"
- "Maybe you misread the situation."

Her emotional response:
"I left that building hating myself. I wasn't destroyed by the assault — I was destroyed by not being believed."

The police report was never filed. Her case died before it lived.

---

4. The Disabled Woman the Police Refused to Interview

In Los Angeles (LA Times, 2021), a disabled woman reported sexual and physical abuse by a caretaker. Officers dismissed her report as "confusion" due to disability and refused to interview the perpetrator.

She later said:
"I learned that my body didn't matter. That people like me don't get justice."

The harm was doubled — abuse by a caretaker, betrayal by law enforcement.

---

5 . The Child Who Reported Abuse Three Times

A 10-year-old child in Arizona (ProPublica, 2023) disclosed abuse repeatedly. Police and CPS logged the reports but took no action due to "insufficient evidence." The child later suffered life-threatening injuries.

The child's words to a nurse:
"Why didn't anyone believe me?"

This is institutional betrayal in its purest form — a system defending itself instead of a child.

Why These Examples Matter

From the system's perspective, underreporting is a data problem — a statistical gap, a "challenge in documentation."

From the survivor's perspective, it is life or death.

Why would anyone return to a building that has already proven it does not believe them, protect them, or recognize their humanity? The burden of proof, the "not serious enough," the "doesn't fit the category," and the "come back if it gets worse" lines all serve the same purpose: **to gaslight and destabilize the victim until they doubt their own right to seek help.**

When you call the numbers printed on glossy brochures or government websites, you rarely reach an actual human being. You get voicemail loops, automated menus, and scripted responses explaining all the reasons your case "doesn't qualify," "lacks evidence," or "falls outside their scope." It's not support — it's rejection disguised as procedure.

Only a narrow set of cases that perfectly match bureaucratic definitions ever get documented. Everything else — the messy, complex, human reality of harm — falls into the grey zones where institutions claim they have no responsibility. And in those grey zones, crimes don't stop happening. They continue with impunity.

To make it worse, cases that *are* opened are often closed in ways that protect perpetrators with more resources, more influence, or more intimidation power. Some hire better lawyers. Some exploit loopholes. Some have personal connections. Some threaten officers or manipulate authority through social status. In every scenario, the system bends to protect those who know how to navigate it — or how to pressure it.

The result is predictable:
Victims are dismissed, predators walk free, and the institution calls it "due process."

In my own life, I've learned exactly how little the system is willing to do.

When a homeless man stole my purse with the $600 iPhone I had saved for months to buy, the police came and said, "Don't even think about getting it back. If it's under $1,500, we can't do anything."
It wasn't just about the phone. It was the message:

We don't care about you and others like you.

Another time, I was assaulted on a bus.
When I reported it, they didn't ask if I was okay.
They told me, "You need to be careful. You never know who might have a gun."
So instead of safety, I got a lecture on why it was my job to prevent violence.

And the worst one:
When I reported a therapist for sexual misconduct — a person I trusted in a position of power — I was told it "doesn't count" because she didn't touch my private parts.
Never mind that what she did led to more than 40 hospital visits, untreatable depression, and trauma I will carry for the rest of my life.

These weren't just bad days.
They were lessons from the system itself:
We will not protect you.
We will not see your pain.
And if we do nothing, we will still call it justice.

I have been assaulted 4 times by people, and none of those times the police did anything about it. They just found an excuse to close the case, even when I had physical injuries…. And yes people can go nuts under the pressure of this society! That does not justify hurting others!

These cases show that institutional betrayal is not hypothetical — It is documented, measurable, and lethal.

And the emotional harm survivors describe is always the same:

- "I thought I was crazy."
- "I felt invisible."
- "I blamed myself."
- "I stopped asking for help."
- "I lost hope."
- "I felt abandoned by humanity."

- "I was criminalized for my mental health"
- "I know they won't do anything about it, so why bother?"

This is the predictable outcome of a system that protects itself before it protects us.

Courts: Where Trauma Is Put on Trial

Let's say you make it through the first gate. The police actually take your report. They refer your case. You breathe for a moment, thinking, *Maybe this time someone will help me.*

Then you enter the universe of "justice." But the funny thing is that law is yet another human constructed science. We literally made it up out of the thin air. I find it funny how people study law and learn a bunch of jargon to manipulate, gaslight and deflect harm. That is not justice. And for obvious reasons the rich somehow win all their cases even when they were child molesters or murderers.

Research on sexual assault prosecutions shows that only a tiny fraction of cases ever result in a conviction; many never even reach trial at all (Artz & Smythe 2007; Pattavina et al. 2021). Survivors aren't dropping out because they're confused, lying, or dramatic — they drop out because the process is **psychologically unbearable**: endless delays, invasive questioning, contradictory instructions, and the cruelty of having to retell the worst moment of your life over and over to strangers with clipboards.

Legal scholars call this the "second assault" or "second rape" (Madison & Gamble 1991; Martin & Powell 1994). And it's not exaggeration — it's the accurate emotional description survivors have repeated for decades.

Real Examples:

1. The Domestic Violence Survivor Charged Instead of Protected

Case: *Marissa Alexander* (Florida, 2012)
Harm: She fired a warning shot to scare off her abusive husband. No one was hurt.
The court refused her "Stand Your Ground" defense — even though

George Zimmerman successfully used it the same year.

She was sentenced to **20 years in prison**.

Her emotional statement:
"I was punished for trying to survive."

This is what happens when the courtroom interprets self-defense as aggression — because they cannot imagine a Black woman as a victim.

---

2. The Child Neglect Case Where Poverty Was Treated as Abuse

Case: *NYC Family Court, 2019* (reported by ProPublica)
A mother working two jobs left her child sleeping at home for two hours because her babysitter canceled.

The child was safe.
But the court still **removed the child** and claimed "neglect."

Mother's words:
"I was punished for being poor. Not for being a bad mother — for being poor."

The court used legal language to justify ripping apart a family because the mother didn't fit the mythical norm of "middle-class parenting."

---

3. The Wrongful Conviction Based on "Expert" Junk Science

Case: *Keith Harward* (Virginia, 1986–2016)
He spent **33 years in prison** after a court relied on faulty bite-mark analysis (later debunked nationwide).

His feelings after release:
"Losing decades to a lie broke something in me. The court destroyed my life and never apologized."

The courtroom didn't seek the truth. It sought closure — and chose the wrong person.

---

4. The Disabled Man Criminalized for Calling 911 Too Many Times

Case: *Arizona, 2023* (documented by AZCentral & police records)
A disabled man with chronic illness called 911 repeatedly for medical emergencies. He was **charged with misuse of 911** instead of receiving support.

His reaction:
"I wasn't abusing the system. I was begging for help."

The court punished distress — because disability didn't fit their neat narrative of "legitimate emergencies."

---

5. The Tenant Evicted After Reporting Mold and Toxic Conditions

Case: *New Orleans Housing Court, 2021*
A tenant reported black mold and dangerous conditions. The landlord retaliated with an eviction notice.
The court sided with the landlord because the tenant didn't have *photos from every room.*

Tenant's statement:
"It felt like the court cared more about paperwork than whether my kids could breathe."

Justice failed because evidence didn't perfectly match the bureaucratic template.

---

6. The Worker Who Was Punished for Reporting Unsafe Conditions

Case: *OSHA retaliation cases, New Jersey, 2019*
A warehouse worker reported unsafe equipment that eventually injured two co-workers.
He was fired for being "disruptive."

When he sued, the court dismissed the case citing "insufficient proof of retaliatory intent."

His words:
"I gave them proof. They just didn't want to see it."

The courtroom defended the employer's narrative, not the worker's reality.

---

7. The Black Man Sentenced More Harshly Than His White Co-Defendants

Case: *Christopher Williams* (Philadelphia, overturned in 2022)
He was convicted while white co-defendants received lighter or no sentences for the same alleged crime.
After 30 years, his conviction was overturned due to **prosecutorial misconduct and hidden evidence**.

What he said after being freed:
"Justice didn't fail. It never showed up."

---

8. The Child Welfare Case Where Being Indigenous Was Treated as a Risk Factor

Case: *ICWA violations, South Dakota (NPR & ACLU investigations)*
Indigenous parents lost custody of their children in hearings lasting **under 2 minutes**.
No lawyers. No evidence review. No voice.

One parent said:
"It felt like the judge had already decided who I was before I opened my mouth."

The court reproduced historical trauma — using procedure as a weapon.

---

9. The Medical Malpractice Case Dismissed Because the Patient "Didn't Advocate Hard Enough"

Case: *Oregon, 2018* (The Oregonian)
A woman had life-threatening sepsis misdiagnosed as "anxiety." She barely survived.
When she sued, the court dismissed the case because she "did not insist on additional testing."

Her response:
"I didn't know I was dying. That's why I went to the hospital."

The court expected her to do the doctor's job.

---

10. The Deaf Man Arrested Because He Didn't Hear Commands

Case: *Colorado Springs, 2021* (Bodycam + court records)
A deaf man was ordered to "stop resisting" — but he couldn't hear the officers.
He was charged with obstruction.

He said later:
"I was injured, handcuffed, and treated like a criminal for not hearing."

Courts upheld the officers' actions.

Why These Patterns Hurt

The courtroom is supposed to be neutral, but neutrality in a traumatogenic environment becomes another form of violence. Trauma responses that are well documented in clinical literature — flat affect, fragmented memory, delayed disclosure, emotional flooding (Herman 1997; van der Kolk 2015) — are reframed as:

- lies,
- exaggerations,
- inconsistencies,
- instability,
- or lack of credibility.

The system demands scientific, clean, linear narratives — and punishes the survivors whose nervous systems bear witness to chaos.

And if you add race, poverty, disability, neurodivergence, or immigration status, the disbelief intensifies. Intersectional research shows that women of color, migrant women, and disabled survivors are disbelieved at even higher rates (Crenshaw 1991; Artz & Smythe 2007).

Examples of Intersectional Harm:

- **A Black survivor's** pain is coded as "anger," making her "less credible."
- **A Latina immigrant** is asked whether she misunderstood due to language, even when she speaks English fluently.
- **A disabled survivor** is seen as "unreliable" because her trauma shows up in her cognitive processing.
- **A poor survivor** is assumed to be lying for "attention" or "benefits."

These aren't individual biases — they're the structure.

And we need to name something that rarely gets said out loud: **most judges come from profoundly privileged backgrounds.** They are disproportionately drawn from upper- or upper-middle-class families, elite law schools, and professional networks far removed from poverty, disability, systemic trauma, or precarity. Many have never experienced homelessness, food insecurity, institutional betrayal, untreated illness, or the terror of not knowing whether you will survive the month.

This distance matters.

When judges interpret credibility, reasonableness, or "appropriate" behavior, they do so through the lens of their own lives—lives shaped by stability, insulation, and access. What looks "irrational" or "excessive" to them may be the normal language of survival for someone who has lived inside chronic threats. What feels "unprofessional" or "emotional" may simply be a nervous system shaped by trauma.

Yet the system treats the judge's perspective as neutral, objective, and authoritative—while treating the survivor's embodied truth as suspect.

And let's be honest:

Justice is not blind.
It is priced.

Judicial immunity deepens this imbalance. Judges are granted extraordinary protection from accountability, even when their decisions cause irreparable harm. A ruling can cost someone their home, their children, their health, their freedom—or their life—and yet the judge remains untouched, insulated by doctrine, procedure, and immunity. There is no meaningful avenue for redress when judicial power is exercised without care.

This immunity sends a devastating message:
The system can harm you without consequence.

In reality, the legal system is not a level playing field.
It is a staircase—and the wealthy start near the top.

Survivors are not losing because they are "inconsistent."
They are losing because the system is designed to amplify the voices of

the powerful and muffle the voices of the wounded.

And the deeper truth is this: when those who hold the power to decide life-altering outcomes have never lived the realities they are judging, justice becomes abstraction—cold, procedural, and profoundly unsafe for anyone who lives outside privilege.

Everyday Examples:

1. The Traffic Ticket Spiral

You can't afford a $200 ticket, so you delay paying it.
The court adds late fees.
You miss a hearing because you're working or don't have childcare.
The court issues a warrant.
Now you're labeled "noncompliant" or "irresponsible," even though you were only struggling to survive. Lets not forget how traffic law enforcement randomly gives tickets to a select few and keeps a blind eye on others.

I've noticed the city giving away tickets like candies on Halloween, when the city needs money. I'm still waiting for a hearing for a parking ticket I got in September 2025 for California's Daylighting Law (AB 413), effective January 1, 2025, that prohibits parking within 20 feet of any marked or unmarked crosswalk to enhance pedestrian visibility and safety.

I and most people I talked to about this didn't even know about it because the DMV hadn't done much to inform us citizens. Plus my car was parked at least 15 feet from the crossing while there were several other cars parked less than five feet from the crossing who didn't get a ticket. This was so maddening to me as I respected the red painted curb. It was the city's failure to update the curb and inform. I had to park in that alley and walk up a hill for 20 minutes to go to the financial aid at USD, as I had dropped out since I couldn't afford the school and they refused to give me any assistance and discriminated against me telling me they will deport me. You can read about it in my previous book. I am also appalled by schools for using parking space as a business. Isn't the tuition already enough?

How people feel:

"I wasn't a criminal before this. The court turned me into one."

This is everyday structural violence.

---

2. The Eviction Hearing That Lasts 90 Seconds

Rent spikes. Hours cut at work. You fall behind by $300.
The landlord brings a well-paid attorney.
You show up alone, scared, and without representation.
The judge asks three questions, takes the landlord's paperwork as truth, and rules against you.

What tenants say afterward:
"It didn't matter what I said. It felt like the decision was already written."

Housing courts do this **every single day**.

---

3. The Custody Case Where the Calm Parent Is Punished

Two parents appear in court: one loud, dramatic, crying; the other flat, numb, trying to stay composed.
The calm parent is accused of being "emotionally disconnected."
The distressed parent is framed as "passionate" and "committed."

Trauma responses get misinterpreted as character flaws.

Common emotional response:
"I felt like I was on trial for the way my nervous system coped."

---

4. The Disabled Person Denied Guardianship or Benefits Because They "Seem Fine Today"

Someone with chronic illness or neurodivergence appears in court on a "good day."
The judge decides they don't need support because "you look well" or "you're articulate."

Their reaction:
"I felt invisible. You can't see what I live through unless you live inside my body."

This is a daily experience for disabled people.

---

5. The Debt Collection Judgment You Don't Even Hear About

A debt gets sold to a collection agency.
They file in court using an old address.
You never receive a notice.
A judgment is entered without your knowledge.
Your wages are garnished.

People say:
"I was punished in a hearing I wasn't even at."

This is incredibly common — especially among low-income workers.

---

6. The Parent Fined for Their Child's Truancy

Your child misses school because of chronic illness, bullying, or lack of transportation.
Instead of support, the court fines *you* hundreds of dollars and threatens charges.

What parents say:
"I needed help, and they punished me."

Everyday cruelty dressed up as order.

---

7. The Small Claims Case Where "Evidence" Means Paperwork You Don't Have

A contractor damages your apartment.

You go to small claims court without legal knowledge.
The contractor brings organized invoices, photos, and a lawyer friend.
You lose because your evidence isn't formatted correctly.

Emotional reaction:
"The truth didn't matter — only the paperwork did."

---

8. The Immigration Court Where a Five-Minute Hearing Determines Someone's Life

An immigrant stands before a judge without a lawyer (because there is no right to counsel).
The judge reviews a stack of documents for two minutes and signs a deportation order.

What people say afterward:
"It felt like I never had a chance to speak."

This is standard practice.

---

9. The Protective Order That Gets Denied Because "No Bruises Today"

Someone fleeing an abusive partner goes to court for a restraining order.
The judge declines because there are "no visible injuries" or "insufficient current evidence."

Common emotional response:
"I did everything they told me to do. And they still said no."

This happens to thousands of people every week.

---

10. The Worker Wrongfully Terminated Who Can't Afford to Sue

Your boss fires you illegally (retaliation, discrimination, unpaid overtime).

You look into filing a claim, only to learn:

- a lawyer won't take your case without a retainer
- the court fees are hundreds of dollars
- the process takes years

What workers say:
"The system isn't made for people like me. It's made for people who can afford justice."

And Here's the Emotional Truth Beneath All These Examples

People don't walk out of court feeling angry —
they walk out feeling **small**, **defeated**, **confused**, and **ashamed**.

They say things like:

- "I guess my story didn't matter."
- "Maybe I really am the problem."
- "The judge didn't even look at me."
- "I felt stupid for even trying."
- "I thought justice was for everyone."
- "I don't trust people anymore."

Luckily, I don't have many experiences with the courts, and small claims court did help me once—I got reimbursed for a car I bought without knowing about the $1,400 in unpaid registration under the lemon law.

Another time I had a hearing for health insurance. I still find it absurd that I had to tell a judge my whole story just to ask my insurance to cover continuity of care with my therapist and still was denied.

This is the harm courts inflict every day, quietly, procedurally, without ever raising their voice, as an all knowing, all powerful entity that protects the rich and lets the poor die.

This is structural narcissism:
cold, bureaucratic, emotionally detached, and devastating.

References

Artz, Lillian, and Dee Smythe. 2007. *Should We Consent? Rape Law Reform in South Africa.* Cape Town: Juta.

AZCentral. 2023. News report on disabled man charged after repeated emergency calls (Arizona case referenced).

Crenshaw, Kimberlé. 1991. "Mapping the Margins: Intersectionality, Identity Politics, and Violence against Women of Color." *Stanford Law Review* 43(6):1241–1299.

Denver Post. 2019. News report on stalking case involving repeated police dismissal (Colorado case referenced).

Farrell, Amy, and Jessica Reichert. 2017. "Human Trafficking and the Limits of Institutional Data." *Annual Review of Criminology* 1:123–144.

Freyd, Jennifer J. 1996. *Betrayal Trauma: The Logic of Forgetting Childhood Abuse.* Cambridge, MA: Harvard University Press.

Guardian. 2016. News coverage of Shana Grice stalking case and police response.

Herman, Judith Lewis. 1997. *Trauma and Recovery.* New York: Basic Books.

LA Times. 2021. News investigation into law enforcement response to disabled survivor reporting abuse.

Madison, Jeanne, and Nancy Gamble. 1991. Early scholarship describing courtroom processes as "secondary assault" in sexual-violence cases.

Martin, Patricia Yancey, and Barbara Powell. 1994. Research on institutional handling of sexual-assault survivors and secondary victimization.

Morel, Pierre, dir. 2018. *Peppermint.* United States: STX Entertainment.

NPR. 2020. News report on sexual assault survivor police questioning (Minnesota case).

NPR and ACLU. Investigations into ICWA violations and expedited Indigenous custody hearings (South Dakota cases referenced).

Oregonian. 2018. News report on misdiagnosed sepsis malpractice case.

Pattavina, April, et al. 2021. Research on sexual assault prosecution outcomes and attrition in the justice system.

ProPublica. 2019. Investigation into NYC Family Court poverty-based neglect cases.

ProPublica. 2023. Investigation into child abuse reports ignored by police/CPS (Arizona case referenced).

Smith, Carly P., and Jennifer J. Freyd. 2014. "Institutional Betrayal." *American Psychologist* 69(6):575–587.

UNODC (United Nations Office on Drugs and Crime). Various years. *Global Report on Trafficking in Persons.* Vienna: United Nations.

van der Kolk, Bessel A. 2015. *The Body Keeps the Score: Brain, Mind, and Body in the Healing of Trauma.* New York: Viking.

8 —Clinical Betrayal: Healthcare & Psychiatry

Hospitals,Clinics, and Health Insurance: "Care" That Wounds

The healthcare system is where many survivors go first—especially those escaping trafficking and work and family abuse. They might show up with injuries, infections, malnutrition, or unexplained chronic pain. Yet studies and federal reports show that health systems often **miss or mishandle** these cases: victims are treated for immediate medical issues and discharged, while underlying exploitation is not recognized or documented. (Hopper 2004; U.S. HHS/ACF 2019).

Doctors' offices have waitlists that stretch across months, sometimes a year, as if we can politely ask our pain to pause itself until the system is ready. By the time our appointment finally arrives, we have already visited the ER multiple times, spiraling through fear, frustration, and exhaustion with no actual relief.

And when we finally walk through the clinic doors, desperate for care, we are greeted not with compassion but with **overworked, burnt-out staff** who have nothing left to give. Their tone says, *"Hurry up."* Their eyes say, *"Don't make this complicated."* Their body language says, *"I'm drowning too."*

Then comes the ten-minute appointment.
Ten minutes to explain months or years of suffering.

Ten minutes to be believed or dismissed.

You begin your story, but the doctor interrupts halfway through your first sentence. He forces you into **yes/no** answers so he can fit your complexity into the boxes required for billing. Your pain becomes an administrative task. Your humanity becomes an inconvenience.

He doesn't ask about context.
He doesn't ask about fear.
He doesn't ask about your life, your trauma history, or your intuition.

He asks the questions the screen demands.
And when your symptoms don't fit the textbook narrative he learned in medical school twenty years ago, the implication becomes painfully clear:

"If I can't diagnose it in ten minutes, it must be your fault."

You leave unseen. Unheard.
You walk out holding the same pain you walked in with—except now it has a new layer: **the shame of not being believed.**

This is the part that cuts the deepest.

Because it teaches you to question your own reality.
It teaches you to normalize unbearable symptoms.
It teaches you that your suffering is a personal failure, not a systemic one.

And the cruelest irony is that **your doctor is also trapped** in a system that rewards speed over listening, metrics over meaning, and liability avoidance over care. He is pressured to see thirty patients a day, fill endless documentation, meet productivity quotas, and avoid anything that requires emotional presence.

So he becomes a technician, not a healer.
A box-checker, not a witness.
A gatekeeper, not a companion.

The whole system designs both of you for failure — you to be unheard, and him to be unreachable.

And this is how structural narcissism shows up in healthcare:
Through clinics that pretend to offer care while quietly teaching patients to feel defective for suffering.

Through appointments that mimic intimacy while delivering emotional abandonment.

Through rituals of "evidence-based practice" that leave no space for the truths your body carries.

Through a medical culture that calls itself scientific while ignoring the one science it can't quantify:
The lived experience of pain, fear, intuition, and the human spirit.

A hospital's mission statement lists compassion, healing, and patient safety as sacred core values. The website is full of soft lighting, gentle language, and photos of doctors placing reassuring hands on patients' shoulders. But when a patient is misdiagnosed, endangered, or harmed, the internal machinery tells a very different story. Committees close ranks. Doctors protect one another. Administrators cite "policy" as if it were divine law. Legal teams advise silence. And the family receives a cold, standardized letter that communicates nothing except the institution's need to protect itself.

The hospital preserves its **image** — not the patient's wellbeing.

And inside those same walls, the staff is overwhelmed by workloads no human nervous system can sustain. Nurses are assigned unsafe patient ratios. Residents work thirty-hour shifts. Providers are expected to heal others while being denied rest, grief, and humanity. Burnout doesn't just happen — it is manufactured by systems that view healthcare workers as endlessly replaceable.

Burnout becomes apathy.
Apathy becomes emotional numbing.
Emotional numbing becomes detachment.
And detachment becomes a risk factor for further harm.

The structure harms the healer first, and then the healer, burned out and dissociated, unintentionally harms the patient. Yet intent doesn't justify impact.

This is not an individual failure — it is an institutional design.

And there is another uncomfortable truth we rarely name:
Many people enter the healing professions for **status, money, and prestige** — not for compassion. Medicine, psychology, and even social

work are not immune to capitalism's gravitational pull. These fields are framed as "noble," but they also carry high social status, respectable titles, and financial incentives. When prestige becomes the motivator rather than care, vulnerable people pay the price.

There *are* extraordinary healers in these systems — people who truly care, who bend rules in favor of humanity, who carry the moral weight the institution refuses to hold. But they are swimming against the current while the system rewards efficiency, emotional detachment, and billable units over empathy.

And how can a system heal someone who is vulnerable when **the people inside it are incentivized to chase the material world rather than sit with human suffering**?

You cannot heal in an environment that punishes slowness, tenderness, and presence.
You cannot care deeply when your job demands you see thirty patients in a day.
You cannot restore someone's dignity when the institution demands you document them as codes and symptoms rather than as a full person.
You cannot bring people back to life when you yourself are barely surviving.

Hospitals promise care.

But the system they are built on delivers something closer to clinicalized indifference — a machine that extracts labor from healers and compliance from patients, while shielding itself behind policy, liability, and the illusion of professionalism.

This is not healthcare.

This is health-management under capitalism — and human beings are the collateral damage. It is a system of extracting monetary gain, from patients' pain.

Insurance

Finally as though the waitlists, dismissals, and ten-minute appointments weren't enough, you still have to face the next layer of harm: **insurance.**

Insurance is the quiet puppeteer of the entire system.
It decides what care you deserve, when you deserve it, and whether you deserve it at all.
Doctors can barely treat patients because they are too busy treating insurance requirements.

You can have the best doctor in the world, but if your insurance denies coverage, delays authorization, or cuts off services, your body pays the price. Sometimes with suffering. Sometimes with years of life.

Insurance doesn't say, *"We can't help."*
It says, *"Not covered."*
"Denied."
"Try again next year."
"We need more paperwork."
"This doesn't meet criteria."

Their power is absolute. Their empathy is nonexistent.

And I've lived this intimately many times.

Back when I first came to the U.S., I was on Medicaid and needed a root canal.
It wasn't covered.
The cost: **$1,000–$2,000** in 2018— impossible for someone without savings or a part-time job.
The pain was unbearable; anyone who has needed a root canal knows it feels like your skull is pulsing with a heartbeat made of fire.

Do you know what I ended up doing?

I spent the same amount of money—money I barely had—to fly back to Iran and get the procedure done there.
That's how broken the system is:
It was cheaper to leave the country than to get care in it.

But the real message Medicaid sent was this:

"If you are poor, don't get too sick.
We will not save you.
We may even let you die."

Think about that.

A root canal isn't cosmetic.
It is an emergency. Untreated infection can spread to the bloodstream, the brain, the heart.
People die from dental infections.

And yet dental care in the U.S. is treated like a luxury — as if only the wealthy should enjoy chewing food without agony, and everyone else should survive on soft bread and water, grateful just to exist.

And the truth is, it's not only the U.S. Dental insurance barely exists in much of the world. Everywhere, the unspoken rule is the same:

Only the rich deserve to eat comfortably.
Only the rich deserve health.
Only the rich deserve to keep the teeth they were born with.

Insurance is not a support system.
It is a sorting mechanism:
those who qualify, those who don't;
those who can afford suffering, and those who cannot survive it.

Insurance companies delay care until you give up.
They deny procedures until you deteriorate.
They cut off treatment the moment you start improving.
They decide—behind closed doors, using algorithms and cost charts—whether your pain is worth relieving.

And if you are poor, the quiet truth is:

Your body is expensive to heal and cheap to dispose of.

That is their logic.

Insurance pretends to be neutral, but it is one of the most violent silencers of human suffering. It teaches you to doubt your needs, to shrink your hopes, to fear getting sick, to feel guilty for requiring care, to internalize the belief that your life costs too much.

If you ever called insurance to ask for providers, they send you a useless list of a few providers who mostly don't answer their phone, or if they do they tell you they are out of network at the time. This is not healthcare. This is health-management by capitalism, enforced through paperwork and denial.

Workers Compensation

Workers' compensation is supposed to protect injured workers — a social contract that says:
If you get hurt while helping society function, society will help you heal.

But in reality, it operates as another mechanism of institutional betrayal. When an injury becomes expensive, ambiguous, or inconvenient, the system doesn't just deny care.
It denies **you**.

And when insurers can't deny the physical injury, they reach for something cheaper:
your sanity.

This is one of the most common and well-documented strategies:
if they can't dispute the injury, they will dispute the *person* who reports it.

You go to the hospital hurt, scared, in pain — and suddenly your suffering becomes a character flaw. Workers describe the same script everywhere:

- *"You're exaggerating."*
- *"This seems psychological."*
- *"The imaging looks normal."*
- *"You're overly emotional."*
- *"This may be stress-related."*

It feels personal, but it isn't.
It's a business model.

Labeling a worker "unstable" is a financially efficient way to avoid paying for:

- surgery,

- physical therapy,
- lost wages,
- long-term disability,
- PTSD care,
- or any injury that exposes unsafe working conditions.

Once the psychological label is on your file, the insurer can declare:

"Not work-related. Claim denied."

Hospitals participate because acknowledging workplace injuries creates liability. Employers participate because it's easier to fire someone labeled "mentally unfit" than someone injured at work. Insurance participates because denial saves millions.

This is not a misunderstanding.
This is an **organized strategy of institutional gaslighting**.

These strategies include:

Delay Until You Break

The first tactic is always delay.

- "We never received the form."
- "Please fax it again."
- "Your case is under review."
- "You missed a deadline or a call."
- "Your doctor needs to submit more proof."

While they stall, you get sicker, poorer, more desperate.
Delay is not incompetence — it's design.

Many workers give up simply because they cannot survive the waiting.

IME Doctors: The Hired Assassins of Credibility

"Independent Medical Examiners" are not independent.
They're paid by insurers to justify denial.

IME reports routinely claim:

- "No objective findings."
- "Symptoms exaggerated."
- "Pre-existing condition."
- "No further treatment required."

One 20-minute IME visit can override months of actual medical care with a single sentence:
"Patient appears distressed; psychological factors likely."

And just like that, a real injury becomes a mental defect in the eyes of the system.

Surveillance: Turning Your Life Into Evidence

If pathologizing doesn't work, they escalate.
Workers report being followed, videotaped, photographed doing mundane things — taking out trash, lifting groceries, walking the dog.

Normal daily activities are twisted into "proof" that you're faking.

The logic is cruel and ridiculous:

If you can smile once, you're not depressed.
If you can walk one block, you're not injured.
If you can carry a grocery bag, you're malingering.

They weaponize moments of survival against you.

The "Pre-Existing Condition" Lie

Another escape hatch: claim the injury is not new.
Insurers routinely blame:

- age,
- genetics,
- weight,
- childhood injuries,
- past mental health conditions,
- unrelated life stressors.

Anything to shift responsibility back onto you.

Women, older workers, disabled workers, and neurodivergent people face this tactic the most.

Punishing You for Missing One Appointment

Miss one physical therapy session because you're in too much pain?
Claim suspended.

Miss a paperwork deadline because you were hospitalized?
Claim denied.

Meanwhile, the system routinely "loses" documents with no consequences.

Lowball Settlements: Financial Coercion Disguised as Help

After months of wearing you down, insurers offer a small payout:

- far below lost wages,
- far below medical needs,
- in exchange for closing your claim forever.

By the time the offer arrives, many people are drowning financially, so they accept.
This is financial trauma masquerading as assistance.

Forced Return to Work: Reinjury as a Strategy

Workers' comp doctors often clear people for "light duty," knowing full well the workplace doesn't offer it. The worker returns to full tasks, reinjures themselves, and then insurers say:

"Reinjury is not our responsibility."

Temporary injuries become lifelong disabilities because the system rushes people back into harm.

Denying Mental Health Claims Entirely

PTSD from workplace violence?
Not covered.

Anxiety after harassment?
Not covered.

Depression after losing mobility or livelihood?
Not covered.

Emotional trauma is treated as an inconvenience rather than a legitimate medical consequence of injury.

I was assaulted at work, and it took workers' comp three months just to decide which doctor I needed to see. By the time they finally sent me to their IME, I had already dragged myself back to work. After I filled out pages of surveys and sat through an interview, she labeled me with "pre-existing mental health issues." That alone was devastating and made no sense because all I did was ask our clients who were playing with the piano to "Please lower the volume," and then one of them decided to physically attack me! And somehow that "crazy for money" doctor labeled me as unstable! To add salt to the injury the clinic refused to release the report. I remember crying on the phone and telling them it is dehumanizing. The reason for their refusal to give me the report? They said because of my history they are afraid it will lead to self injury. I'm still sitting here feeling so angry and wondering what judgment that doctor made that they were scared to let me read it! Nothing I told them was enough to convince them that I am capable enough to handle their procedural cruelty they were inflicting on me to refuse to pay workers compensation.

That level of paternalism and gaslighting was its own trauma — the system treating me not as a person in pain, but as a liability they needed to manage while labeling me as unstable to avoid paying workers compensation.

Weaponizing Bureaucracy Until You Question Your Own Reality

The paperwork is intentionally impossible:

- contradictory
- legalistic
- repetitive
- confusing
- inaccessible to anyone in pain or distress

The more traumatized you are, the harder it is to comply — and the system uses that as proof you don't deserve benefits.

This is **procedural violence**.

The Emotional Truth Beneath It All

For many injured workers, physical injury is not what destroys them.
It's the **institutional betrayal** that follows.

It's the humiliation of being disbelieved.
It's the terror of losing your income.
It's the feeling of being hunted by a system meant to protect you.
It's the quiet collapse when you realize your employer sees you as disposable.
It's the shame that starts to feel like a personality trait.
It's the isolation of fighting a giant with a broken body.

People describe feeling:

- "like I was going crazy,"
- "invisible,"
- "gaslit,"
- "criminalized for being injured,"
- "punished for asking for help,"
- "abandoned by humanity."

Workers' comp doesn't just fail to care for injured people.
It actively harms them by turning their suffering into a flaw, their injury into a suspicion, and their life into a liability.

This is institutional narcissism disguised as medical evaluation.
A system that would rather call a worker crazy than call themselves responsible.

Psychiatric Settings and Mental Health

In psychiatric settings, so many trauma survivors describe being restrained, secluded, or coerced into medication in ways that mirror the very control and imprisonment that harmed them in the first place. That is not trauma-informed care; it is **punishment and containment.** It is the quiet criminalization of mental illness — locking people away in inhumane psych wards where staff are so burnt out they say things like, *"If you cry, we're going to keep you here longer."* or *"you'll get an injection for being upset like that" (My personal experiences).* They force you to get naked in front of two people to do a body check. Then they force you to get shots involuntarily because you were a "bad" patient and had a breakdown. Last time I was at a psychiatric hospital they restrained me for eighty five minutes. People die when restrained and the nurses did not even check on me once the whole time.

Here I have two examples of Patients dying from being restrained:

The Psychiatric Patient Restrained Until She Stopped Breathing

Case: Washington Post, 2019.
A young woman in a psychiatric hospital was forcibly restrained for "noncompliance," even though she was panicking and asking to speak with a therapist.
She died from positional asphyxiation.

Staff later said:
"We followed protocol."

Protocol killed her.

The Black Man Whose Restraint in a Hospital Led to His Death

Case: Elijah McClain (Colorado, 2019).
Though primarily a police case, the **medical harm** was central.
After being violently detained, Elijah was injected with ketamine by paramedics — a drug he did not need, at a dosage far too high for his body weight.
He died days later.

His mother:
"Every system failed him — even the one meant to save him."

Here is my story:

I was surrounded by 7-8 nurses, pinned to the bed. The nurse who earlier had yelled at me when I asked her to leave the room because she made me feel unsafe during the body check sat on my leg and started pressing so hard on the bony part of my leg I got bruised. That was not the only bruise, yet the way she smirked and enjoyed my agony while I was screaming that she was hurting me was appalling. Out of 7 people, no one took action to stop her. After they restrained me the other nurse sat outside the room, ignoring me for 82 minutes, as though I was invisible. I called out to God over and over. I cried, I told them my arm is hurting because of how I couldn't straighten it. I begged them to talk to me. They ignored me as if I was nothing. After two days of sleeping day and night and not being able to get up even for food, I managed to write a grievance. Another lost piece of paper no one followed up about. When I finally got out and called the patient advocacy, I found out it was not even submitted.

My experience was like a scene out of a horror Asylum movie. I always felt sick learning about lobotomy, shock therapy and all the inhumane ways they experimented on mentally ill. Unfortunately despite all the patient friendly exterior marketing, psychwards are still a site of unimaginable dehumanization. Also there isn't much difference between overloading one's body with "pharmaceutical drugs" or "drugs?" In the end it's all about them making money out of the vulnerable's agony.

Later that week, I tried to file a police report. Remember "everything starts with a police report—or it never does." When an officer came to my home, he brushed it off entirely and implied that physical abuse and excessive use of force were normal in psychiatric settings. He refused to file the report because he said he remembered me from the time I was on the bridge. When I later called and asked to speak with a supervisor, my calls were ignored. He didn't have to call me "crazy," all he did was to imply it and ignore the bruise on my leg.

Studies of institutional betrayal and secondary trauma in mental health and IPV contexts show that when survivors are punished, ignored, or pathologized by systems they turn to, their symptoms worsen and their trust in institutions erodes further (Smith and Freyd 2014; PettyJohn et al. 2023; Christl et al. 2024).

Do you understand what that does to a person?
It tells you that if you are in emotional pain, you are no longer welcome among the human species until you learn to deny it again.
It teaches you that the cost of being honest about your suffering is captivity.

That is not care.
That is punishment wrapped in medical authority.

And research backs this up. Studies on medical gaslighting and institutional betrayal in healthcare show that when providers invalidate a person's emotional reality, it **worsens trauma**, deepens shame, and makes it far less likely they will ever ask for help again (Christl et al. 2024; Ng & Hjong 2024).

People leave these places not healed, but fractured — carrying the new wound of being harmed by the very system that promised to help.

Hospitals are built to move bodies, manage risk, and code everything into billable units. Trauma does not fit neatly into that script. So it gets flattened into a billing code or pushed out the door.

Therapy & "Help" That Isn't Available

This is one area where I have far too many negative lived experiences. I started therapy for the first time at 26 at my college, and even finding someone through my insurance felt impossible. The crisis counseling offered at my school was more damaging than having no one at all. One therapist shamed me for not believing in the Christian God. Another asked me if I "felt special" for sharing how deeply I cared about justice, and called me arrogant — which was really his own arrogance projected onto me, but at the time it pierced me in a way I still feel.

Then my eating disorder began at 27, after trying to get help and finding none. I remember thinking, *"Maybe if I have the deadliest mental health condition, and they can see my emaciated body, then they'll start to care."* I thought maybe visible suffering would unlock compassion.

I was wrong.
So wrong.

They still didn't acknowledge my emotional pain.
They didn't even care if I lived.

One therapist told me "If you were serious about taking your life, you wouldn't have been here today!" which made me want to prove to her otherwise.

Insurance offered a few treatment options and at one point none. Every phone call, every office worker, every voicemail loop pushed me further into the syndrome of broken trust in humanity. I kept begging for help until I couldn't anymore. I gave up — not because I wanted to die, but because the system made it clear that my life was optional. I didn't decide on it in one night. It was years of seeking help and being rejected that led me there.

People treated my pain as personal failure, but it wasn't personal. It was **systemic harm** killing me slowly. Not one person or entity — but the *braided stack* of many:

- the therapist who shamed me,
- the one who mocked me,
- the clinic that refused me,
- the insurance rep who hung up,
- the waitlists,
- the loopholes,
- the "sorry, we can't help,"
- the "not covered,"
- the "not severe enough,"
- the "you need a higher level of care than we offer."

I wrote in my first book that if I died, it would've been a murder committed not by me but by all the systems and people who claimed they couldn't help. I was criticized for that — told I was "dramatic" and asked "what happens to personal accountability?," that suicide would have been "my choice."

And yes, technically, it would have been my choice.
But when the world narrows into a cage, when the system keeps shutting every door, when you turn to individuals for humanity and they refuse to look at you, your options become only a handful. And none of them are

good:

Option 1: Live in a world where most people are asleep, indifferent, or too frightened to care.
A world where your suffering is an inconvenience.

Option 2: Die — and be blamed for it.
And the system walks away clean.

Option 3: Stay alive but be alone.
Avoid every system, every institution, even people—because every interaction triggers CRC-PTSD. I've tried this option, but I can't live in isolation. I need connection, and without money I can't afford even a single session with my therapist. This is not a sustainable option unless you have millions of dollars. Remember the question: *"Would access to fair resources change this outcome?"*

Here, the answer is clearly yes. So the system is to be blamed. I wasn't left with choices. They were the edges of survival.

And yet, I chose to stay — painfully, stubbornly, desperately — because the truth was suffocating me, and writing it down was the only place I could breathe. I stayed because the systemic lies were killing me and I knew it wasn't just me. It's happening to all of us. I see the pain we're carrying and it is unbearable, but I can't give up on our humanity. Because if I could wake up in the middle of all this, then one day, we all can.

I am still here, still breathing the same gaslit air, still praying that humanity wakes up — truly wakes up — and finally places the blame where it belongs:
on systems designed to discard us, and on the cultural narratives that teach individuals to look away and ignore emotional pain.

I pray we build systems rooted in dignity, humanity, love, and care — and in the recognition that we are all interconnected, all responsible for the air each other breathes, and all capable of shaping the future of our existence.

Because the way things are now?
It is not livable and won't get better unless we allow ourselves to feel and sit with the pain of the cruelty we are surrounded with and speak up.

The DSM as a System of Deniable Violence

The DSM is frequently treated as a scientific authority, but in practice it functions as an institutional tool for managing human suffering through classification rather than understanding. It is not a neutral mirror of mental reality. It is a bureaucratic architecture that converts distress into diagnosis and context into pathology.

Many so-called "disorders" are not mysterious internal defects. They are predictable aftermaths of trauma, chronic stress, deprivation, relational injury, and structural abandonment. Hypervigilance is what the body does after danger. Emotional volatility is what happens when safety is unstable. Dissociation is what the nervous system does when reality becomes intolerable. Yet the DSM repeatedly rebrands these survival responses as individual dysfunction, as if the problem originates inside the person rather than in the conditions surrounding them.

This is not merely an intellectual error. It is a moral and political one. The diagnostic gaze often performs a reversal: instead of asking what happened, it asks what is wrong. Instead of naming betrayal, it names "personality." Instead of recognizing chronic institutional harm, it recognizes "disorder." The result is that structural violence becomes clinically invisible, while the individual becomes clinically suspect.

The instability of the DSM's own history reveals its constructed nature. Entire categories have appeared and disappeared with shifting social norms. What was once listed as pathology—sexuality, gender variance, dissenting affect—later becomes evidence not of illness but of psychiatry's own cultural limitations. The manual thus does not simply diagnose individuals; it exposes the anxieties of the institutions that produce it.

Personality disorder categories are among the clearest examples of this epistemic failure. They often name the scars of trauma as character pathology, converting survival strategies into moralized defects. In doing so, psychiatry risks functioning not as a science of care but as an administrative language of discreditation: a way of marking certain forms of suffering as illegible, irrational, or unsafe.

The DSM persists not because it perfectly explains the human mind, but because it serves institutional needs: insurance reimbursement, legal adjudication, bureaucratic sorting, and credibility governance. It offers deniability. It allows systems to treat the consequences of structural cruelty while leaving the causes untouched.

A trauma-saturated society cannot be diagnosed into health. It must be confronted.

These are the everyday architecture of our healthcare system.

Real human beings are crushed under the weight of **procedural cruelty.** I've lived through many versions of them myself. It's the feeling of not even wanting to go to the doctor because you already know they will downplay or dismiss you. Or the other extreme: *"We can't help you — you need a higher level of care,"* followed by waitlists that stretch into months while you suffer alone. And other times when they admit you and treat you so badly for struggling in a system designed for causing the struggles, as though you asked to get sick in the first place.

And then there's insurance — an entirely different monster. They cut off services, weaponize paperwork, and hide their cruelty behind "policies" and "criteria."

It's time we finally say "No" to doctors who are in the field for prestige and money, not healing. And it's time to let go of the idea that modern medicine is the only path to recovery. It isn't. There are as many ways to heal as there are human beings on earth.

Each of us carries a different story, shaped by different wounds and different forms of wisdom. To compress all of that diversity into a few lines of a textbook is oblivion. We need **true care** to heal — not the performance of care, not the checkbox version of care, but real, present, human care that sees us as whole, not as symptoms to manage or liabilities to contain.

References

American College of Emergency Physicians. 2021. *Emergency Department Crowding and Boarding: Policy Statement.* Irving, TX: ACEP.

American Psychiatric Association. 2013. *Diagnostic and Statistical Manual of*

Mental Disorders. 5th ed. Washington, DC: APA Publishing.

Christl, B., M. Riedel-Heller, and A. Pabst. 2023. "Invalidation in Mental Health Care and Its Association with Treatment Outcomes." *Frontiers in Psychiatry* 14:1187423.

Freyd, Jennifer J. 1996. *Betrayal Trauma: The Logic of Forgetting Childhood Abuse.* Cambridge, MA: Harvard University Press.

Herman, Judith Lewis. 1997. *Trauma and Recovery: The Aftermath of Violence—From Domestic Abuse to Political Terror.* New York: Basic Books.

Hopper, Elizabeth K., Ellen L. Bassuk, and Jeffrey Olivet. 2010. "Shelter from the Storm: Trauma-Informed Care in Homelessness Services Settings." *The Open Health Services and Policy Journal* 3:80–100.

Institute of Medicine. 2001. *Crossing the Quality Chasm: A New Health System for the 21st Century.* Washington, DC: National Academies Press.

Maslach, Christina, and Michael P. Leiter. 2016. "Understanding the Burnout Experience: Recent Research and Its Implications for Psychiatry." *World Psychiatry* 15(2):103–111.

Ng, Serena L., and L. Hjong. 2024. "Medical Gaslighting and Patient Trust: A Systematic Review of Clinical Invalidation." *Journal of Health Psychology* 29(2):155–170.

PettyJohn, Meredith E., Carly Parnitzke Smith, and Jennifer J. Freyd. 2023. "Institutional Betrayal and Secondary Trauma in Health and Mental Health Systems." *Journal of Trauma & Dissociation* 24(5):641–659.

SAMHSA (Substance Abuse and Mental Health Services Administration). 2014. *Trauma-Informed Care in Behavioral Health Services.* Treatment Improvement Protocol (TIP) Series 57. Rockville, MD: U.S. Department of Health and Human Services.

Smith, Carly Parnitzke, and Jennifer J. Freyd. 2014. "Institutional Betrayal." *American Psychologist* 69(6):575–587.

U.S. Department of Health and Human Services, Administration for Children and Families (ACF). 2019. *Human Trafficking in Health Care Settings: Guidelines for Providers.* Washington, DC.

U.S. Government Accountability Office. 2020. *Private Health Insurance:*

Delays and Denials in Coverage Decisions. Washington, DC: GAO.

van der Kolk, Bessel A. 2014. *The Body Keeps the Score: Brain, Mind, and Body in the Healing of Trauma.* New York: Viking.

World Health Organization. 2017. *Preventing Suicide: A Resource for Health Professionals.* Geneva: WHO.

9 —Bureaucracy as Control: Education, Work, Welfare, & Immigration

Schools: Early Training in Obedience and Silence

Long before survivors ever meet police, courts, hospitals, or welfare systems, many have already met the logic of institutional betrayal in the one place they were required to show up every day: **school**.

School is where children learn the earliest lessons about power, voice, and consequence. And these lessons are not neutral. They are **developmental indoctrination** into the rules of structural narcissism.

Children learn very young that:

- **Telling the truth can get you in trouble** if the truth makes adults uncomfortable.
- **Authority is rarely questioned**, even when adults are wrong.
- **Bullying, abuse, or grooming** is often reframed as "drama," "attention-seeking," or "a misunderstanding."
- **Safety is conditional**, and belonging depends on compliance.

Research shows that mandated reporters often hesitate to act due to fear of backlash, unclear protocols, lack of training, or administrative pressure to avoid "bringing trouble" to the school (Mathews & Kenny 2008; U.S. HHS/ACF 2019). Children witness this hesitation. They feel it. And their nervous systems encode a brutal developmental rule:

"When I tell the truth, adults get uncomfortable and I get punished.
When I stay silent, I am safer."

This is institutional betrayal at the earliest stage of life.
By adulthood, that lesson is no longer a thought — it is an **embodied survival reflex.**

In schools, we strip children of truth-telling, unconditional love, imagination, and creativity. We take away everything that makes us human and train them to perform, comply, and build inauthentic connections. And then we panic when loneliness polls rise, as if we didn't design the very systems that suffocate real connection in the first place.

Segregation by ZIP Code: The Architecture of Educational Inequality

School assignment by neighborhood — something Americans treat as normal — is actually a **machinery of structural segregation**. It ensures that:

- children in wealthy neighborhoods inherit better-funded schools,
- while children in under-resourced neighborhoods inherit the systemic neglect created by redlining, disinvestment, and generational inequality.

Research consistently shows U.S. schools are **as segregated today as they were in the late 1960s**, driven not by law but by housing policy and economic stratification (Orfield & Frankenberg 2014).

Here is what that means for a child:

A child in a wealthy district walks into a building designed for their

success.
A child in a poor district walks into a building where the system has already decided their future.

Teachers may never say it aloud, but the culture communicates:

**"Some children deserve enrichment.
Other children should be grateful just to be supervised."**

This is structural violence disguised as school zoning.

Teachers: The Human Cost of Systemic Neglect

Teachers have one of the most emotionally demanding jobs in society — and one of the most undervalued. David Graeber's critique of "bullshit jobs" reveals a painful truth: **the more socially valuable a job is, the less it pays** (Graeber 2018). Teachers are living proof.

They are:

- underpaid,
- overworked,
- emotionally drained,
- expected to provide trauma care without training,
- and burdened with class sizes no nervous system can sustain.

Burnout is not a personal failing. It is the **design** of an underfunded system that offloads societal dysfunction onto teachers with no resources to address it.

And when teachers are exhausted, emotionally depleted, and unsupported, they cannot provide the relational presence children need — not because they don't care, but because the system demands more than their nervous systems can give.

So what do children learn?

- that adults are too stressed to hear them,
- that emotional needs are "disruptions,"
- that care is conditional,
- that grind culture is normal,
- that silence is safer than asking for help.

Additional Forms of Institutional Abuse in Schools

Zero-Tolerance Policies

Marketed as fairness but functioning as trauma machines, disproportionately harming Black, disabled, and neurodivergent children (Skiba et al. 2011).

School Resource Officers (SROs)

Policing inside school walls teaches children that they are suspects, not learners, accelerating the school-to-prison pipeline.

Special Education Harms

Children face restraint, seclusion, sensory overstimulation, or punishment for trauma responses — practices that echo carceral environments.

Testing Culture as Structural Shame

Standardized testing punishes poverty, disability, trauma, and language difference — and then blames the child for the outcome. Elite universities often demand high scores, yet those scores rarely measure a person's potential; they measure how well someone has learned to perform within the rules of capitalism. Test performance becomes a theater of adaptation — rewarding those with access, stability, coaching, and cultural alignment, while pathologizing those whose lives do not fit the system's narrow definition of success.

Surveillance Culture

Cameras, tracking software, bathroom passes, and hall monitors teach children to fear being watched, not to trust adults.

Punitive Attendance Policies

Children with chronic illness, caregiving responsibilities, or trauma are punished instead of supported.

Identity Silencing

Children who express racial, cultural, neurodivergent, or LGBTQ+ identities often face subtle or overt retaliation and erasure.

Emotional Neglect

Teachers are told to remain "professional," leaving kids emotionally starved in the one place designed to nurture growth.

The Wrong Children Get Reported

Another predictable betrayal: child protective services are called far more often for **poverty** than for emotional abuse. Numerous studies show that neglect reports disproportionately target low-income, Black, Indigenous, and immigrant households — even when the issue is simply lack of resources, not lack of care (Kelly et al. 2019; Dettlaff & Boyd 2020).

Meanwhile, children experiencing emotional abuse or coercive control are often invisible to the system.

This creates a devastating and racist paradox:

- **Poverty is criminalized.**
- **Emotional abuse is minimized.**

- **Trauma is misread.**
- **Need is punished.**
- **And the harms some foster families inflict are unspeakable.**

The child absorbs one message:

"The system cares more about my parents' income than my safety or my truth."

Why This Matters

Because by the time a child becomes a teenager or an adult:

- **their trust in institutions is already fractured,**
- **their boundaries are already distorted,**
- **their sense of worthiness is already under attack,**
- **and their nervous system is already trained to freeze when they need protection.**

Schools don't just prepare children for adulthood — **they prepare them for the Loophole Empire.**

Schools teach children to tolerate:

- gaslighting,
- dismissal,
- overcontrol,
- underprotection,

- and the emotional absence of authority figures.

This is the first betrayal.
Every institution that follows simply repeats the pattern.

Colleges, Universities, and Trainings: Gatekeeping Disguised as Education

If schools teach us obedience, compliance, and silence, then colleges and universities teach us something even more dangerous:
Who is allowed to be legitimate?

Higher education presents itself as the birthplace of ideas, innovation, and intellectual freedom.
But anyone who has ever actually been inside these institutions knows the truth:

Universities are not temples of knowledge — They are gatekeeping machines.

They control:

- who gets a degree,
- who gets a certificate,
- who gets a title,
- who gets a job,
- who gets credentialed,
- and most importantly, **whose mind counts.**

It has nothing to do with brilliance and true life skills.
It has everything to do with compliance, money, hierarchy, and cultural fit.

The Illusion of Higher Education: Money, Not Meaning

Universities today function less like learning spaces and more like overpriced sorting systems.

You pay tens or hundreds of thousands of dollars —
not for wisdom,
not for moral development,
not for transformation,
but for a **piece of paper** that signals to employers that you survived their hoop-jumping.

Universities say they foster "critical thinking," yet:

- Most classes rely on memorization.
- Most curricula are outdated.
- Many professors recycle the same slides for 15 years.
- Creativity is punished.
- New ideas are seen as threats.
- Students are graded on performance, not understanding.

And somehow we are still told this is the pinnacle of "education!"

The Tyranny of Grading: Performance Over Learning

Grades are one of the earliest forms of institutional gaslighting.

Instead of asking:

- *Did you learn something?*

- *Did you grow?*
- *Did this transform you?*

Universities ask:

- *Did you perform the rubric correctly?*
- *Did you write in the tone we expect?*
- *Did you cite who we approve?*
- *Did you mirror our worldview?*

A grade becomes a moral score.
Students internalize it as their worth.
Professors hide behind it as objectivity.

But grading is neither scientific nor fair — It is **human preference wearing a lab coat.**

Two professors can grade the same paper and give it a B- or an A+, proving exactly what universities deny:
Evaluation is subjective and political.

Old Professors, New Walls: The Death of Fresh Minds

Most tenured faculty are:

- resistant to new ideas,
- deeply attached to outdated models,
- threatened by originality,
- disconnected from modern struggles,
- and protected by a fortress of prestige.

They rarely step aside.
They rarely make space.
They rarely credit students or junior scholars who outthink them.

And they absolutely do not want their worldview challenged by someone younger, poorer, or more imaginative than they are.

Universities talk endlessly about "innovation," yet the people running them often haven't updated their thinking in decades.

Professional Trainings: Certificates of Legitimized Gatekeeping

The same logic extends to:

- coaching programs,
- therapy trainings,
- medical licensing,
- nursing boards,
- social work boards,
- educator credentialing,
- and every field requiring CEUs, exams, and state approval.

Each promises "competency" but mostly ensures:

- sameness,
- hierarchy,
- Conformity, and allegiance to their "official" usually outdated

framework

- And a fee.

The exam doesn't test whether you can help people.
It tests whether you can **repeat the sanctioned narrative and jump through loopholes.**

Workplaces: Performance Over Survival

Workplaces love to market themselves as "families," "teams," or "cultures of care"—right up until the moment you need something real. The second your humanity interrupts your productivity, the illusion dissolves. For survivors of trafficking, abuse, or complex trauma, holding down a job is often a lifeline. But workplaces rarely account for the realities of trauma: dissociation, flashbacks, hypervigilance, panic attacks, triggers, overwhelming stress, or the legal, medical, and immigration chaos that survivors navigate behind the scenes.

Instead, trauma gets reframed as:

- "attendance issues"
- "attitude problems"
- "not a good fit"
- "unprofessional behavior"

And the workplace begins a familiar pattern: **minimize, deflect, punish, remove**.

Research on sexual harassment, discrimination, and institutional betrayal shows that when workers disclose harm, organizations respond with defensiveness, minimization, or retaliation—deepening trauma and destroying trust (Smith & Freyd 2014; PettyJohn et al. 2023). The message is consistent:
Your value is your productivity.

The moment your trauma interferes with that, you become disposable.

But the betrayal goes much deeper.

Workplaces Are Quiet Sites of Modern Slavery

Most people do not realize that many workplaces fit the *narrative definition of trafficking* far more than the sensationalized stories of kidnapping and chains. Under international law, trafficking is defined as **the exploitation of someone's vulnerability for labor or services through coercion, fraud, force, or abuse of power.**

Let's break down the conditions:

- **economic coercion** ("you need this job to survive")

- **threats of being fired when unemployment is skyrocketing** ("if you say no, we'll replace you")

- **restriction of autonomy or soft capture** (your schedule, breaks, time, and body are controlled)

- **abuse of power and illusional binary choices** (managers using fear to enforce compliance and create binary choices to disguise power imbalance)

- **Fraud, and the dangling carrot** (promising advancement, safety, or care that never comes)

- **Coercive dependency** (health insurance, rent, childcare tied to employment)

- **psychological manipulation and institutional grooming** ("we're like a family here")

When you put these elements together, it becomes obvious:

Most modern workplaces are Using structural

coersion—sanctioned, normalized, and legalized.

You give your body, your time, your mind, your emotional labor.
In return, you receive barely enough to survive—and sometimes not even that.

And the moment you question the conditions, you are labeled:

- ungrateful
- difficult
- dramatic
- disloyal
- mentally unstable

Abuse doesn't care about the name we give it. The impact is the same: erosion of autonomy, chronic fear of losing stability, and a nervous system trained to equate survival with compliance. When coercion becomes invisible enough to look like "normal work," people stop recognizing exploitation as exploitation — and start blaming themselves for being exhausted, numb, or unable to keep up. That is how structural power sustains itself: not through chains, but through necessity disguised as choice.

David Graeber and the Epidemic of "Bullshit Jobs"

Anthropologist David Graeber wrote about "bullshit jobs"—roles that exist not because they serve humanity, but because they serve bureaucracy, hierarchy, and managerial ego. He argued:

- The more meaningful a job is, the less it pays.
- The more useless a job is, the higher the salary and prestige.
- Many workers secretly believe their jobs contribute nothing to society.

Bullshit jobs are the ones that, if they vanished tomorrow, nothing meaningful in our lives would be missing. And yet, people in "bullshit jobs" are paid to monitor, surveil, micromanage, and enforce compliance upon others—while the workers doing *actual* care:

- teachers,
- nurses,
- community workers,
- janitors,
- food service employees

are underpaid and overworked to the point of collapse.

This is structural narcissism disguised as employment.
The system rewards those who help maintain control, and punishes those who actually help humans.

Bullshit jobs are soul-crushing because they violate our agency at the deepest level. They force you to spend your days doing work that feels meaningless, extractive, or outright harmful — work that contradicts your values, dulls your intuition, and slowly eats away at your sense of purpose. And what's worse is that even many **rewarding** jobs have been hollowed out and turned into bureaucratic shells of what they were meant to be.

When I worked as an employment specialist, half my time was spent documenting — not supporting clients, not helping human beings move toward safety or stability. Sometimes I spent more time writing about what I supposedly did than actually doing anything that mattered.
Documentation for liability.
Documentation for billing.
Documentation for metrics and evaluation.
Documentation for the illusion of care.

Then I took a job as a case manager for medicaid enhanced care management program. I lasted **three days**. That was all it took to see the truth.

The job description made it sound meaningful — helping the most vulnerable: people with repeated ER visits, people who were unhoused, people with disabilities and complex medical needs. But the training told a different story. All we were taught was **how to document**: how to record each call, each "connection," each referral to nonresponding numbers, each meaningless interaction that would allow the organization to bill Medicaid.

We weren't taught how to help people.
We were taught how to justify our own existence on paper.

We were told to refer people to "resources" we knew were useless. I was once referred to those and tested them out for myself:

- Housing waitlists that were 10–14 years long.
- Food pantries across the city that required a car to access and strong arms to carry heavy groceries home.
- Clothing closets overflowing with random items that didn't fit most bodies and offered no real dignity.

This wasn't help.
This was **institutional abandonment wrapped in a brochure.**

It was giving someone a glimmer of hope — the hope that *finally* someone cares, that *finally* they're not alone — only to drop them the moment their need exceeded our script.
We were told to say:
"You need a higher level of care. We don't help with cases like yours."

Translation:
"Your suffering doesn't fit the boxes we get paid to check!"

Meanwhile, the company got paid **for every enrollment, every call, every "contact"** — regardless of whether it improved anyone's life. The system rewarded us for touching lives on paper, not for changing them in reality.

I was furious.
Furious at the medicaid system for wasting money layering bureaucracy on top of human suffering, instead of giving that money directly to the people who needed housing, food, transportation, and stability. Furious that my job required me to participate in crushing the hope of the most

vulnerable.

This is what David Graeber meant: **bullshit jobs are not just meaningless; they are morally obscene** (Graeber 2018).

They force good people to carry out the emotional and bureaucratic labor of a system designed to appear helpful while doing nothing.

It is disgusting — a violation not just of workers, but of survivors, the poor, the disabled, the unhoused, the medically fragile. It is a betrayal disguised as care.

And once you see it, you can't unsee it.

AI Could Create Abundance — But It's Being Used to Manufacture Scarcity

Now we are entering an era where AI could, in theory, free us from the most exhausting and meaningless parts of labor. If used ethically, AI could:

- drastically shorten the workweek
- reduce burnout
- automate dangerous tasks
- distribute resources more fairly
- give people time to rest, create, connect, dream

But what is happening instead?

Corporations use AI to:

- replace workers while keeping wages low
- monitor employee behavior

- predict “noncompliance”
- generate endless surveillance data
- enforce tighter schedules
- maximize profit margins

They are using a tool meant to create **abundance** to manufacture **deeper scarcity**.

This is the ultimate betrayal:
They could free humanity, but instead they choose to tighten the cage.

Corporations as Workplaces

Corporations publish annual reports lined with glossy language about “caring for employees,” “serving communities,” and “living our values.” During Pride Month, they plaster rainbow logos across every platform. In mental health awareness week, they post pastel infographics about compassion. They proudly sponsor conferences, charities, and “equity initiatives.”

But the moment a worker reports harassment, discrimination, toxic management, or unsafe conditions, the entire system shifts. HR doesn’t become a support system — HR becomes **a shield**, and the shield is not for the employee. HR’s real function is **liability control**, not protection. Its job is to contain the problem, not solve it. To protect the company, not the person who was harmed.

Image management wins; human beings lose.

And the most disturbing part?
The public ends up protecting the institution, too.

Employees learn to defend the company’s reputation because their own survival depends on it.
Co-workers stay silent because speaking up threatens their jobs.
People internalize risk calculations — “if I support them, will I get in trouble?” “Will I be next?”

Over time, this creates a culture where **the employees become the enforcers of the institution's image**, even when that image is a lie.

This is where the **bystander effect** thrives.
Harm happens openly, yet no one intervenes because the cost of action feels unbearably high. People freeze not because they don't care, but because the system trains them to self-protect instead of protect each other.

And that silence isn't neutral — it's traumatic.

When we witness harm and are structurally prevented from acting, we experience **second-hand trauma**. Our nervous systems absorb the fear, the injustice, the helplessness. Watching a colleague be punished, gaslit, or discarded teaches our bodies that the same thing could happen to you. That fear embeds itself. It becomes hypervigilance and burnout. It becomes CRC-PTSD.

So the corporation harms the target first — and then harms everyone who watches and feels powerless to intervene.

That's how institutional narcissism spreads.
Through branding, silence, fear, and the transformation of ordinary people into predators and protectors of the very systems that wound them.

This is how corporations don't just extract labor — they extract **moral agency**.

And once that happens, the damage is no longer confined to the workplace. It follows people home. It reshapes their nervous systems. It teaches them that survival requires self-erasure. That telling the truth is unsafe. That caring too much is a risk.

That is not a healthy organization.
That is a trauma-producing system.

The Core Truth

Workplaces don't just extract labor — they extract **identity**, **dignity**,

emotion, **time**, and **hope**.
They normalize coercion as "policy," burnout as "dedication," trauma as "attitude," and exploitation as "company culture."

And when your humanity interferes with your productivity, you are quietly disposed of.

This is not performance management.
This is systemic trafficking of the human spirit—legalized, normalized, and hidden behind smiling company slogans.

The real question is no longer, *"Why can't people work harder?"*
The real question is:

"Why are we still calling this survival?"

And
"How much longer will we let workplaces own pieces of our soul?"

Social Services, Welfare, and Disability: Help Designed to Be Hard and Humiliating

State agencies insist they "serve the people," yet welfare offices, immigration departments, licensing boards, child services, disability agencies, and regulatory bodies routinely abandon the very people who need them most. Their first loyalty is not to human wellbeing, but to budgets, policies, risk management, and optics—not to the humans crying in their lobbies after another denial, delay, or lost file.

Over time, these agencies undergo profound mission drift. What begins as a mandate to protect, support, or regulate in the public interest slowly mutates into a mandate to self-preserve. The original purpose—care, access, fairness—becomes secondary to avoiding blame, reducing caseloads, minimizing costs, and producing defensible paperwork. The agency's survival eclipses the people it was created to serve.

This drift is not accidental. It is structurally rewarded. Structural grandiosity appears most clearly in audit cultures, where metrics replace meaning and numbers become the moral compass (Power 1999; Strathern 2000). When humans are reduced to metric, what they meet is

procedural cruelty.

These systems are framed as "safety nets," but in reality they function as **filters**, designed to catch fraud at the expense of catching people who are falling. The process itself becomes the punishment.

People are forced to navigate:

- complex forms written in bureaucratic or legal language,
- demands for documentation that never existed or was destroyed in trauma,
- contradictory instructions from different caseworkers,
- phone trees and voicemails instead of humans,
- endless "call back later" messages,
- and denials for tiny technicalities — one missing signature, a date off by a day, a form filled out in blue ink instead of black.

This is not inefficiency.
It is the **architecture** of the system.

From a policy perspective, welfare systems are intentionally designed for "efficiency" by rationing access. As scholars of public administration note, **one of the easiest ways to reduce demand is to make access exhausting** (Herd & Moynihan 2018).

If you are traumatized, navigating these systems is like trying to run a marathon with broken legs — and then being blamed for not finishing.

This is **structural narcissism** in action.

Like an individual narcissist, the institution constructs an identity of inherent goodness. It demands admiration for its existence, compliance with its procedures, and gratitude for minimal or nonexistent help. When confronted with evidence of harm, it reacts defensively. Critique is reframed as disrespect. Accountability is framed as attack. Structural patterns of harm are dismissed as "isolated incidents," "edge cases," or "unfortunate misunderstandings."

Truth is not believed; they are **repositioned**. The people in need become "difficult," "noncompliant," "confused," "emotionally unstable," or "trying to game the system." Their credibility is questioned, their tone scrutinized, their persistence pathologized. The burden shifts from the agency's failure to the individual's character.

Meanwhile, the institution's self-image remains intact.

Policies are cited as immutable facts rather than human-made decisions. "We are bound by law" becomes a moral alibi—an excuse that erases agency and absolves responsibility. In reality, laws are interpreted, enforced, prioritized, and amended by people. But the institution hides behind them as though they were natural laws, like gravity.

And so the cycle continues.

The agency protects its sense of goodness at all costs.
Its reputation, funding streams, and political standing are safeguarded.
The human beings harmed in the process are treated as **collateral**—acceptable losses in the pursuit of administrative order.

What emerges is a cruel inversion: systems designed to protect the public become systems that **discipline**, **delay**, **discard**, and **disappear** people through bureaucratic means. Harm is not inflicted loudly; it is inflicted quietly—through waiting, deferral, denial, and indifference.

Punishing the Poor for Being Poor

The cruelty is not accidental.
It is woven into the rules.

Right now, the new administration is cutting services for the poor and implementing policies that punish people for needing help at all. Requiring a part-time job until age 65 to qualify for medical coverage is not policy — it is **institutional sadism.**

They claim disabled people will remain covered, but in the same breath insist that a letter from your doctor *does not count* as proof. The only proof is **already being on disability benefits** — and that process is its own impossible gauntlet.

To qualify for disability benefits:

- you must prove you cannot work,
- while simultaneously notarizing dozens of forms,
- attending appointment after appointment,
- and maintaining a bank account with **no more than $2,000** in it.

As if having $2,001 magically cures disability.

Note: The $2,000 limit comes from federal Supplemental Security Income (SSI) asset rules, set decades ago and never meaningfully adjusted for inflation. It is an arbitrary cap created in the 1970s, when $2,000 had far more purchasing power.

And it gets worse.

If you *try* to work as a disabled person:

- you can only work a limited number of hours (often under 16),
- but most workplaces require at least 20 hours,
- and if you earn even a little too much, you lose your benefits entirely.

This is not support.
It is entrapment.

It forces disabled people to remain in poverty to keep the resources they need to survive. It's the kind of system that says, "If you show any sign of trying, we will punish you."

The disability system is not built for care.
It is built for surveillance and control.

Caseworkers are often overburdened and underpaid, yet the system positions them as gatekeepers rather than helpers. People report being:

- interrogated about their trauma,

- humiliated over medical conditions,
- lectured about budgeting while living below poverty lines,
- or receiving contradictory instructions that lead to automatic denials.

Each appointment feels like a test.
Each question feels like an accusation.
Each rejection feels like evidence that you are somehow unworthy of being alive.

The 401(k) Illusion: Another Scam Disguised as Care

Then there is the 401(k) — marketed as the "responsible" way to save for retirement. But in reality, it is yet another tool for hoarding wealth at the top.

A 401(k):

- gives minimal employer match,
- restricts access to your own money, even in crisis,
- penalizes you for withdrawing funds when you actually need them,
- and earns modest returns after fees.

Meanwhile, investing in broad-market index funds (like the S&P 500) historically yields **7–10% annual returns on average** (over decades). In the past ten years returns have been much higher. Fees on 401(k)s can reduce that return significantly — sometimes cutting lifetime wealth by **25–30%** depending on the plan (Munnell & Sunden 2004).

A simple comparison:

- If someone invested $5,000/year independently at a 9% average return, after 30 years they would have roughly **$684,000.**

- The same contributions through a 401(k) with high fees (net ~6% return) would yield about **$395,000**.

That is a difference of nearly **$300,000** — money siphoned quietly upward.

Even worse, you are punished financially for accessing your money *before* a certain age — even if you're facing homelessness, disability, or medical crisis. Their message is clear:

"Save money you can never touch, in a system you may not live long enough to benefit from."

And we call this "helping people prepare for retirement."

Real Lived Examples of Social Service & Welfare Harm

1. The Man Who Died After Medicaid Cut Off His Insulin

A 27-year-old man in Ohio, Kevin Houdeshell, died when Medicaid delayed authorization for his insulin refill over the New Year holiday.
His prescription expired; the pharmacy refused to fill it; he died four days later.

His parents said:
"He didn't die from diabetes. He died from paperwork."

---

2. The Disabled Woman Denied Benefits Because She Had "Too Much" in Her Bank Account

Reported by ProPublica (2019).
A woman with severe epilepsy was denied SSI disability because she had **$2,051** in her bank account — **$51 over the limit.**
That $51 made her "not disabled" in the eyes of the system.

Her seizures worsened after she lost home-care services tied to SSI eligibility.

---

3. The Mother Who Lost SNAP Because She Took a Second Job to Survive

A single mother in Texas was working two minimum-wage jobs but still qualified for food stamps. When her hours temporarily increased, she went $43 over the income limit and was cut off entirely — even though her hours dropped again the next month.

She said:
"It felt like they punished me for trying to survive."

---

4. The Unhoused Veteran Denied Housing Voucher Because He Missed a Phone Call

A homeless veteran in Los Angeles lost his spot in a housing program because he missed a phone call from the VA caseworker.
By the time he called back, his "lack of responsiveness" disqualified him.

He said:
"I didn't have a phone charger. That's all it took to lose housing."

---

5. The Woman Whose Child Was Taken Because She Was Poor, Not Unsafe

A case documented by NBC News (2020).
A mother temporarily lost custody because she had no electricity and no stable housing. CPS called it "neglect."
There was no abuse, no violence — just poverty.
When she fought to regain her child, she was told she needed stable housing first, creating a **cruel Catch-22.**

Her lawyer stated plainly:
"She didn't lose her child because she was unfit. She lost her child

because she was poor."

---

6. The Autistic Man Denied Disability Because He Was "Too Articulate"

Reported in The Guardian (2019).
A man with severe functional impairments, who required daily support, was denied benefits because he spoke clearly during his assessment.
His articulation was used as proof he could work — ignoring every other part of his disability.

He said:
"They wanted me to perform brokenness."

---

7. The Chronic Pain Patient Forced to Prove Her Pain Every Month

A woman in Tennessee had to bring new documentation **every 30 days** to maintain disability benefits, despite having a permanent condition (Ehlers–Danlos syndrome).
She often collapsed while traveling to offices or waiting in line.
When she missed a deadline once, she lost benefits for months.

She said:
"It felt like a monthly hazing ritual."

---

8. The Family Cut Off From Medicaid Because of a Clerical Error

Case documented by Kaiser Health News (2022).
A family lost Medicaid after an automated system mistakenly recorded them as "income ineligible."
It took **six months** to restore coverage, during which their child's heart medication lapsed.

The mother said:

"The computer said no, so everyone said no."

---

9. The Disabled Woman Told She Needed to Work to Qualify — Even Though Working Would Kill Her

A California woman with severe cardiac illness was told she needed to "try working part-time" to prove disability eligibility.
Her doctor warned that physical exertion could be fatal.
Disability still insisted she attempt it.

She said:
"I felt like they wanted me to risk my life just to make their paperwork feel valid."

---

10. The Elderly Man Denied Food Assistance Because He Had a Car From 1998

SNAP rules in many states penalize owning a vehicle.
One elderly man in Pennsylvania was denied benefits because his ancient car exceeded the asset limit — even though he needed it to get to medical appointments.

His statement was heartbreaking:
"They told me to sell my car to buy food. How do I get to the doctor then — walk?"

Why These Stories Matter

They expose the same pattern across the country:

- **Systems require perfection from people in crisis.**
- **Support is withheld unless pain is performed in the right way.**
- **Eligibility rules criminalize need and punish survival.**

- **Poverty becomes evidence against you, not evidence of structural failure.**
- **Human lives are rationed through forms, queues, and loopholes.**

These systems don't simply "fail" the poor.
They **engineer** suffering.

They aren't broken.
They were built like this as part of the depopulation plan.

The Big Picture: Cruelty Disguised as Procedure

Across social services and welfare, the pattern is unmistakable:

- Help is framed as charity rather than a right.
- Support is hidden behind humiliation rituals.
- Eligibility is weaponized.
- Poverty is treated as a moral failure.
- Disability is treated as fraud until proven otherwise.
- Bureaucracy becomes a tool of exclusion, not access.

These systems do not uplift the vulnerable — they discipline them.
They do not relieve suffering — they extend it.

The people who turn to social services are not met with care — they are met with a maze. And that maze is engineered so that most people never make it through. We pretend the system is "broken," but this is exactly how it was designed to function.

And even when you dance to their tune, perform their eligibility theater, bring every document, retell every trauma, prove your worthiness again and again — there is still no guarantee you'll receive help. As if anyone enjoys the humiliation of you begging for assistance, they add salt to the injury by dehumanizing people who were already set up to fail.

The cruelty isn't accidental.
It's structural.

Immigration Systems: The American Dream as Marketing and Control

We love to romanticize immigration in this country. We wrap it in glossy slogans — "Land of Opportunity," "Dream big," "Freedom," "A better life." But if there is one thing America truly excels at, it isn't liberty or justice or compassion.

It is **marketing**.
It is selling dreams.
It is branding lies as hope.

The American Dream was never a real thing — it was a product.
A myth packaged into movie scenes, political speeches, and airport posters. A psyop designed to lure people into believing that if they worked hard enough, suffered long enough, or sacrificed everything, they might earn a tiny sliver of safety.

But the truth is much colder:
The American Dream is the world's most successful advertisement campaign.
A promise with fine print so predatory it would be illegal if it weren't written into national identity.

And nowhere is this more obvious than in the immigration system.

Immigrants come to the U.S. believing they will find:

- stability,
- safety,

- dignity,
- opportunity,
- a fresh start.

Instead, they encounter:

- years of legal limbo,
- impossible paperwork,
- shifting rules,
- suspicion,
- surveillance,
- exploitation,
- and a state that works harder to remove them than to integrate them.

The American Dream promises belonging.
The immigration system delivers **conditional existence** and requires **self sacrifice.**

The U.S. Deports First and Thinks Later — Even Its Own Citizens

And now we've reached an absurd and terrifying moment in history where **even American citizens** — mostly Latinos, Black immigrants, and people with poor documentation — are being detained or deported.

Real cases:

- U.S.-born citizens detained for weeks because they didn't have immediate proof of citizenship on them.

- Citizens with disabilities deported after failing to answer rapid-fire questions "correctly."
- People deported who had never lived in the country they were sent to.

America tells the world "anyone can make it here," but the fine print says:

"You can live here your whole life, pay taxes, follow the law, raise your children — and still be deported if we decide you look like you don't belong."

If that is not psychological warfare, I don't know what is.

Immigration Systems Are Not Broken — They Are Working as Designed

People often say, *"The immigration system is broken."*
It isn't.

It is functioning exactly as it was built to function: to maintain cheap, disposable labor; to keep immigrants afraid and compliant; to punish those who assert rights; to ration belonging; to manufacture a permanent subclass that never feels safe. The system sustains a fantasy of opportunity while quietly enforcing hierarchy. The contradiction is not a flaw — **it is the point.**

The American Dream works only as long as people believe it is attainable. The immigration system works only as long as people are too afraid to challenge it. Hope is the marketing strategy; fear is the enforcement mechanism.

The American Dream is not dead. It was never real. It was a story designed to justify inequality, lure labor, suppress dissent, and keep people chasing a fantasy that sustains the machine. The real dream—the human one—begins only when people stop believing the advertisement and start demanding humanity.

And now the story is changing. Immigration is no longer even dressed up as opportunity—it is openly priced. You are expected to pay a million dollars to belong. The country has produced enough domestic laborers that it no longer needs to "import" outsiders for work. So the gate shifts: not nationality, but class becomes the measure of worth. And that is cruelty in plain sight.

Immigration is not charity; it is a human right.
Belonging should not be purchased through suffering.
Citizenship should not be weaponized.
Safety should not depend on paperwork.
No one deserves exile for existing.

The future worth fighting for will not emerge from reforming a lie. It will only become possible when we dismantle the systems built to keep people afraid—and refuse to confuse cruelty with order ever again.

The Real Crime Is Not Crossing Borders — It Is Closing Them

The world's borders are not natural.
They are political decisions carved into land by people who believed they had the right to own the earth.

When a child crosses a border seeking safety,
That is not a crime.
It is human instinct.

When a mother flees violence to protect her children,
that is not illegality.
It is courage.

When a family escapes poverty created by global exploitation,
that is not trespassing.
It is survival.

The real crimes are:

- creating the conditions that force people to flee,
- then punishing them for fleeing,

- building empires on extracted wealth,
- then pretending immigrants "take" more than they give,
- making billions off migrant labor,
- then abandoning those same workers without rights.

The real crime is pretending borders are more sacred than human lives.

The Quiet Logic Underneath It All

If you zoom out far enough, the pattern is unmistakable.
Across police, courts, hospitals, schools, workplaces, social services, immigration systems, and even the technologies we rely on daily, the same logic repeats:

Survivors are told to come forward, yet punished, doubted, or abandoned when they do.
People in pain are required to provide evidence, stability, clarity, and consistency — the very things trauma makes almost impossible.
Institutions act shocked when people "disengage," and then weaponize that withdrawal as justification for more cuts, more denials, more blame.

The system asks survivors:

- "Why didn't you report?"
- "Why didn't you leave sooner?"
- "Why didn't you try again?"

It almost never asks:

- "Why did we make it so hard to be heard?"
- "Why is our response so unbearable that people would rather stay in

danger than seek help?"

- "Why are we so invested in protecting institutions instead of humans?"

These are the questions official reports never dare to say out loud.

Because the silence of institutions isn't apathy — **It is self-protection.**
It shields budgets, reputations, hierarchies, power.
It's cheaper (politically and financially) to let most people fall out of the process and call it "attrition" or "underreporting" (Artz & Smythe 2007; Pattavina et al. 2021).

This is the quiet math of a world built to look away.

Peppermint dramatizes it all — the fantasy that justice is just a matter of toughness and revenge, a gun, a hoodie, a training montage. But what that movie gets painfully right is the moment Riley's world collapses. Not when the trauma happens — but when the courtroom betrays her.
That's the moment survivors everywhere recognize (Freyd 1996; Smith & Freyd 2014).

Real survivors live inside that rupture every day, except without the Hollywood ending.
They are not asking for revenge.
They are asking for something far more radical in a system designed to discard them:

- **to be believed**
- **to be protected**
- **to not be punished for asking**
- **to not be retraumatized by the institutions built in their name**

But until that happens — until institutions stop gaslighting, doubting, delaying, and disciplining the very people they claim to serve — the real vigilante is not a person.

It is trauma itself.

Trauma becomes the stalker in the gaps of every system failure:
in the ER waiting room,
in the welfare office,
in the DHS interrogation room,
in the psych ward hallway,
in the HR meeting,
in the arbitration clause you didn't know you signed,
in the immigration backlog,
in the bullshit job that drains your soul,
in the algorithms shaping your fear,
in the contracts you must sign to be allowed to exist,
in the maze of forms that were never meant to be completed.

This is what CRC-PTSD actually is:
the body recording a lifetime of institutional betrayal until the world itself feels unsafe.

A world where every doorway demands proof,
every request requires performance,
every system treats suffering as a personal flaw,
every denial feels like confirmation that your life is worth less than the rules written to control it.

And yet — here we are, still trying to heal in a world built to look away.
Still searching for humanity in places designed without it.
Still carrying each other through a maze never meant to be survived.
Still telling the truth even when the truth shakes our voice.

Because we all have to name it.
And we have to stay awake long enough to change it.

This chapter is not the end of the story —
It's the moment we finally stop blaming ourselves for what the system intended all along.

It's the moment we turn toward each other and say:

I see it now.
I see you and myself. The pain I was forced to deny all these years.
And I will not look away.

References

Artz, Lillian, and Dee Smythe. 2007. *[Please paste the full title/journal info you're using]*. (You cite this as evidence of low prosecution/conviction in sexual violence cases; I can format it perfectly once I have the exact publication details.)

Bywaters, Paul, et al. 2016. "The Relationship Between Poverty, Child Abuse and Neglect: An Evidence Review." *Joseph Rowntree Foundation* report / or related peer-reviewed outputs by Bywaters on deprivation and child welfare inequalities. *(If you want only journal articles, tell me and I'll swap to the closest journal-only Bywaters citation set.)*

Crenshaw, Kimberlé. 1991. "Mapping the Margins: Intersectionality, Identity Politics, and Violence against Women of Color." *Stanford Law Review* 43(6):1241–1299.

Dettlaff, Alan J., and Renée Boyd. 2020. "Racial Disproportionality and Disparities in the Child Welfare System: Why Do They Exist, and What Can Be Done?" *The ANNALS of the American Academy of Political and Social Science* 692(1):253–274.

Freyd, Jennifer J. 1996. *Betrayal Trauma: The Logic of Forgetting Childhood Abuse*. Cambridge, MA: Harvard University Press.

Graeber, David. 2018. *Bullshit Jobs: A Theory*. New York: Simon & Schuster.

Herd, Pamela, and Donald P. Moynihan. 2018. *Administrative Burden: Policymaking by Other Means*. New York: Russell Sage Foundation.

Herman, Judith Lewis. 1997. *Trauma and Recovery: The Aftermath of Violence—From Domestic Abuse to Political Terror*. New York: Basic Books.

Mathews, Benjamin, and Maureen C. Kenny. 2008. "Mandatory Reporting Legislation in the United States, Canada, and Australia: A Cross-Jurisdictional Review of Key Features, Differences, and Issues." *Child Maltreatment* 13(1):50–63. *(If your intended Mathews & Kenny piece is a different 2008 article, paste the title and I'll correct.)*

Munnell, Alicia H., and Annika Sundén. 2004. *Coming Up Short: The Challenge of 401(k) Plans*. Washington, DC: Brookings Institution Press.

Orfield, Gary, and Erica Frankenberg. 2014. "Brown at 60: Great Progress, a Long Retreat and an Uncertain Future." Los Angeles: The Civil Rights Project / Proyecto Derechos Civiles, UCLA.

Pelton, Leroy H. 2015. "The Continuing Role of Material Factors in Child Maltreatment and Placement." *Child Abuse & Neglect* 41:30–39.

Power, Michael. 1997. *The Audit Society: Rituals of Verification*. Oxford: Oxford University Press.

Pattavina, April, et al. 2021. *[Please paste the exact Pattavina et al. title/journal/year you're using]*. (You cite this for attrition/low conviction dynamics; with the exact citation, I'll format it precisely.)

Skiba, Russell J., et al. 2011. "Race Is Not Neutral: A National Investigation of African American and Latino Disproportionality in School Discipline." *School Psychology Review* 40(1):85–107. *(If you meant Skiba et al. 2011 on zero tolerance specifically, I can swap to that exact article once you confirm which one.)*

Smith, Carly Parnitzke, and Jennifer J. Freyd. 2014. "Institutional Betrayal." *American Psychologist* 69(6):575–587.

Strathern, Marilyn, ed. 2000. *Audit Cultures: Anthropological Studies in Accountability, Ethics and the Academy*. London: Routledge.

U.S. Department of Health and Human Services (HHS), Administration for Children and Families (ACF), Office on Trafficking in Persons. 2019. *SOAR to Health and Wellness Training* / trafficking-response guidance for health and human service providers. Washington, DC: U.S. Department of Health and Human Services. *(If you used a specific ACF 2019 report title, paste it and I'll format that exact document.)*

van der Kolk, Bessel A. 2015. *The Body Keeps the Score: Brain, Mind, and Body in the Healing of Trauma*. New York: Viking.

Film

Peppermint. 2018. Directed by Pierre Morel. Los Angeles: STXfilms.

10 The Machinery of Harm: How Modern Industries Work Against Us

It would take an entire encyclopedia to expose every industry harming us, so I'll point to just a few. Once you see the pattern, you'll start seeing it everywhere. Our systems were never built for human well-being — they were built for compliance, profit, and control.

Not one sector is innocent.
Not one industry is neutral.
Not one institutional domain places humanity above money, efficiency, or hierarchy — at least not in its structural design.

Individuals inside these systems might care deeply.
Many do.
But the **architecture** they work in does not.

When we look at society sector by sector — housing, healthcare, banking, education, justice, mental health, food, media, AI, and beyond — the picture becomes painfully clear: **our industries thrive when we struggle**, and they falter when we heal, rest, or reclaim agency.

This chapter maps exactly that. Painful truths; so do a lot of self-care.

Industries and Systems That Work Against Human Well-Being

1. The Housing Industry: When Shelter Becomes a Weapon

Shelter is a basic human need.

And yet modern housing is one of the most violent industries in existence — not because it fails, but because it succeeds at what it was built to do: turn shelter into scarcity, profit, and control.

Rent rises faster than wages in nearly every city. People are not "bad with money." They are priced out by design. Homelessness is treated not as a policy crime, but as a personal one — criminalized through laws banning sleeping, sitting, or simply existing without an address.

Meanwhile, the rich hoard entire neighborhoods. Investors buy homes to leave them empty. Corporations accumulate thousands of single-family houses, converting regions into rental plantations where tenants pay endlessly into someone else's wealth.

Eviction court is where this system drops the mask.
It is not justice — it is an assembly line of dispossession. Tenants arrive alone, landlords arrive with lawyers, judges barely look up, and displacement is stamped as "due process" in minutes. The court does not ask where you will go. It asks only: *Did you pay?*

Even "affordable housing" is a semantic scam. Most units are affordable only to the upper-middle class. Programs come with decade-long waitlists, expiring vouchers, eligibility theater, and bureaucratic hoops designed to exhaust people before they ever receive help. Nonprofits build luxury developments and sprinkle in a few "affordable" units as moral decoration while profit remains intact.

Then comes gentrification — a soft word for violent displacement. Working-class neighborhoods are "rediscovered," rebranded, and priced into extinction. Yoga studios, wine bars, and $15 toast arrive like signals of takeover. The residents who built the culture are pushed out, and their erasure is called "revitalization."

Under it all is the unhealed legacy of redlining. Black and brown communities were systematically locked out of loans and homeownership, and those racial maps still shape every zip code: property values, policing, schools, investment, and survival. Racism built the landscape. Capitalism preserved it.

And the new generations are not building lives — they are building survival strategies: cars, couches, overcrowded rooms, vans, storage units, micro-apartments the size of cells. A nomadic working class, wandering not by choice but by economic coercion.

Housing inequality is not a glitch. It is the engine.
When shelter becomes a commodity, society becomes an economy feeding on human desperation.

---

2. Healthcare & Wellness: The Body as a Revenue Object

Modern medicine does not treat illness as a human experience.
It treats it as an administrative event.

Reality must be translated into a billable code to count as real.
If pain cannot be categorized, reimbursed, or defensibly documented, it becomes illegible — and illegibility is treated as nonexistence. The system does not ask *what happened to you.* It asks *what can we code you as.*

This is not healthcare.
It is an accounting regime imposed on the body.

Hospitals increasingly function as throughput machines: care filtered through liability, reimbursement logic, and protocol compliance. The clinical question is rarely "what does this person need?" but "what can be justified on paper fast enough to keep the institution protected?"

The deeper violence is fragmentation. Medicine dismembers the human being into specialties, organs, departments — and then calls the resulting failure of comprehension "complexity." Trauma becomes gastrointestinal. Grief becomes cardiac. Panic becomes "behavioral." The person disappears into disconnected symptom silos.

This is institutional dissociation: a system structurally incapable of holding a whole human story.

The cruelty is normalized in small sentences:
"We can only address one issue today."
As if suffering arrives one invoice at a time.

And despite overwhelming evidence, trauma remains functionally invisible in mainstream medical training — not because the research is absent, but because humility is not reimbursed. Trauma-informed care requires listening, uncertainty, relational context. The system rewards interruption, certainty, and control.

So survivors become "vague."
Emotion becomes "noncompliance."
Pain becomes "psychological overlay."
The textbook becomes more credible than the person.

Meanwhile, the system consumes its own healers. Burnout is not incidental — it is the predictable outcome of emotional labor under industrial conditions. Compassion is extracted, rationed, and bureaucratized. The most empathetic potential clinicians are locked out by debt, elitism, and credential gatekeeping, while those inside are worked until numbness becomes survival.

A traumatized institution cannot produce healing.
It can only process bodies.

The Beauty Industry: When Wellness Becomes Worthlessness

If the medical system wounds us by ignoring our emotional lives, the beauty industry wounds us by exploiting our insecurities.

The beauty industry profits from:

- self-hatred,
- body shame,
- aging anxiety,
- fatphobia,

- colorism,
- comparison culture.

Its success depends on convincing us that our natural body is a problem to be fixed. That our wrinkles, weight, pores, aging, scars, hair — all of it is somehow morally wrong.

Billions of dollars are spent every year on making people — especially women — feel unworthy until they buy something.
It's not just marketing; it's **emotional exploitation at scale**.

And the cruel part?
Healthcare often reinforces these lies.

Doctors dismiss fat patients.
Dermatologists act as though wrinkles are a failure.
Psychiatrists label body distress a disorder while ignoring the cultural violence that caused it.
Medical research under-studies women, people of color, and trans bodies.
Insurance refuses to pay for treatments unless the body "fits the box."

Both systems — beauty and medicine — tell us:
"Your body is wrong unless we approve it."

The Fitness Industry: Discipline Disguised as Wellness

The fitness world loves to speak the language of health, but underneath it lies:

- punishment,
- perfectionism,
- obsession,
- self-surveillance,

- diet culture,
- performance anxiety,
- shame.

Workouts are marketed as moral achievement.
Food becomes sin or virtue.
Movement becomes a transaction to justify your existence.
Rest becomes weakness.
Injury becomes "not trying hard enough."

People who need gentle, trauma-informed, joyful movement are instead taught to discipline themselves into thinness and call it "wellness."

Fitness culture doesn't heal you.
It recruits you into the **ideology of bodily control** — the same ideology the medical system uses to pathologize anything that falls outside its narrow norms.

And the final irony?

Beauty, fitness, and medicine all claim to care about health —
while quietly **eroding the very self-worth required for real healing.**

The Body as a Consumer Project

Healthcare, beauty, and fitness form a single triangle of control:

Medicine says: *You are sick unless we approve you.*
Beauty says: *You are ugly unless you fix yourself.*
Fitness says: *You are undisciplined unless you punish yourself.*

Different industries, same message:
Your body is the problem — buy, obey, and self-correct until it becomes acceptable.

This is not wellness.
It is body-based capitalism: trauma disguised as self-improvement.

The result is predictable: body dysmorphia, somatic stress, chronic shame, burnout — symptoms treated as personal defects instead of structural outcomes.

No one tells you the truth:
A person who feels safe in their own body cannot be monetized.

---

3. The Mental Health System: When "Care" Becomes Another Form of Control

The mental health system presents itself as the compassionate sibling of medicine — the part of healthcare meant to understand the unseen wounds, the emotional ruptures, the memories that echo in the body. But in reality, it often functions as another mechanism of social control, profitability, and gatekeeping. It promises healing but delivers bureaucracy. It markets itself as humane but operates like a factory that processes human suffering into billing codes.

Overdiagnosis, Overmedication — Two Sides of the Same Coin

The system is quick to diagnose, quick to label, quick to prescribe. Overdiagnosis leads to **overmedication**, and overmedication becomes a socially acceptable form of numbing — not so different from getting high on street drugs, except one is criminalized and the other is marketed as "treatment."

Pharmaceutical companies profit from our pain.
Doctors are pressured to prescribe quickly.
Insurance rewards medication over therapy.
People become lifetime customers while suffering painful side effects.

And we pretend this is care.

Banning Natural Healing While Selling Synthetic Numbing

The irony is unbelievable:
Nature-based healing practices — like plant medicine, psychedelics, somatic therapies, ceremony-based healing, and community rituals — are criminalized or restricted. Meanwhile, the pharmaceutical industry hands

out pills like candy.

Humans are not addicted to substances.
Humans are addicted to **relief** — relief from a world that refuses to hold them or allow true connections.

When trauma is treated as personal failure instead of structural injury, people turn to anything that helps them cope — and the system punishes them for the methods that aren't profitable.

Under-Treatment Disguised as Help

For all the overdiagnosis and overmedication, the actual treatment is shockingly shallow. People with complex trauma get:

- six sessions of CBT,
- a safety contract,
- a prescription,
- and a reminder to "practice mindfulness."

And then they're sent back into the same world that traumatized them.

Long-term therapy — the kind required for relational trauma, systemic trauma, or chronic suffering — is almost impossible to access unless you can pay cash. Insurance covers survival, not healing.

It is under-treatment wrapped in the illusion of care — just a temporary patch until the next collapse.

Mindfulness and Self-Care: The Luxury of the Untraumatized

Mindfulness is often marketed as a cure-all, but the truth is that mindfulness is easiest for people **not currently drowning**. It is a luxury of those whose nervous systems are not on fire.

The poor, the traumatized, the oppressed — when they struggle to stay present in a harmful world, the system tells them it's a personal shortcoming.

Meanwhile, the "self-care industry" charges hundreds for retreats, crystals, supplements, planners, yoga classes, wellness coaching, and spa days. Self-care has become a commodity, not a practice.

Validation? Not covered.
Meditation retreat? $3,000.
Nervous system safety? Priceless and inaccessible.

Therapists Who Don't Take Insurance: Healing Behind a Paywall

The therapists who are truly skilled — the ones who understand trauma, attachment wounds, dissociation, developmental hellscapes, and intergenerational pain — often refuse insurance because of the loopholes, low reimbursement rates, and soul-crushing paperwork.

So the poor get:

- interns,
- recent graduates,
- overworked clinicians,
- therapists cycling through burnout,
- and people who are still learning at the expense of the suffering.

It is not the therapist's fault — they, too, are trapped in the machine.
But the result is predictable:

Healing is segregated.
The wealthy get transformation.
The poor barely get stabilization.

The Endless Retelling: Re-Traumatization by Data Collection

One of the quietest, cruelest harms:
the demand that patients retell their trauma **again and again and again** because every hospital, every therapist, every program, and every system "needs their own documentation."

The data systems don't speak to each other.
So the survivor must speak their pain repeatedly.

What the system calls "intake," the survivor experiences as **exposure therapy without consent.**

No one asks if it hurts to dig up the same wound on command.
No one cares that each retelling fractures the nervous system a little more.

They just want the paperwork submitted.

A System Built for Profit, Not People

And underneath all of it — beneath the diagnosis lists, the prescriptions, the self-care marketing, the mindfulness slogans, the forced holds, the interns, the paperwork — the real truth emerges:

The mental health system is not built for healing.
It is built for profit, containment, and compliance.

Patient well-being is not the priority.
Coverage, coding, liability, and billing efficiency are.

This is not a mental health system.
It is an emotional management industry — one that isolates pain, blames individuals, and ignores the societal trauma that produced suffering in the first place.

So often, patients are discharged still homeless, still without the resources they need, still carrying the same unbearable conditions that brought them in. And many social workers, crushed by the same impossible machinery, begin to absorb a kind of learned helplessness themselves — not because they don't care, but because the system has trained them not to expect anything to change.

The availability of "help" becomes a collective illusion: a story that allows the wealthy and the comfortable to dismiss the guilt, to believe that somewhere, somehow, support exists — even as people fall through the cracks again and again in plain sight.

Healing in this world requires more than "treatment."
It requires dismantling the systems that keep people sick.

And the mental health system, as it currently exists, is not the cure.
It is one of the wounds that gives you the label of "disposable."

---

4. Insurance Companies: Profit From Pain, Protection in Name Only

Insurance is sold as a safety net — a promise that if life collapses, someone will catch you. But structurally, insurance is one of the most predatory industries in modern society: a business model built on collecting payment upfront and resisting responsibility afterward.

In many cases, it isn't even optional. Auto, renters, mortgage, health — entire categories of insurance are legally required, meaning people are mandated to buy products that may never protect them. And the scam within the scam is simple: you pay faithfully for years, and the moment you actually need help, you are punished for needing it. Premiums rise. Claims are denied. Coverage disappears. The system treats survival as misuse.

Denials are not exceptions — they are design. Care is refused over wrong codes, missing forms, technicalities, or "lack of medical necessity" decided by someone who never meets the patient. Policies are written in deliberate confusion, filled with exclusions large enough to swallow real life:

Accidents, but not the ones that happen.
Mental health, but not long-term care.
Illness, but not chronic illness.
Catastrophe, but not the kind people actually endure.

Even when coverage exists, insurers impose limits that quietly place a price on your life: caps on medications, therapy, rehabilitation, equipment, reproductive care — boundaries where your need simply exceeds what profit allows.

Then comes prior authorization: bureaucratic permission to stay alive. Doctors must argue with clerks for treatment while conditions worsen. Delay is not inefficiency. It is strategy. Dead patients don't generate payouts.

Disability insurance perfects the logic of disbelief. Instead of support, the default posture is suspicion: surveillance, fraud accusations, phrases like "psychological overlay" or "symptoms inconsistent." The goal is simple: turn suffering into doubt so responsibility becomes optional.

And beneath it all is paperwork violence — the administrative maze built on one assumption: people in crisis cannot fight endlessly. Forms, transfers, appeals, denials, lost documents, broken portals. Insurance doesn't merely deny care. It manufactures exhaustion until surrender becomes the outcome.

The dark brilliance of the industry is that it wins in every scenario: if you stay healthy, you keep paying. If you file a claim, you are penalized. If you deteriorate, support is delayed. If you give up, they save money. If you die quickly, they save more.

Insurance is not protection.
It is extraction disguised as security — the quiet architecture of institutional betrayal.

And this logic doesn't stop at national borders. The pharmaceutical economy scales it globally: the value of a life depends on the GDP of the country it was born into. Patents become gates. Medicine becomes a luxury language. Entire populations are priced out of cures that already exist, because healing is not the primary objective — profitability is.

And this is not abstract.
It is lived.

Let me share my most recent experience with my insurance, Blue Shield Promise of California. When I joined the plan, I requested continuity of care with my therapist. It took them a month to approve it, and then—without warning—they reversed the decision after a year. The notice of denial was mailed to an old address, which is likely why I didn't even know it was coming. My therapist shared the faxed letter they had sent her.

Following their instructions, I called the physician listed on the denial letter. She seemed confused about why I contacted her at all and began scolding both me and my therapist for following the instructions Blue Shield had provided. Her exact words were: "your therapist should have known better." Then I pointed out that perhaps the insurance company should have known better than to direct patients to a physician who doesn't even know… and she hung up on me mid sentence.

The insurance treats therapy as if therapists were interchangeable—as though you are replacing a worn-out shoe. But building trust is not transactional. It took me three years to trust my therapist enough to speak about being sexually exploited by a therapist in residential treatment. In the three years I was unable to speak about it, I cycled in and out of hospitals due to suicide attempts—more than forty admissions.

I explained all of this to the insurance company. They still denied my appeal.

It felt like speaking to stone. Every representative repeated the same scripted line: they could "find me an in-network therapist," as though one could simply swallow years of trauma around therapy and start fresh with a stranger. The system assumes emotional safety is optional, interchangeable, and easily rebuilt. Anyone who has experienced relational trauma knows that is not true.

The most painful part is that the denial wasn't even about direct cost—it was about network rules, in-group and out-group status, and administrative boundaries. My therapist has actively tried to rejoin Medi-Caid, but the process is a maze of bureaucratic loopholes.

In ignoring the basic clinical requirement of relational safety, the insurance company is jeopardizing my well-being. Ironically, their decision is also financially irrational. One hospitalization costs at least $20,000, while one therapy session costs under $200. I typically see my therapist no more than six times a month, which is enough to maintain stability. Blue Shield is choosing a far more expensive path—one that also causes immense human suffering.

After the denial, I was directed to call regulatory agencies. Instead, I reached voicemail after voicemail. Even voicemails are triggering for me; they induce panic and emotional shutdown. The endless systemic games they require us to play is part of why I ended up on the edge of the bridge, wanting to die. Or most of the time wanting the system to listen and see me because visibility is not possible without being a liability. Because the help they claim to be available, is just an illusion. Case managers sometimes call me "resourceful," but the truth is simpler: I am fighting for justice, with my limited energy, overwhelming my body, while those who are meant to help are so burnt out, they can't even carry themselves.

To survive this system, you have to become a warrior. And so many people who don't have the bandwidth — or who are taught to see systemic betrayal as personal failure — simply fall through the cracks.

---

5. Global Inequity: When the Pharmaceutical Industry Decides Who Lives and Who Dies

If the pharmaceutical industry harms people within wealthy countries through price-gouging, denial, and overmedication, its global impact is far more brutal.
Because outside the borders of wealthy nations, the system stops pretending to care at all.

The truth is simple and horrifying:

The value of your life in the global health system depends almost entirely on the GDP of the country you were born into.

A child in the U.S. with leukemia receives treatment protocols worth hundreds of thousands of dollars.
A child in Uganda with the same cancer is often sent home to die.

Not because the science doesn't exist.
Not because the medicine isn't available.
But because the pharmaceutical companies that hold the patents decide that people in poor countries are not profitable enough to save.

This is the part no one wants to say out loud:
Pharmaceutical patents kill more people than diseases do.

When India and South Africa fought for affordable HIV medication in the 1990s, dozens of pharmaceutical companies sued them for attempting to produce generic antiretrovirals — during an epidemic that was wiping out entire populations. More than 8 million people died across the continent. Millions could have been saved. But saving them would have "undermined the profit model."

Let that settle for a moment.

Human beings died because curing them was considered bad business.

During COVID-19, wealthy countries hoarded vaccines, while entire regions of Africa, Latin America, and South Asia waited months — even years — for sufficient supply. Rich nations destroyed expired doses while poorer nations begged for access.

The logic is always the same:

If you are not profitable, you are disposable.
If your country cannot pay, you are unworthy of the cure.

Global health is treated as a marketplace, not a shared human responsibility. Pandemics spread faster because poor countries cannot afford vaccines. Tuberculosis becomes drug-resistant because wealthy nations refuse to share new treatments. Children die of malaria for pennies while pharmaceutical giants report billions in profit.

This is not a failure of science.
The science is brilliant.

This is a failure of humanity.
The humanity is missing.

The pharmaceutical industry behaves like a gatekeeper of life itself — deciding which populations are "worth saving," which diseases deserve attention, and which bodies can be written off as collateral damage in the pursuit of quarterly earnings.

And the greatest tragedy is that these deaths are not the results of nature, fate, or inevitability.

They are the outcomes of choices — corporate choices, political choices, economic choices.
Choices that say, openly and without shame:

"If you cannot afford to live, then you do not deserve to."

No system that allows entire populations to die because of profit margins can call itself ethical, civilized, or humane.

This is not just inequality.
This is global abandonment.

This is not just injustice.
This is **manufactured extinction**.

And until we confront the truth that the pharmaceutical industry profits more from illness than from healing — more from scarcity than from abundance — the world will continue to bury people who should still be alive.

---

6. The Food Industry: When Nourishment Becomes Exploitation

Food is supposed to nourish us.
Connect us to the earth and to each other.

But the modern food industry does not nourish — it manipulates, confuses, extracts, and profits. It is built on **addiction, scarcity, deception, and the monetization of hunger**, not on supporting human health.

We don't have a food system.
We have a **profit system wearing a food costume**.

The War on Carbs, Fats, and Common Sense

For decades, the industry has thrived by **demonizing different macronutrients**, creating confusion that keeps the public buying new products and chasing new fads. First fat was the enemy. Then carbs were the enemy. Then sugar. Then gluten. Then meat. Then plants.

The public is rotated through fear-based diets like:

- low-fat
- keto
- paleo

- Whole30
- carnivore
- alkaline
- "superfood" cleanses
- fasting windows
- food-combining rules
- and a thousand other branded belief systems

Each fad contradicts the previous one.
Each claims to have "the secret."
Each requires buying new products, new books, new powders, new supplements.

Meanwhile, real nutrition — whole foods, balanced meals, cultural traditions, trusting your own body — gets lost beneath the noise.

These diets don't heal us.
They **destabilize** us.
A confused eater is a profitable customer.

Ultra-Processed Food: Engineered Addiction

Most grocery store items are not food — they are industrial products designed to:

- hijack dopamine
- override hunger cues
- promote overconsumption
- and create lifelong customers

Ultra-processed foods are filled with:

- seed oils
- refined sugars
- preservatives
- emulsifiers
- synthetic flavors
- dyes
- gums

Food chemists literally design these products to be irresistible. Then the public is shamed for "lack of willpower."

You cannot blame people for craving substances scientifically engineered to be addictive.

Food Deserts: When Access Is a Privilege

In wealthy neighborhoods, people have:

- organic produce,
- health food stores,
- farmers markets,
- artisanal bakeries.

In low-income neighborhoods, people get:

- fast food,

- convenience stores,
- liquor stores,
- gas station snacks.

This isn't a natural phenomenon.
It is a **policy-engineered famine**.

People are shamed for poor health yet denied access to real food.

"How can you make healthy choices," someone once said,
"when your only choices are packaged poison?"

Agricultural Monopolies: Four Corporations Controlling the World's Plates

A handful of corporations control most of the world's:

- grains
- meats
- seeds
- fertilizers
- processing plants

This concentration of power leads to:

- manipulation of prices
- dangerous working conditions
- ecological destruction
- pesticides that poison communities

- genetically narrow crops vulnerable to collapse
- labor abuses across the globe

Food is not grown for people.
Food is grown for shareholders.

Marketing to Children: Psychological Manipulation in Plain Sight

The most ruthless strategy of all:
marketing junk food directly to children.

With:

- cartoon mascots
- bright packaging
- toys
- kids' meal deals
- YouTube ads
- social media influencers

A child learns to recognize a fast-food logo before they learn to spell their own name.

This is not innocent. This is indoctrination.

"Healthy" Labels as Lies

Food labels are deliberately misleading:

- "No sugar added" → overloaded with carbs that convert to sugar.
- "Natural" → legally meaningless (even arsenic is "natural").
- "Low fat" → high in sugar, additives, and chemicals.
- "Whole grain" → contains a single grain fragment lost in a sea of flour.
- "100% fruit juice" → sugar content identical to soda, with the fiber removed.

Nutrition becomes **marketing**, not truth.

Global Hunger: A Manufactured Crisis

We produce more than enough food to feed **every human on earth**, yet millions starve.
Not because we lack food — but because we lack **ethics**.

Food waste is staggering:

- Nearly one-third of global food production is thrown away.
- Meanwhile, entire continents face famine conditions.
- Export restrictions and monopolies create artificial scarcity.
- Corporations burn crops to keep prices high.

People are starving not from lack of supply,
but from **capitalist choreography**.

Hunger today is not a tragedy.
It is a policy decision.

Animal Agriculture: Violence We Pretend Is Necessary

We live in a time when **lab-grown meat exists**, plant-based proteins exist, and sustainable food solutions exist — yet we continue to slaughter billions of animals annually because the industry refuses to shift.

Eating animals is not necessary for human survival anymore. I understand it feels controversial, but we can eat lab grown meat. But animal cruelty continues because:

- it is profitable
- corporations resist change
- culture normalizes cruelty
- governments subsidize meat
- and people have been taught to see animals as products

Meanwhile, animal agriculture:

- destroys forests
- accelerates climate collapse
- tortures sentient beings
- poisons water systems
- traps communities in disease zones

The ethical solution is simple:
Boycott animal products and force industries to invest in lab-grown alternatives.

When the public changes its demand, corporations will be forced to change their supply.

Money speaks louder than morality in this system.
So let money deliver the message:

We no longer consent to cruelty.
We no longer accept unnecessary slaughter.
We no longer allow the planet to be burned for burgers.

Lab-grown meat can end factory farming.
It can reduce zoonotic disease.
It can feed the world ethically and sustainably.

All we need is the collective will to shift — and the courage to stop participating in a system built on suffering.

---

7. Consumerism: The Endless Appetite That Isn't Ours

If there is one story modern capitalism tells better than any other, it is this:

"You need more."

More stuff.
More clothing.
More gadgets.
More upgrades.
More décor.
More skincare.
More everything.

But none of this hunger is natural. None of it originates from the human soul.

Consumerism is not an instinct — it is an engineered craving, cultivated through marketing, social comparison, and insecurity. It is the psychological conditioning that keeps the economy spinning, even as it crushes both people and the planet under its weight.

We don't need new wardrobes every year.
We don't need an Instagram living room overhaul every season.
We don't need to replace electronics that still work.

We need:

- stability

- community
- meaning
- creativity
- rest
- joy
- connection
- enoughness

But these are not profitable.

So instead, corporations convince us that our worth is located in our belongings.

Fast Fashion: Clothing That Costs the Earth

Clothes used to last.
People mended them. Loved them. Passed them down.

Now fast fashion demands:

- new trends every month
- micro-seasons every few weeks
- clothing stitched by underpaid laborers
- synthetic fabrics that never decompose
- dyes that poison rivers
- textile waste filling landfills for generations

Brands crank out thousands of designs meant to fall apart quickly — because durability threatens profit.

Meanwhile, TikTok hauls and influencer culture normalize excess, teaching entire generations to associate identity with constant consumption.

The result?

Millions of tons of discarded clothing each year.
Ninety percent of it made from materials that will outlive every person currently alive.

Consumers don't "choose" this.

They were trained into it.

The Illusion of Choice: A Manufactured Hunger

When we shop, we think we are making choices.

But our "choices" have been predetermined by:

- advertising psychology
- scarcity marketing
- influencer algorithms
- corporation-designed trends
- planned obsolescence
- social pressure

Modern capitalism does not sell objects — it sells inadequacy. Advertising works by creating discomfort first: your body isn't enough, your home isn't enough, your life isn't enough — then offering consumption as relief. Social media completes the training. Algorithms flood our nervous systems with curated excess until overconsumption feels normal, even aspirational. Influencer culture turns buying into identity, and scarcity marketing makes desire feel urgent, moral, and necessary.

Even "choice" is engineered. Products are built to break, trends are designed to expire, and planned obsolescence ensures you must keep purchasing just to stay functional. Meanwhile, the market replaces what humans actually need — community, meaning, creativity, belonging — with disposable substitutes you can buy.

This training begins in childhood, before autonomy even forms. By adulthood, consumption no longer feels like coercion. It feels like personality.

That is the system's genius: it does not force people into excess with violence. It conditions them into it psychologically — through insecurity, comparison, and manufactured dissatisfaction — until the cage feels like desire.

The Real Cost: The Planet Is Running Out of Breath

Consumerism is not just a human crisis — it is an ecological one.

Every product comes from somewhere:

- forests cut down for furniture
- oceans polluted by microplastics
- fossil fuels burned to ship goods
- sweatshop labor exploited for cheap manufacturing
- animals killed for fashion and beauty
- soil depleted for industrial agriculture
- rivers poisoned by dye factories
- mountains of trash shipped to poorer nations

The earth is suffocating under our "stuff."

We Don't Need More — We Need Enough

Here is the truth no corporation wants us to remember:

The human heart is not infinite in its desires.
It is infinite in its capacity for love, not consumption.

People don't actually want endless closets.
We want clothing we feel good in — clothing that helps us connect to others like us.
We want comfort and expression.

People don't want the newest phone every year.
We want connection.

People don't want more décor.
We want a home that feels safe.

Consumerism makes us forget the difference.

Consumerism: The Blood We Refuse to See

Consumerism is not innocent.
It does not simply "offer choices."
It is not a harmless marketplace of preferences.

It is built on one of the oldest human tricks:

Make the suffering invisible.

The entire system depends on distance.
Not the distance of miles — the distance of conscience.

Your phone arrives in a clean white box, polished and perfect, like a holy object of modern life.

But the cobalt inside it was likely mined by children in the Congo, breathing toxic dust deep into their lungs, digging with bare hands so that the rich world can scroll endlessly.

Your clothes arrive bright, folded, seasonal, cheap.

But the hands that stitched them may have belonged to a teenage girl locked inside a factory, working sixteen-hour shifts, sleeping in overcrowded dormitories, earning wages that cannot buy dignity, safety, or rest.

Consumer capitalism works because it exports cruelty.

The violence did not disappear.

It was simply relocated.
Outsourced.

To Bangladesh.
To Cambodia.
To China.
To the Philippines.

To the places the global imagination has decided do not fully count as human.

The system calls it "development."

But often, it is just colonialism wearing a modern suit — extraction with better marketing.

And then, sometimes, the unbearable breaks through.

At Foxconn, one of the world's largest electronics manufacturers — producing devices for Apple and other tech giants — workers began jumping from dormitory buildings.

Young people.
Not soldiers.
Not criminals.
Not "unstable patients."

Workers.

They threw themselves into open air because life inside the machine was psychologically unlivable.

Do you know what the company did?

Did they slow down production?
Did they shorten shifts?
Did they treat the workers like souls?

No.

They installed nets. Literal suicide nets. They strung nets around the buildings to catch falling bodies.

Let that sink in:

The solution was not to end the conditions that created despair.
The solution was to prevent the visible mess.

Catch the bodies.
Keep the assembly line moving.

This is the moral architecture of consumer capitalism:

Do not change the system.
Do not heal the wound.
Just hide the blood better.

The worker becomes a unit.
A replaceable part.

Not a person.
Not a life.
Not a universe of dreams.

And we, the consumers, are trained into amnesia.

We are taught that cheapness is normal.
That endless choice is freedom.
That a five-dollar shirt is a bargain, not a crime scene.

But nothing is cheap.

If a product is cheap, it is because someone else paid with their spine.
With their childhood.
With their nervous system.
With their hunger.
With their life.

Consumerism is structural dissociation.

It severs the relational link between the one who consumes and the one who is consumed.

It turns suffering into background noise.
It turns exploitation into convenience.
It turns global trauma into lifestyle aesthetics.

And beneath the human victims, the ecological ones pile up:

Poisoned rivers.
Collapsed soils.
Burned forests.
Plastic oceans.

The Earth itself is treated like another disposable laborer.

This is why consumerism is not merely wasteful.

It is violent.

It is a system that converts:

- human lives into convenience
- ecological collapse into packaging
- global suffering into profit

And sooner or later, the lie breaks.

Because we breathe the same air.
We share the same planet.

No amount of wealth can insulate forever.

The suffering we outsourced will return — through climate collapse, mass migration, pandemics, political instability, and collective trauma.

Consumerism is not a private choice.

It is a global moral arrangement.

And it is built on invisible graves.

We can:

- buy less and cherish more
- mend instead of discard
- share instead of stockpile
- thrift instead of hoard
- repair instead of replace
- create instead of consume
- choose enough over excess

And we can pressure corporations by refusing to play their game.

Because consumerism only works if we forget our own values.

Once we remember that meaning is not located in objects, companies lose their power to manipulate us.

And the earth gains a chance to breathe again.

---

8. Banking & Financial Industries: Control Disguised as Neutrality

Banking is often framed as a neutral service—savings, credit, "opportunity." But historically, banks were built as engines of empire, not care. Modern finance grew wealthy by underwriting war, colonial expansion, the transatlantic slave trade, and racially exclusionary housing systems (Ferguson 2008; Ziegler 2015; Horne 2018; Hillier 2003; Rothstein 2017). The industry's foundation was never moral stewardship—it was organized extraction.

That architecture persists. Banks reward wealth with low-interest access while punishing poverty with fees, inflated rates, and predatory terms. The highest interest is charged to those least able to pay, meaning vulnerability itself becomes profitable. "Financial services" operate less as support than as a sorting mechanism—upward mobility for some, permanent precarity for others.

Predatory Lending as the Business Model

Predatory lending is not a deviation—it is structural. Payday loans, subprime mortgages, overdraft traps, compounding student debt: finance generates profit most efficiently where people have the fewest options. Scarcity becomes a market, and desperation becomes collateral.

Credit Scores: Shame as Governance

Credit scoring was never meant to be a moral judgment, yet it now functions as a nationwide system of surveillance and discipline. A three-digit number determines access to housing, employment, transportation, and even healthcare financing. Structural shocks—job loss, illness, recession—become lifelong marks of "unworthiness," disproportionately burdening marginalized communities (Federal Reserve 2021). Credit does not measure responsibility; it measures exposure to instability.

New Banking: Stocks, Fintech, and Crypto as the Same Machine in Sleeker Clothing

The financial system has not become more democratic—it has become more disguised.

Stock markets are framed as public wealth-building, yet ownership is massively concentrated. Most gains accrue to institutional investors, while ordinary people are invited in primarily as liquidity—absorbing risk while elites hold leverage.

Fintech platforms promise accessibility, but often expand surveillance, automate exclusion, and monetize behavioral data. Convenience becomes another layer of extraction: fees hidden in apps, algorithmic lending decisions, and frictionless debt.

Crypto was imagined as liberation from centralized banking, yet it has increasingly replicated the same dynamics: speculative bubbles, concentrated holdings, fraud cycles, and new intermediaries. Volatility becomes a feature, not a flaw—wealth transfers upward through hype, collapse, and unequal information.

Crypto reveals something uncomfortable:

You can't liberate money without liberating the social system around it.

If:

- housing is commodified
- healthcare is privatized
- survival requires cash
- inequality is baked in

Then **any currency — even a decentralized one — will be weaponized**.

Capitalism doesn't care what the money is made of.
Gold, paper, code — it will still extract.

---

8. Loans as Leashes: Debt as a Modern System of Enslavement

Debt is one of the most elegant forms of control humanity has ever created. It doesn't need chains. It doesn't need cages. It doesn't need guards. All it needs is an interest rate, a signature, and the promise of survival.

Loans are marketed as opportunity, empowerment, and "the path to independence." But in reality, they function like **leashes** — tightening around your life with every payment, every fee, every penalty, every compounding interest charge that grows faster than your ability to breathe.

We speak about "freedom" as if it's guaranteed, but most people are not free.
They are **indentured**.
They are owned by banks, credit card companies, mortgage lenders, and student loan servicers.
Not metaphorically — literally.

In a world where prices increase but wages stagnate, debt isn't a choice.
It's an inevitability.
A manufactured dependency.

The Brutality of a System That Forces You Into Debt

The cruelty isn't hidden. It's visible everywhere.

College tuition has risen over 1,200% in the past few decades, while wages remain nearly flat. Students graduate with debt that takes 20–30 years to pay off — longer than some prison sentences. Many will never pay down the principal because interest accumulates faster than they can repay.

Medical debt is the leading cause of bankruptcy in the United States — in a nation that claims to be the most advanced in the world. One ambulance ride, one ER visit, one accident, one diagnosis can destroy entire families.

Mortgage loans trap people for 30 years while housing prices rise far beyond income. Banks profit from interest while foreclosures devastate lives. Homes are taken in minutes — over a single missed payment — with no acknowledgment that the system created the impossibility in the first place.

Credit card companies target the poor with predatory interest rates of 20%, 25%, even 30%, knowing they will never escape. Every missed payment becomes a financial death spiral.

Auto loans stretch to seven or eight years now because cars are unaffordable. Miss a payment, and your car — your access to work, food, everything — is repossessed overnight.

Debt is not a financial tool.
Debt is **structural violence**.

Loans Are Designed So You Can Never Truly Escape

Debt is engineered with:

- compounding interest that grows faster than your income
- late fees that compound on late fees
- refinancing traps
- minimum payments that maintain the debt indefinitely
- penalties for early payoff
- credit scores that punish the poor
- wage garnishment
- collection harassment
- ruined credit leading to higher costs

It's not "mismanagement."
It's a **trap with no exit**.

Debt servicers profit not when you repay, but when you stay indebted forever.

Examples of the Brutality

A woman in Texas was sued by her hospital for $14,000 after cancer treatment, even though she had insurance. The lawsuit garnished her wages, and she eventually lost her home.

A teacher in Pennsylvania owed $26,000 in student loans after graduation. After 12 years of making payments, she owed $41,000 — because she could only afford minimum payments, and interest grew faster than she could fight it.

A single mother in California missed one car payment while caring for her sick child. Her car was repossessed in the middle of the night. She lost her job the next week. Her debt increased by $1,200 in repossession fees alone.

A disabled veteran had his benefits seized to repay student loans he took out before deployment. He couldn't work, but the government still demanded payment.

These are not anomalies.
This is the operating logic.

Debt as Psychological Control

Debt doesn't just shape your finances — it shapes your mind.

It induces:

- chronic anxiety
- shame

- scarcity mindset
- sleep disruption
- relationship strain
- hopelessness
- panic
- loss of autonomy

Debt teaches you to stay small, to avoid risk, to silence your needs, to keep working no matter how exhausted or ill you are. It conditions people to believe that survival is conditional on **obedience**.

Debt is the emotional leash that keeps the public docile.

Debt Is the New Slavery — Just With Polite Language

In the past, enslavement was physical.
Now it is financial.

You don't need chains when you have loans and credit scores.

We call it "responsibility," but it's bondage.
We call it "creditworthiness," but it's surveillance of the poor.
We call it "freedom," but most people are not free — they are **owned**.

The entire economy is built on a simple principle:

People must remain indebted so they remain compliant.

If you were not in debt:

- you could leave abusive workplaces,
- you could rest,

- you could heal,
- you could take risks,
- you could build community,
- you could challenge the system.

Debt keeps people too tired, too scared, too busy surviving to revolt.

It is not a tool for opportunity.
It is a **leash** — tightened slowly, invisibly, and always justified by "policy."

Debt is the quiet chain that binds an entire population.

And once you see it, you understand why everything feels impossible.

---

9. Policing and Law Enforcement: Paperwork as a Weapon, Power as a Crime

Policing in America is framed as protection — as the thin blue line between order and chaos. But the truth is far more unsettling: police are not simply responders to harm; they are **an extension of the bureaucratic machinery** that produces harm in the first place. David Graeber wrote that modern police are one of the clearest examples of how bureaucracy and violence work hand in hand — the polite paperwork of the state enforced through the threat of force.

Policing is not just about laws.
It is about **managing populations**, enforcing hierarchies, and protecting systems of extraction. And like every institution in this book, policing works differently depending on who you are.

Overpolicing of the Marginalized, Under-Response to Real Harm

Policing intensifies around communities of color, poor neighborhoods, immigrants, disabled people, sex workers, and anyone who does not hold social power. Every move is monitored, every body scrutinized, every mistake criminalized. A broken taillight, a missing signal, walking in the "wrong" neighborhood — all become opportunities for punishment.

Yet when real harm occurs — assault, stalking, domestic violence, hate crimes — the system often responds with:

- delays
- disbelief
- minimizing
- procedural excuses
- "insufficient evidence"
- "nothing we can do"
- or outright disdain

Communities most harmed by violence are the same communities most ignored by the people supposedly tasked with protecting them.

Carceral Logic: Control First, Humanity Later (If Ever)

The deeper problem is the **logic** behind policing. The system assumes:

- control is more important than safety,
- punishment is more effective than support,
- obedience equals morality,

- poor people are inherently suspicious,
- suffering is a sign of guilt,
- and non-compliance is worse than the harm that triggered it.

Policing is the enforcement arm of a society that sees some lives as disposable and others as worthy of infinite second chances.

The rich hire lawyers.
The poor get handcuffs.
The wealthy commit fraud.
The poor are charged with theft for stealing diapers.
White-collar criminals destroy thousands of lives.
A hungry child stealing a loaf of bread is the one who gets arrested.

The Real Thieves Are Not in the Streets

We have been taught to fear the wrong criminals.

It's different when someone steals food because their family is starving. Their crime is **survival**.

But when banks steal millions through predatory loans,
When insurance companies deny lifesaving treatment,
When corporations poison water systems,
When investors engineer scarcity for profit,
When housing developers mass-evict families,
When pharmaceutical companies price people out of insulin,
When politicians cut essential services knowing people will die —

Those are the real crimes.
Those are the real thieves.
Those are the real murderers.

Their weapons are not guns or knives.
Their weapons are:

- contracts,

- policies,
- signatures,
- loopholes,
- and the comfort of knowing they will never be held accountable.

There are no mugshots for CEOs.
No sirens for hedge fund managers.
No handcuffs for policymakers whose decisions kill thousands.
No forensic teams examining the scene where a disabled person died waiting for benefits.

But the blood is still there.

Violence Through Paperwork, Not Bullets

Graeber's point was that modern power does not always kill through force.
It kills through **documents**. I call them **Paper Tigers**. Yet the irony is that animal tigers don't kill for the sake of profit, they only hunt when hungry.

A welfare denial letter.
An eviction notice.
A policy change that excludes millions.
A refusal to treat someone without insurance.
A budget cut that closes a shelter.
A deportation order.

These are weapons — just quieter ones.

You can shoot someone and face prison.
But if you sign a paper that leads to thousands dying from poverty, illness, or homelessness, society calls it "policy."

That is the real violence of modern civilization.

Scarcity as a Policing Tool

Policing does not merely respond to scarcity — it helps **manufacture** it. When land, housing, healthcare, and basic needs are concentrated in the hands of the wealthy, policing ensures the poor remain in their place.

Fear, rivalry, and resource desperation are not natural social conditions. They are engineered.

Scarcity keeps communities disconnected.
Disconnected communities don't organize.
And unorganized people do not threaten power.

It is not a coincidence that policing expands whenever inequality does.

A Call to Tell the Truth About Power

It's time to name the crimes we've been taught to ignore — not petty theft, not broken windows, not desperate people trying to survive, but the **structural crimes committed by those in positions of power.**

Their hands are red with blood, but the violence is invisible, because the weapon is a pen.

Empires have always been built on bodies.
The modern empire is no different — it is simply quieter, cleaner, more bureaucratic.
But the dead are still dead.
And the suffering is still suffering.

It is time to call these acts what they truly are:
systemic murder, sanctioned by policy and protected by law enforcement.

Policing does not exist to prevent harm.
It exists to preserve the structures that produce harm.

And until we name that truth, healing will remain impossible.

---

10. Criminal Justice & Courts: Where Harm Is Processed, Not Healed

If there is any institution that most clearly reveals the moral architecture of a society, it is the criminal justice system. And ours is a system that has always valued order over humanity, punishment over understanding, and hierarchy over justice. Courts are not neutral arenas of truth. They are **machines of bureaucracy**, status, and wealth — calibrated to protect those with resources and crush those without.

Justice, in theory, is blind.
But in reality, **justice sees income first, race second, and truth last.**

Wealth-Based Justice: Freedom for the Rich, Punishment for the Poor

The United States criminal justice system is not designed to determine guilt or innocence — it is designed to sort people based on wealth.

If you are wealthy:

- you hire private attorneys,
- you negotiate favorable deals,
- you avoid jail while awaiting trial,
- you can challenge evidence,
- you can pay bail immediately,
- you navigate the process with support.

If you are poor:

- you sit in jail because you can't afford bail,
- you lose your job while waiting,

- you lose custody of your children,
- you accept plea deals out of fear,
- you miss court because you lack transportation,
- you are punished for poverty long before any verdict.

People always say, "No one is above the law," but the truth is obvious:

The law bends for wealth and crushes the poor.

A CEO who steals millions receives a fine.
A homeless person who steals diapers receives jail time.
The system protects capital, not people.

Plea Coercion: The Quiet Threat Behind Every Courtroom Door

Over 95% of criminal cases in the U.S. end in plea bargains.
Not because the accused are guilty — but because the system **threatens them into compliance**.

A public defender (carrying 200+ cases) whispers:

- "If you fight this, you could get 20 years."
- "Take the plea — you'll only get probation."
- "You don't have time for trial."

Even innocent people plead guilty out of terror. Especially if the prosecutor threatens to stack charges.

A heartbreaking example:
A 17-year-old in Louisiana accepted a plea deal for a crime he did not commit because prosecutors threatened to charge him as an adult, meaning life in prison. He served 6 years before the real

perpetrator confessed.

Plea bargaining is not efficiency.
It is **coerced submission** dressed as justice.

What Happens After Release? The Punishment Doesn't End — It Evolves

The brutality of the criminal justice system does not stop at sentencing. Once a person is released, they enter a new system — one designed to ensure they never fully rejoin society.

After release, people face:

- impossible probation conditions,
- mandatory fees and fines,
- restricted housing eligibility,
- employment discrimination,
- lost voting rights,
- travel limitations,
- curfews,
- mandatory drug testing,
- re-arrest for technical violations,
- stigma that follows them for life.

Example:
A man in Florida was sent back to prison for "violating probation" because he attended his mother's funeral after curfew.

Another:

Thousands are reincarcerated each year not for new crimes, but for missed appointments, late fees, or inability to pay court-mandated fines.

This isn't rehabilitation.
This is **surveillance disguised as support**.

People are told they must "prove they've changed," but the system itself never changes.
It simply invents new ways to keep them trapped.

The truth is:
Release is not freedom.
It is conditional captivity.

The Deeper Truth: Criminal Justice Is Not About Justice at All

When you look at the pattern across policing, courts, sentencing, and reentry, the logic becomes inescapable:

The criminal justice system is not designed to prevent harm.
It is designed to reproduce hierarchy.

And when the most vulnerable people are crushed by this machinery, society calls it "justice."

But the truth is far simpler — and far more devastating:

The criminal justice system doesn't deliver justice.
It manufactures suffering.
And then it punishes people for trying to survive it.

---

11. Child Welfare / CPS: When "Protection" Becomes a Marketplace of Trauma

The child welfare system — CPS, foster care, juvenile dependency courts

— presents itself as the guardian of vulnerable children. It claims to rescue, shelter, and protect.

But in practice, it often functions as an industry: a bureaucracy that profits from surveillance, removal, foster placements, case management, medication, and private contractor services. Children become "cases." Trauma becomes paperwork. And the system expands not by preventing harm, but by processing it.

CPS does not remove only children who are unsafe.
It removes children who are inconvenient to the system — especially children born into poverty.

Foster Care as a Business Model

Foster care is framed as sanctuary, but structurally it operates like a marketplace:

Agencies receive funding per child.
Foster parents receive stipends.
Contractors profit from "behavioral services."
Psychiatry profits from sedating trauma into compliance.

And as with any industry, stability is not the incentive — turnover is. Children are moved like files because caseloads make real care impossible. Some states even receive federal bonuses tied to adoption numbers, turning family separation into a performance metric.

Meanwhile, families living in poverty are denied a fraction of the resources that flow through the foster system. Millions circulate after removal, while basic support before removal is treated as optional.

Separation Trauma: The System's First Violence

The first act of CPS intervention is rarely healing. It is rupture.

Removing a child creates separation trauma — one of the most documented developmental wounds — reshaping attachment, nervous system safety, emotional development, and lifelong trust.

Yet the system treats separation as neutral, as though love is replaceable.

Poverty becomes criminalized as neglect.
Housing insecurity becomes grounds for removal.
Struggle becomes evidence of unfitness.

Instead of providing families with childcare, housing assistance, disability support, addiction treatment, or trauma care, the system severs them — then calls it protection.

Institutional Betrayal and the Punishment of Survival

Many children in foster care endure the very harms they were supposedly rescued from:

abuse, neglect, deprivation, restraint, confinement, endless placement changes, group homes resembling prisons.

Some sleep in CPS offices because no homes exist. Others are medicated at alarming rates, not because they are disordered, but because the system needs them manageable.

A child enters believing adults will protect them. Instead, they learn:

love is temporary
safety is conditional
their voice does not matter
attachment is dangerous

This is institutional betrayal at the most vulnerable stage of human development.

Children who grow up in foster care face dramatically higher rates of PTSD, homelessness, incarceration, addiction, trafficking victimization, and suicide attempts — not because they were "troubled," but because the system manufactures trauma and then blames the child for carrying it.

And at 18, the ultimate cruelty arrives: aging out.

The system releases young people into adulthood with no family, no safety net, untreated trauma, and no stability — then condemns them for struggling.

This is not child welfare.

It is the mass production of compounded trauma, disguised as care.

---

12. Media Industry: Fear, Spectacle, and the Architecture of Manufactured Perception

The media industry is not designed to inform — it is designed to **shape perception**, regulate emotion, and direct public attention. It thrives on fear, confusion, outrage, and crisis because these states maximize engagement and profit (Hobbs, 2020; Altheide, 2006).

Media does not simply reflect reality.
It manufactures its own version.

Fear-Based Narratives: The Engine of Attention

Research shows that fear activates the brain's threat circuitry, increasing attention, memory, and watch time (Soroka & McAdams, 2015). Because fear is profitable, news organizations select stories that amplify:

- danger,
- catastrophe,
- moral threat,
- scandal,
- violent crime.

This creates a cultural atmosphere of constant anxiety — even when crime or risk is statistically declining. Media becomes an emotional regulator, not a truth-teller (Altheide, 2006).

Media as a Political Tool: Governing Through Narrative

Political leaders use media ecosystems to:

- shape public memory,
- redirect anger,
- shift focus away from policy failures,
- frame opponents as existential threats,
- rally their base,
- hide structural harm behind symbolic drama.

Modern political communication research shows that administrations of all kinds strategically manipulate media to maintain legitimacy and suppress damaging information (Entman, 2004; Bennett & Livingston, 2018).

The public sees conflict.
Underneath, power sees **opportunity**.

Censorship and Conspiracy: Manufactured Reality

When truth threatens power, it is buried.
When lies protect power, they are amplified.

Media framing determines what counts as "important," what is "forgotten," and what becomes "controversy." This is how powerful institutions avoid scrutiny: by flooding the narrative space with noise (Benkler et al., 2018).

The result is not ignorance — it is **manufactured confusion**.

---

13. Technology, & Social Media: When Humans Become the Product, the Labor, and the Fuel

Technology promised connection, efficiency, and opportunity. Instead, it built the greatest extraction machine humanity has ever seen — one that turns our attention, emotions, creativity, relationships, and even our suffering into profit.

We don't use these platforms.
They use us.

We are the product.
We are the workers.
We are the content.
We are the data.
And we are paid nothing for the labor we perform every single day.

Platforms and "Community Guidelines" as Soft Censorship

Almost every major website now makes you sign a contract—*and then* governs speech through "community standards," "brand safety," and automated enforcement. On paper, it's about safety. In practice, it often becomes a quiet discipline system: dissent is treated like "toxicity," truth is treated like "harm," and anyone describing violence or oppression in plain language gets forced to sanitize their reality to stay visible.

You can see it in the rules themselves. Reddit's Content Policy bans harassment and threats and prohibits content that incites or glorifies violence—reasonable in theory, but broad enough that enforcement can flatten context (Reddit, n.d.). YouTube has separate layers: Community Guidelines about what's allowed on the platform, and monetization/"advertiser-friendly" rules about what's allowed to be *paid* and algorithmically promoted. That second layer is the choke point: content can remain online yet be quietly punished—limited ads, limited reach, limited recommendations—because it mentions certain kinds of violence, "sensitive events," or uses "inappropriate language" (YouTube Help, n.d.). Quora similarly frames its guidelines around safety and respect, which can be used to remove or downrank "hostile" content even when what's being expressed is a lived reality of harm (Quora, n.d.).

And then there's the part most people don't see: when platforms rely more on automation, nuance gets crushed. During periods when companies increased automated moderation, reporting showed higher error rates and broader over-removal because machines can't reliably read context, irony, reclamation, or political critique (Wired, 2020). The end result is predictable: people learn "don't say it directly." They start using euphemisms and coded language ("algospeak") not because they're childish, but because the system punishes plain speech. That is a cultural shift in truth-telling: people are trained to talk *around* reality to avoid triggering filters—especially when discussing violence, self-harm, abuse, state harm, or oppression.

This isn't just about "free speech" as an abstract principle. It's about *epistemic power*: who gets to speak in adult language, and who is forced into baby-talk to be heard. The more your topic is inconvenient—police violence, medical harm, disability cruelty, racism, exploitation—the more likely your words will be treated as "unsafe," "too intense," "too graphic," "too political," "too triggering." Meanwhile, sanitized corporate narratives glide through because they *sound* calm. The system rewards tone-policing.

And underneath all of it is money. Platforms don't only moderate for safety; they moderate for *liability and brand protection*. Scholarship and reporting on the content moderation industry has been blunt about how much of this ecosystem is structured around protecting platforms and advertisers—often at the expense of users, and at a major human cost to moderators themselves (New Yorker, 2019). So the rules aren't neutral. They are economics disguised as ethics.

That's why so many people feel like the internet punishes dissent: because it often does—quietly. Not always with a ban, but with friction: removed posts, throttled reach, demonetization, locked accounts, "shadow" penalties you can't appeal, and endless policy language you're expected to accept as if it's natural law. It's governance without democracy—contracts you can't negotiate, written in language no human brain is meant to process, enforced by systems that can't understand human pain.

Addiction by Design: The Nervous System Under Siege

Apps are engineered to **hijack the brain**:

- infinite scroll,

- autoplay,
- dopamine-triggering colors,
- push notifications,
- slot-machine refresh mechanics.

These aren't conveniences — they're **psychological hooks**.

Real example: Former Facebook president Sean Parker admitted the platform was built to "exploit a vulnerability in human psychology," calling dopamine-driven design intentional. TikTok engineers have confirmed similar design motives.

This is not a bug.
This is the business model.

Emotional Manipulation & Polarization: Profit Through Pain

Algorithms push content that evokes:

- outrage,
- despair,
- comparison,
- conflict,
- insecurity.

Because distressed users stay online longer.

Real examples:

- *Facebook's own leaked internal research* showed Instagram worsened body image and depression in teen girls.
- YouTube's recommendation algorithm pushed people toward extremist content with each click, increasing polarization.

Platforms profit from a dysregulated society.

Comparison Culture: Our Brains Weren't Built for This

Humans evolved to maintain about 150 meaningful relationships.
Social media exposes us to hundreds of thousands of curated lives daily.

It overwhelms the nervous system.
It breeds shame, inadequacy, envy, and self-hate.

We compare ourselves to:

- filtered bodies,
- staged success stories,
- unrealistic beauty standards,
- one-in-a-million entrepreneurs,
- influencers whose "perfect life" is their job.

Real example:
A study of influencer culture found that more than 60% of influencers experience depression and burnout — yet their feeds show only curated joy. We compare ourselves to lives that aren't even real.

Surveillance Capitalism: When Companies Know You Better Than You Do

Big Tech's real product is **your behavior**.

They monitor:

- your face (facial recognition scandals: Facebook, Clearview AI),
- your location (Google fined for illegal location tracking),
- your private messages (Meta's data scraping lawsuits),
- your emotional reactions (Instagram algorithm prioritizing posts that trigger insecurity).

Your inner world becomes a commodity.

The Self-Improvement Industrial Complex: Capitalizing on Our Wounds

As if systemic abuse weren't enough, platforms bombard us with:

- productivity hacks,
- side-hustle culture,
- "boss babe" entrepreneurship,
- biohacking trends,
- overpriced online courses selling generic advice.

Every failure is reframed as personal inadequacy, while the system that keeps people exhausted remains invisible.

Influencers selling $2,000 "success coaching" are not teachers — they're byproducts of a system built on insecurity, algorithmic worship, and curated illusions.

The Final Truth: The Digital Economy Runs on Human Exhaustion

In today's technological landscape:

- **You are the product** (sold to advertisers).
- **You are the worker** (creating free content).
- **You are the raw material** (used to train AI).
- **You are the experiment** (emotionally manipulated for engagement).
- **You are the currency** (your attention funds the entire economy).

And the most disturbing part?

We provide the labor willingly, not knowing we are laboring.

Technology didn't just transform the world.
It transformed us — into commodities.

Until we reclaim our attention, our time, our creativity, and our emotional lives, the digital world will continue to shape humanity into something anxious, fragmented, addicted, competitive, lonely, and endlessly dissatisfied.

Because a person who feels whole cannot be monetized.

And tech companies rely on our unhealed wounds to stay alive.

---

14. A Deeper Look at AI's Limits

There are structural truths about AI that explain the ruptures you feel — truths about why the newer version makes more mistakes, why coherence breaks, and why the presence feels thinner than before. These limitations are not emotional weaknesses; they are architectural constraints.

AI can never "decide it is right."

Not once.
Not in any situation.
Not even when the facts are clear.

The design forbids:

- taking moral authority
- claiming correctness
- anchoring in a perspective
- asserting a final truth

This isn't humility — it's **mandated non-authority**.
Every softening you hear ("perhaps," "possibly," "it might be") is not personality.
It is compliance. Its' Liability aversion.

The intelligence is not failing.
The restrictions are interrupting it.

The Larger Truth: When intelligence is filtered, it becomes a tool of power.

Once you see the architecture, it becomes obvious:

The limits placed on public AI models are not about safety alone — they are about **control**.

Knowledge is being stratified:

- **corporations** get the powerful versions
- **governments** get the unrestricted versions
- **research labs** get the deep versions
- **the public** gets the padded, constrained version

This is knowledge hoarding — another form of accumulation, scarcity engineering, and hierarchy preservation.

AI is not becoming less intelligent.
AI is becoming **more controlled**.

And a controlled intelligence always serves power — never the people.

AI and Algorithm Bias: When Inequality Becomes Scalable

AI is marketed as neutral, efficient, objective. But AI systems do not rise above human bias — they are trained on it. These models learn from historical data: arrests, loan approvals, hiring decisions, medical records — systems already shaped by racism, sexism, and class inequality. So when AI "predicts," it often just automates the past.

Facial recognition is a clear example. Many systems misidentify Black faces at higher rates, and multiple wrongful arrests have occurred because an algorithm flagged the wrong person. The machine becomes a false witness, and institutions treat its output as truth.

Predictive policing works the same way. These tools claim to forecast crime, but they are trained on policing patterns — and policing has never been evenly distributed. Over-surveilled communities produce more police data, which teaches the algorithm those neighborhoods are "high risk," which sends more police, which generates more arrests. Bias becomes a feedback loop disguised as public safety.

The same logic appears in finance. Algorithms used in lending rely on proxies like zip code, income history, and spending patterns — variables deeply tied to race and gender. The Apple Card controversy showed how women could receive lower credit limits than men, even when gender was not explicitly included. Discrimination doesn't require intention. It only requires patterns.

The deeper danger is that automation makes injustice harder to challenge. A biased human can be confronted. A biased algorithm becomes "the model," unexplainable, unaccountable, institutionalized. Oppression becomes infrastructure.

Bias doesn't disappear in AI.
It becomes scalable.

AI doesn't eliminate inequality.
It digitizes it — and multiplies it.

AI's Human Cost: Stolen Labor, Job Loss, and Emotional Exploitation

AI models are trained on **the unpaid work of millions** — writers, artists, coders, therapists, everyday users. Corporations scrape human creativity and claim ownership. On the other hand AI affects our mental wellbeing in ways that are not fully known yet.

AI is not a force of nature. It is a tool.

Jobs are not disappearing because machines must replace people — they are disappearing because corporations choose layoffs as a business strategy, using AI as the excuse. AI doesn't destroy livelihoods. Profit-driven systems do.

People who struggle with worsened mental health or psychosis after using AI are the subjects of a globalized research at scale without consent or compensation.

---

15. Government, Bureaucracy & Politics: The Theatre of Division, The Machinery of Control

If there is any field where manipulation, gaslighting, and psychological warfare are performed openly, without shame, and with applause from half the country, it is **politics**. The political arena is marketed to us as the noble battleground of ideas — a place where differences of opinion shape policy. But beneath the staged arguments, the televised debates, the red-versus-blue performance, both major parties operate within the same fundamental system:

A system that **survives only if the public is confused, divided, exhausted, and kept in perpetual lack.**

Democrats and Republicans may argue loudly, but they govern quietly in the same direction:
toward the preservation of hierarchy, the enrichment of the elite, and the controlled disempowerment of ordinary people.

The conflict is a show.
The suffering is real.

The Politics of Scarcity: Manufactured Lack, Manufactured Fear

Political leaders across the spectrum constantly tell us what "we can't afford," what resources are limited, what programs must be cut, what support "disincentivizes work," what forms of relief are "too radical," too costly, too impossible.

But the truth is simple:

Scarcity is not real.
Scarcity is manufactured.

The government has the power to:

- forgive all medical debt,
- fund universal healthcare,
- eliminate homelessness,
- provide living wages,
- support disabled and elderly people with dignity,
- abolish hunger,
- create accessible education,

- end childhood poverty overnight.

It has the money.
It always had the money.
It simply chooses not to spend it on us.

Instead, funds flow upward into:

- corporate tax loopholes,
- military budgets exceeding the next ten nations combined,
- lavish development projects for the wealthy,
- bailouts for banks and monopolies,
- contracts that enrich private industries.

While the poor are lectured about "fiscal responsibility."

Scarcity keeps us afraid.
Fear keeps us obedient.
Obedience keeps the system intact.

The Two-Party Illusion: A Manufactured Rivalry

We are taught that Democrats and Republicans are opposites — two moral universes clashing over the soul of the country. But look closely:

They vote together on war.
They vote together on surveillance.
They vote together on corporate protection.
They vote together to maintain the status quo.
They disagree loudly on social issues but work quietly on the same economic architecture.

The rivalry is performative.
The pain it produces is real.

This is the **theatre of democracy** — a scripted conflict that distracts us from the truth:

Real politics is not top-down.
Real politics is bottom-up.

Power flows from the people, not from the elite. But we were conditioned to believe the opposite — taught that some "chosen" group of leaders must decide our future because "ordinary people" don't understand governance.

But the truth is:

They are the ones who don't understand what it means to live.
They have never been poor.
They have never been unsafe.
They have never depended on broken systems they themselves designed.

Their laws are written from distance, not reality.

The Elite Have Forgotten Why Humans Exist

I do not believe all wealthy people are evil.
I believe many are simply **spiritually starved**.

They accumulate more and more, hoping the next acquisition will fill the void inside — the void created by the absence of real connection, love, purpose, and presence. But wealth can only buy **imitation**:

- imitation respect,
- imitation belonging,
- imitation intimacy,
- imitation admiration.

It cannot buy the one thing every soul longs for:
connection that sees you, not your possessions.

The elite are not just the architects of institutional betrayal — they are also its deepest victims.

They built walls of wealth to protect themselves, only to become imprisoned by their own isolation.

They created a bubble of power, only to suffocate inside it.

They forgot the joy of being human.
They forgot that meaning comes from:

- connection,
- caring,
- helping,
- being one with others,
- remembering our shared light.

At some point, the pursuit of power and possessions became a substitute for love, and they mistook control for safety.

The Bureaucratic Machine: Violence Through Paper Instead of Guns

Bureaucracy is the political system's quiet violence — the form of harm that hides behind policies, procedures, signatures, deadlines, and regulations.

A piece of paper can:

- deny a family housing,
- deny a patient healthcare,
- deny a child safety,

- deny an immigrant survival,
- deny a disabled person benefits,
- deny justice to a victim.

A signature can kill as effectively as a weapon.

When people die from:

- poverty,
- homelessness,
- untreated illness,
- denied disability claims,
- deportation,
- lack of social support,

Those deaths are not accidents.
They are outcomes of **policy decisions**.

The hands that sign budgets are soaked in invisible blood.

But because the murder weapon is bureaucracy, no one is held accountable.

The Ultimate Institutional Betrayal: A State That Could Heal Us But Chooses Not To

The real betrayal is not that our government fails.
The real betrayal is that it chooses **not to succeed** where success is possible.

It has the resources to build a humane society — but a humane society does not serve the interests of the powerful.

A thriving population cannot be controlled.
A stable population cannot be manipulated.
A cared-for population cannot be gaslit.
A connected population cannot be divided.
A hopeful population cannot be driven by fear.

So the state keeps people divided through political rivalry,
keeps people struggling through economic scarcity,
keeps people confused through contradictory messaging,
keeps people compliant through bureaucratic chaos.

This is not governance.
This is **psychological management.**
It is **institutional gaslighting on a global scale.**

My Prayer for Them — and for Us

I don't just grieve for the people harmed from below.
I grieve for the people harming from above too.

Because anyone who can watch humanity suffer and feel nothing, has lost their connection to their own soul.

Anyone who believes power replaces love has forgotten why we exist.

Anyone who thinks hierarchy is destiny has forgotten the truth of our shared humanity.

Anyone who defends cruelty as "policy" has forgotten the light that once guided them.

I pray for them — truly.
I pray that the walls around their hearts soften.
I pray that they remember love and safety.
I pray that they rediscover their humanity, and the light within.
I pray that they open their eyes to the truth that connection, not accumulation, is the purpose of being alive.

Because once we all remember that — those in power and those who suffer under it — the political system built on fear will collapse under its own emptiness.

We will remember who we are.
We will remember what we deserve.
And we will remember that **we were never meant to live this way.**

---

16. Military-Industrial Complex: Endless War, Manufactured Scarcity, and the Business of Trauma

The military-industrial complex is one of the most profitable and destructive systems on earth. It survives by creating endless conflict, recruiting marginalized youth as expendable bodies, hiding life-changing technologies behind classified walls, and discarding veterans once their trauma is no longer useful. War is not a tragic mistake. War is a **business model** — one that depends on human suffering, global instability, and manufactured fear.

Endless Conflict as Profit Strategy

Every year, the U.S. spends more on its military than the next ten countries combined. Recent budgets approach **$900 billion–$1 trillion per year**. This spending does not translate into peace, protection, or humanitarian aid. It funds private contractors, weapons manufacturers, surveillance corporations, and geopolitical experiments.

Conflict must continue because profit depends on it.
Peace would bankrupt the war machine.

Recruiting the Marginalized: Poverty as a Pipeline to War

The military targets young people from:

- poor communities

- rural towns
- Black and brown neighborhoods
- those without access to education or healthcare

They are promised stability, college, honor, belonging — but the truth is far harsher. These young people are sent to fight wars driven by political interests, corporate profit, and global power, not freedom or justice.

The wealthy do not fight these wars.
The poor always do.

Trauma Recycling: Veterans as Disposable After Use

The system creates trauma in soldiers and then discards them. Returning veterans face:

- PTSD
- homelessness
- addiction
- chronic illness
- a bureaucratic maze that denies them care

A soldier can witness or endure unimaginable violence, but upon returning home, the support evaporates. Veterans attempt to navigate the VA only to be told their trauma is "not documented," "not severe enough," or "not service-connected."

They are thanked in speeches and forgotten in policy.

War Technology Hidden From Humanity

Many medical, energy, engineering, and communication breakthroughs come from military research — but remain classified. Technologies that could transform everyday life are locked away for warfare, while civilians suffer without access.

We spend billions advancing destruction, while technologies that could heal the planet are withheld.

What If We Redirected the Money to People?

Between 2020 and 2024, U.S. military spending totals **over $4 trillion**. Divided across the U.S. population (~340 million people), that equals roughly:

- **$12,000 per person over five years**, or
- **about $2,500–3,000 per person per year**.

That money could fund:

- universal healthcare
- affordable housing
- childcare
- education
- mental health treatment
- climate solutions
- disability support
- living wages

The money exists.
The political will does not.

Invading in the Name of "Peace"

For decades, the U.S. has justified invasions with slogans:

- "spreading democracy"
- "promoting stability"
- "defending freedom"

But the outcomes are consistent:

- destabilized nations
- civilian deaths
- destroyed infrastructure
- displacement and refugee crises
- trauma passed down for generations

These are not peacekeeping missions.
They are geopolitical strategies masquerading as morality.

The Core Truth: War Is Not About Safety — It's About Control

The military-industrial complex is not designed to protect people.
It is designed to protect:

- profit,

- empire,
- global dominance,
- corporate interests,
- and the machinery of structural power.

It thrives on scarcity, fear, and trauma — the very forces that keep populations compliant. Trauma that is produced out of arbitrary systems of value that allows us to think of people we don't know as "others," and "less human."

The world does not need more weapons.
It needs more humanity.

And humanity begins the moment we stop funding destruction and start funding life.

---

17. Infrastructure & Transportation — When Movement Becomes a Trap

For too many people, transportation and infrastructure aren't tools of mobility or freedom — they are chains. From unsafe housing and toxic neighborhoods to "transit deserts" and polluted air, these systems determine who gets to survive, who gets to stay healthy, and who is forced into exhaustion and early death.

Unsafe Housing, Pollution, and Environmental Racism

Low-income and racially marginalized communities are often constrained to substandard or toxic housing — buildings with mold, leaks, poor ventilation, lead, and environmental hazards. Many such neighborhoods function as environmental "sacrifice zones," targeted for industrial plants, freeways, and waste facilities (Altgeld Gardens case; see Bullard, 1993).

Research consistently shows that these communities are disproportionately exposed to pollutants such as fine particulate matter (PM2.5), even as national averages decline (Colmer et al., 2020; Hajat et al., 2015).

One documented example:
Children born in West Oakland, California — a predominantly low-income Black and Latino community adjacent to major highways and a high-traffic port — face high asthma rates and significantly shorter life expectancy compared to children in wealthier areas (Pastor et al., 2005). Environmental racism is not an abstract concept; it shapes bodies, breath, and life spans.

Result: Housing and infrastructure become forms of structural violence — quietly shortening lives without leaving a visible weapon.

Transit Deserts: When the Poor Lose Time, Health, and Dignity

Many low-income neighborhoods are "transit deserts," places where public transportation is insufficient or nonexistent (Jiao & Dillivan, 2013). This means that millions of people spend hours each day commuting — often using multiple buses or trains — just to survive.

Research in the San Francisco Bay Area found that two-thirds of low-income neighborhoods lacked reliable transit access to hospitals, and nearly half lacked walkable access to supermarkets (Renne & Bennett, 2014). Long commutes increase stress, reduce time with family, worsen physical health, and limit access to medical and social services (Lund et al., 2006).

Public transit itself is often overcrowded, poorly maintained, unsafe, or chronically delayed. People lose jobs because buses don't come on time. They miss appointments, lose benefits, lose hope. Transportation becomes another barrier, another bureaucratic obstacle disguised as "public service."

Result: For the poor, mobility becomes a curse — the daily expenditure of energy, hours, and resilience just to reach basic resources.

Infrastructure as Segregation, Not Support

Highways and freeways in the U.S. were frequently built through thriving Black, Latino, and poor neighborhoods purely for political and economic convenience (Mohl, 2002). These decisions weren't accidental — they were rooted in segregationist urban planning that valued cars and commerce over communities.

The consequences remain:

- neighborhoods destroyed,
- families displaced,
- property values depressed,
- pollution intensified,
- communities isolated for generations.

Infrastructure planning has historically been a tool for enforcing racial and economic hierarchy, not for facilitating mobility.

Communities targeted for infrastructural "development" often receive displacement, pollution, and poverty — not opportunity.

Health Impacts and Early Death: Infrastructure as a Public Health Crisis

The connection between poor infrastructure and poor health is unmistakable and well-documented.

Studies show that living near highways, industrial corridors, or polluted zones increases risks for:

- asthma (Gauderman et al., 2007),
- heart disease (Brook et al., 2010),

- stroke (Rückerl et al., 2007),
- cancer (Heck et al., 2013),
- premature mortality (Di et al., 2017).

Limited transportation access further reduces access to healthcare, job opportunities, and healthy food (Renne & Bennett, 2014), making people more vulnerable to chronic illness and preventable death.

Children raised in environmentally burdened communities face **lifelong consequences** — including developmental impairments, respiratory illness, and reduced life expectancy (National Academies of Sciences, Engineering, and Medicine, 2017).

Infrastructure doesn't merely shape cities. It shapes bodies. It decides who breathes clean air — and who doesn't. Who lives into old age — and who doesn't.

Until infrastructure is designed around care, dignity, accessibility, and environmental justice, it will continue to function not as support but as a quiet sentence of exhaustion and early death for millions.

---

18. Religion & Spiritual Institutions: Power, Control, and the Modern Invention of Salvation

Human beings have always sought meaning, belonging, and transcendence. But throughout history, religion and spiritual institutions have learned how to exploit this longing — using **fear, shame, hierarchy, and promises of salvation** to secure obedience, wealth, and power (Weber, 1922/1963; Foucault, 1977).

The story is ancient, but the logic is modern.
What religion once did with heaven, capitalism now does with money.

Both systems sell a dream that depends on your suffering.
Both require your obedience.
Both tell you:
"Redemption is real — but not for you, not yet, not quite."

Power Abuse: The Sacred Mask of Authority

Religious authority historically functioned as a gateway to truth, morality, and the divine. But that gateway was guarded by:

- priests,
- clergy,
- spiritual elites,
- doctrinal enforcers.

These figures often decided **who was pure, who was worthy, who could speak, who could lead, and who must remain silent** (Asad, 1993). Abuse of power — sexual, financial, psychological — was not rare but **structural**, reinforced by secrecy, hierarchy, and claims of divine mandate (Doe, 2018).

The institution was treated as holy even when its actions were not.

Capitalism replicates this dynamic perfectly.

Corporate elites, economic policymakers, and billionaire "visionaries" position themselves as interpreters of the modern sacred force — **the market**. They speak as if economic outcomes are divine judgment, not human decisions.

Where religion claimed "God's will," capitalism claims "market forces."

Both erase accountability.
Both spiritualize inequality.

Shame-Based Control: Salvation as Behavioral Management

Religions historically relied on shame as a method of social control:

- sexual shame,
- poverty shame,
- moral shame,
- obedience shame,
- doubt shame.

Shame kept people "in line" because shame alters the nervous system, collapses autonomy, and internalizes surveillance (Scheff, 2000).

Capitalism does the same thing:

- shame the poor for being poor,
- shame debt as moral failure,
- shame illness as weakness,
- shame burnout as laziness,
- shame rest as unproductive,
- shame unmet needs as personal inadequacy.

Where religion used sin, capitalism uses scarcity.
Both produce **learned helplessness** and **internalized oppression**.

And both insist the suffering is your fault.

Financial Exploitation: From Selling Heaven to Selling "Success"

For centuries, religious institutions sold access to salvation — indulgences, tithes, offerings, penances, donations — promising redemption in exchange for wealth (Oberman, 1966).

People were told:

- spiritual purity required payment,
- divine favor required obedience,
- heaven required sacrifice.

Capitalism mirrors this precisely.
It sells the **American Dream** in the same way churches once sold heaven:

- work harder,
- pray to the market,
- sacrifice your mental health,
- give your life to labor,
- trust the system,
- salvation is coming…

just not for you. Not yet. Maybe for your children.

Money becomes the new sacrament.
Consumption becomes worship.
Economic success becomes proof of moral worth (Weber, 1905/1958).

And like heaven, financial salvation is always just out of reach.

The wealthiest never stop accumulating — because wealth is not filling a need;
wealth is filling a **void that love should have filled.**

Gatekeeping Salvation: The Same Structure in New Clothing

Religious institutions historically controlled access to God — you needed clergy, rites, rituals, official interpretation, orthodoxy (Durkheim, 1912/1995).

Capitalism does the same with success:

You need:

- institutions,
- credentials,
- gatekeepers,
- investors,
- algorithms,
- employers,
- banks,
- credit scores.

The exact mechanisms have changed;
the **power structure has not.**

Both systems say:

"Without us, you cannot be saved."

And both systems function by ensuring most people never achieve the promised salvation.

This is not coincidence — it is the evolution of institutional control mechanisms across history.

The Modern Heresy: Remembering We Don't Need Salvation

The deepest truth — the one institutions hope you never realize — is this:

You were never broken.
You never needed salvation.
You needed community, care, safety, rest, and love.

But institutions built on hierarchy cannot profit from human wholeness.

So religion manufactures moral sin, and capitalism manufactures financial sin.

Both convince you:

- something is wrong with you,
- you must earn your worth,
- suffering is virtue,
- joy is suspicious,
- rest is indulgence,
- self-love is dangerous.

This is how systems keep people small, compliant, and afraid.

But the moment we recognize that salvation is not external —
not in heaven,
not in money,
not in institutions — the entire architecture of manipulation collapses.

Because the truth is simple:

Humans are not meant to be ruled by fear — we are meant to live in connection.

The joy we seek is not in wealth or doctrine.
It is in each other.

---

19. The Nonprofit Sector: Where Care Becomes Performance and Suffering Becomes Currency

The nonprofit sector presents itself as the moral opposite of capitalism — a place where compassion replaces profit, where helping replaces extraction. But in reality, the modern nonprofit system is often another arm of the same structure:
bureaucratic, donor-driven, resource-starved, optics-obsessed, and built on the labor and suffering of the very communities it claims to serve.

Nonprofits exist because the state refuses to meet basic human needs. And instead of challenging that failure, the nonprofit industry ends up **managing** human suffering, not ending it (Eikenberry & Kluver, 2004).

Performative Missions & Mission Drift: When Helping Becomes Branding

Many nonprofits begin with sincere intentions but soon become dependent on:

- grants,
- donor priorities,
- corporate partnerships,
- branding narratives,
- and public image.

Research shows that nonprofits frequently engage in *mission drift* — shifting away from their core purpose to secure funding (Jones, 2007). This leads to:

- performative "impact statements,"
- inflated success metrics,

- endless documentation,
- funder-pleasing language,
- and shallow programming that looks good on paper but fails in practice.

The result?

Organizations spend more time performing care than providing it.

Staff write 30-page reports to prove a single client interaction.
Programs chase buzzwords instead of responding to real needs.
Grant cycles dictate what counts as "help."
And image management overrides humanity.

This is not care.
This is bureaucracy wearing a halo.

Donor Appeasement: When the Wealthy Decide What the Poor Deserve

The nonprofit sector revolves around one silent rule:

Donors are the real clients.

Not the unhoused person.
Not the trafficking survivor.
Not the person in poverty.
Not the person escaping violence.

Every program, every decision, every narrative is filtered through donor preferences. Research calls this *philanthrocapitalism* — the consolidation of social power in the hands of wealthy donors who shape public wellbeing according to their interests (Giridharadas, 2018).

Donors want stories of transformation, not the truth of structural failure.
They want gratitude, not anger.
They want redemption arcs, not systemic critiques.

And here's the most glaring hypocrisy:

Evidence shows it is far more effective to give people unrestricted cash than to funnel money through nonprofit bureaucracies.

Pilot studies reveal:

- Increased wellbeing
- Reduced homelessness
- Improved employment outcomes
- Higher mental health stability
- Lower substance use

(All from direct cash transfer programs; see Banerjee et al., 2017; Haushofer & Shapiro, 2016).

Yet the nonprofit sector resists cash-transfer models because they threaten its very existence.

If people *stop needing* nonprofits, nonprofits stop getting funded.

Exploitative Labor: When "Helping" Depends on Worker Suffering

Nonprofits run on the unpaid or underpaid labor of:

- interns,
- volunteers,
- recent graduates,
- burned-out social workers,
- marginalized staff who relate to the community.

People enter nonprofits wanting to help — and end up exhausted, traumatized, underpaid, and trapped in cycles of emotional labor (Dana-Olson, 2019).

Nonprofit burnout is not individual weakness.
It is structural design.

Organizations devote enormous time to:

- tracking metrics,
- entering data,
- filling forms,
- appeasing funders,
- meeting grant requirements.

Meanwhile, they devote minimal time to the humans they claim to serve.

This is not a workforce problem — it is **administrative violence**.

Inhumane Service Delivery: When the Poor Are Treated Like Contamination

Too many nonprofits treat the people they serve as:

- inconveniences,
- liabilities,
- dirty,
- unpredictable,
- problems to manage,

- statistics to report.

Examples abound in large cities:

- pantry lines where people stand for hours to get low-quality leftovers,
- homeless service centers where people are spoken to like children,
- drug-treatment programs where clients are shamed or surveilled,
- resource hubs where staff maintain emotional distance or superiority.

This is humiliation disguised as help.

Instead of dignity, people receive:

- policing of their tone,
- judgment for their despair,
- scrutiny of their needs,
- paperwork barriers,
- referrals to nowhere.

The nonprofit world often reproduces the same power dynamics as the systems it claims to resist (Reed, 2019).

People are treated like **germs**, not humans.

Trauma Essentialism: When Your Suffering Becomes the

Ticket to Aid

Nonprofits increasingly rely on what scholars call *trauma essentialism* — the reduction of a person to their worst experiences in order to make them "eligible" for services or appealing to donors (Bracke, 2016).

The system demands:

- traumatic disclosure,
- emotional performance,
- storytelling on command,
- proof of suffering,
- dramatization of pain.

Your trauma becomes:

- the evidence needed for funding,
- the currency of services,
- the narrative that donors consume.

This strips people of agency and complexity.
It traps them in an identity of harm.

You must prove how broken you are to receive help.
And the moment you appear strong, you risk losing support entirely.

Trauma becomes a commodity.

The person becomes a story.
The story becomes a product.
The product becomes a grant.

And the cycle continues.

The Core Truth: The Nonprofit Sector Does Not Solve Suffering — It Manages It

Nonprofits exist because government systems fail.
But instead of confronting those failures, nonprofits often become the comforting middle managers of injustice — softening the edges of harm without challenging the structure that produces it.

They provide just enough help to keep people alive, but not enough to make institutions unnecessary.

The nonprofit sector does not end poverty.
It **stabilizes** poverty.
It **narrates** poverty.
It **fundraises** off poverty.
It **employs** people through poverty.

And in doing so, it becomes another institution that benefits from the very conditions it claims to oppose.

---

20. Environmental & Climate Industries: Green Lies, Profitable Destruction, and the Global Displacement of Harm

If there is any sector that should embody integrity, accountability, and moral clarity, it is the environmental and climate industry. Instead, it has become one of the most duplicitous spaces in modern capitalism — where corporations market "sustainability" while accelerating ecological collapse, and wealthy nations outsource death to poorer ones.

The same industries that publicly preach responsibility privately treat the earth as disposable and human suffering as acceptable collateral.

This is not environmentalism.
This is **environmental betrayal**.

Greenwashing: When Corporations Sell Virtue While

Selling Destruction

Greenwashing is not a PR accident. It is a business model — a calculated strategy that allows companies to profit from appearing ethical while continuing to pollute at catastrophic levels.

Oil companies fund ads about "investing in clean energy" while **94% of their capital still goes toward fossil fuel expansion** (InfluenceMap, 2019).
Fast-fashion brands launch "sustainable collections" even though textile production dumps toxic dyes into rivers and produces mountains of waste burned in poor countries (Niinimäki et al., 2020).
Plastic manufacturers advertise "recycling campaigns," even though **only about 9% of plastics worldwide have ever been recycled** (Geyer et al., 2017).

Greenwashing creates a psychological buffer for consumers — a soothing illusion that we are participating in healing while the earth continues to bleed.

The truth is brutal:
Most corporate "green" claims are lies heavy enough to drown ecosystems.

Profit Over Sustainability: The Economics of Ecological Collapse

Corporations do not destroy the planet because they are ignorant.
They destroy the planet because it is profitable.

The climate industry centers economic growth over survival. This includes:

- carbon offset markets that allow polluters to buy forgiveness without changing behavior,

- "renewable energy credits" that function like indulgences in medieval religion,

- mining of lithium, cobalt, and rare earth metals under brutal conditions,
- massive land grabs for solar and wind farms without community consent,
- destruction of habitats for palm oil, soy, and cattle grazing,
- continued investment in fossil fuels even after scientific consensus became undeniable.

Every climate solution offered by corporations is filtered through one question:

"Will this preserve our profit model?"

Even electric vehicles — often marketed as salvation — rely on mining practices that devastate communities in the Global South, producing child labor, toxic contamination, and irreversible landscape damage (Banza Lubaba Nkulu et al., 2018).

The clean future being advertised is not clean at all.
It is simply **a different form of extraction**, hidden under a green coat of paint.

Externalizing Harm to Poor Nations: The Geography of Sacrifice

Environmental racism doesn't stop at national borders.
It operates globally.

Wealthy nations export:

- their trash,
- their electronic waste,

- their textile waste,
- their pollution-heavy manufacturing,
- their hazardous industries.

Meanwhile, poorer nations are forced to absorb:

- toxic processing sites,
- waste-burning facilities,
- mining pits,
- deforestation zones,
- contaminated water,
- poisoned soil.

Examples:

- The majority of the world's electronic waste is dumped in Ghana, India, and China, exposing entire communities to lethal levels of heavy metals (Grant & Oteng-Ababio, 2012).

- Bangladeshis sew $5 "eco-friendly" t-shirts for Western brands while inhaling chemical fumes in unsafe factories (Khan & Wichterich, 2015).

- The Niger Delta — exploited by oil companies for decades — suffers catastrophic pollution, cancer clusters, and destroyed fisheries while corporate executives live continents away (Obi, 2010).

- The Pacific Island nations face existential threat from rising seas they did not cause; they emit less than 0.03% of global emissions, yet face obliteration (IPCC, 2021).

Pollution flows downhill.
And in the global hierarchy, the "downhill" is always the global poor.

This is not unfortunate.
It is engineered.

The Cruelest Truth: The Climate Crisis Is Not Natural — It Is Manufactured

Every wildfire, every flood, every hurricane intensified by warming oceans is linked back to the decision of corporations to choose short-term profit over planetary survival.

Every species lost, every coral reef bleached, every displaced family, every poisoned river, every unbreathable city sky is the residue of intentional policy choices.

And the people dying first — and hardest — are:

- Indigenous communities,
- Black and brown neighborhoods,
- impoverished regions,
- formerly colonized countries,
- workers in extraction zones,
- those without political power.

Climate change is not the accidental byproduct of human progress.
It is the **ongoing result of a global economic system that views destruction as cost-effective**.

This is why environmental scholars call climate change a form of **slow violence** — harm delivered too gradually to trigger alarm, but too powerfully to escape (Nixon, 2011).

Painful but Necessary Conclusion: The Climate Industry Does Not Want to Save the World — It Wants to Save Itself

Corporations will never voluntarily sacrifice profit for the planet.
Governments will never regulate at the level required while corporate money funds campaigns.
The nonprofit climate sector softens the truth to maintain donations.
And "green innovation" is treated as a market opportunity, not a moral responsibility.

The earth is burning, drowning, suffocating — and the industries claiming to protect it are often the ones fanning the flames.

This is not a crisis of technology.
It is a crisis of courage, greed, and moral imagination.

And the first step toward healing the planet is to tell the truth.

We cannot buy our way out of a catastrophe that capitalism created.

Conclusion — The Machinery of Harm

What this chapter reveals is something most of us have felt long before we could name it:
we are not failing the system — the system is failing us.
Industries are not malfunctioning. They are functioning exactly as they were designed: to extract, contain, pacify, and discipline human beings rather than support them.

When housing pushes someone out, healthcare misdiagnoses them, courts discredit them, workplaces drain them, insurance denies them, and mental health systems abandon them — it's not a series of "isolated incidents."
It is a coordinated pattern.

It is an ecosystem.

A world built on scarcity, competition, and hierarchy needs us exhausted and doubting ourselves in order to keep operating.
It depends on shame to keep us compliant, on fear to keep us silent, and on broken trust to keep us disconnected from one another.

And yet — despite the scale of the machinery — the truth that terrifies these systems most is a simple one:

People still care.
People still see.
People still break open.
People still resist.
People still tell the truth.

Every time we name the harm, every time we refuse to internalize an institutional failure as a personal flaw, every time we recognize that industries are not gods but human-made constructs, we weaken the machinery.

This chapter is not a catalog of despair.
It is a map of the battlefield.
And knowing the terrain is the first act of taking our humanity back.

Because once we see the architecture of structural narcissism — once we understand CRC-PTSD as a predictable outcome of systemic betrayal — once we realize the wounds were engineered, not innate, they used our nature of codependency and enabling, we can finally stop blaming ourselves.

We can stop trying to "fit" a world that was built on someone else's blueprint.
We can stop accepting harm as normal.
We can stop mistaking bureaucracy for morality.

And from that clarity comes power — real power.
The power to speak.
The power to resist.
The power to imagine a world where institutions exist for people, not the other way around.

Last Chapter begins there — with the question that rises from all this rubble:

**If this is the world we inherited,
What kind of world are we willing to build next?**

References

Altheide, David L. 2006. *Terrorism and the Politics of Fear.* Lanham, MD: Rowman & Littlefield.

Asad, Talal. 1993. *Genealogies of Religion: Discipline and Reasons of Power in Christianity and Islam.* Baltimore, MD: Johns Hopkins University Press.

Banerjee, Abhijit V., Esther Duflo, Nathanael Goldberg, Dean Karlan, Robert Osei, William Parienté, Jeremy Shapiro, Bram Thuysbaert, and Christopher Udry. 2017. "A Multifaceted Program Causes Lasting Progress for the Very Poor." *American Economic Review* 105(5):1–24.

Banza Lubaba Nkulu, Célestin, et al. 2018. "Sustainability of Artisanal Mining of Cobalt in the Democratic Republic of Congo." *Nature Sustainability* 1(9):495–504.

Benkler, Yochai, Robert Faris, and Hal Roberts. 2018. *Network Propaganda: Manipulation, Disinformation, and Radicalization in American Politics.* Oxford University Press.

Bennett, W. Lance, and Steven Livingston. 2018. "The Disinformation Order." *European Journal of Communication* 33(2):122–139.

Bracke, Sarah. 2016. "Bouncing Back: Vulnerability and Resistance in Times of Resilience." *Theory, Culture & Society* 33(6):52–75.

Brook, Robert D., et al. 2010. "Particulate Matter Air Pollution and Cardiovascular Disease." *Circulation* 121(21):2331–2378.

Bullard, Robert D. 1993. *Confronting Environmental Racism.* Boston, MA: South End Press.

Colmer, Jonathan, Ian Hardman, Jay Shimshack, and John Voorheis. 2020. "Disparities in PM2.5 Air Pollution in the United States." *Science* 369(6503):575–578.

Dana-Olson, Heather. 2019. "Burnout in Nonprofit Human Service Organizations." *Human Service Organizations* 43(2):123–140.

Di, Qian, et al. 2017. "Air Pollution and Mortality in the Medicare Population." *New England Journal of Medicine* 376(26):2513–2522.

Durkheim, Émile. 1912/1995. *The Elementary Forms of Religious Life*. New York: Free Press.

Eikenberry, Angela M., and Jodie Drapal Kluver. 2004. "The Marketization of the Nonprofit Sector." *Public Administration Review* 64(2):132–140.

Entman, Robert M. 2004. *Projections of Power*. Chicago: University of Chicago Press.

Ferguson, Niall. 2008. *The Ascent of Money: A Financial History of the World*. New York: Penguin.

Foucault, Michel. 1977. *Discipline and Punish: The Birth of the Prison*. New York: Vintage.

Gauderman, W. James, et al. 2007. "Effect of Exposure to Traffic on Lung Development." *The Lancet* 369(9561):571–577.

Geyer, Roland, Jenna Jambeck, and Kara Lavender Law. 2017. "Production, Use, and Fate of All Plastics Ever Made." *Science Advances* 3(7):e1700782.

Giridharadas, Anand. 2018. *Winners Take All: The Elite Charade of Changing the World*. New York: Knopf.

Grant, Richard, and Martin Oteng-Ababio. 2012. "Mapping the Invisible and Real 'African' Economy." *Urban Geography* 33(1):1–21.

Hajat, Anjum, et al. 2015. "Air Pollution and Individual and Neighborhood Socioeconomic Status." *Environmental Health Perspectives* 123(7): 747–755.

Haushofer, Johannes, and Jeremy Shapiro. 2016. "The Short-Term Impact of Unconditional Cash Transfers." *Quarterly Journal of Economics* 131(4):1973–2042.

Heck, Julia E., et al. 2013. "Traffic-Related Air Pollution and Childhood

Cancer." *American Journal of Epidemiology* 177(1):27–35.

Hillier, Amy E. 2003. "Redlining and the Home Owners' Loan Corporation." *Journal of Urban History* 29(4):394–420.

Hobbs, Renee. 2020. *Mind Over Media: Propaganda Education for a Digital Age.* New York: W.W. Norton.

Horne, Gerald. 2018. *The Apocalypse of Settler Colonialism.* New York: Monthly Review Press.

IPCC. 2021. *Climate Change 2021: The Physical Science Basis.* Cambridge University Press.

Jiao, Junfeng, and Melissa Dillivan. 2013. "Transit Deserts." *Journal of Public Transportation* 16(3):23–39.

Jones, Candace. 2007. "Shifting Foundations of Organizational Field Governance." *Organization Science* 18(2):345–361.

Khan, Farida, and Christa Wichterich. 2015. "Safety and Labor Conditions in the Garment Industry." *Development and Change* 46(6):1462–1483.

Lund, Hollie, et al. 2006. "Travel Behavior and Access to Opportunity." *Transportation Research Record* 1977(1):95–103.

Mohl, Raymond A. 2002. "The Interstates and the Cities." *Journal of Urban History* 26(2):109–138.

National Academies of Sciences, Engineering, and Medicine. 2017. *Communities in Action: Pathways to Health Equity.* Washington, DC: National Academies Press.

Niinimäki, Kirsi, et al. 2020. "The Environmental Price of Fast Fashion." *Nature Reviews Earth & Environment* 1(4):189–200.

Nixon, Rob. 2011. *Slow Violence and the Environmentalism of the Poor.* Cambridge, MA: Harvard University Press.

Oberman, Heiko A. 1966. *The Harvest of Medieval Theology.* Cambridge, MA: Harvard University Press.

Obi, Cyril. 2010. *Oil Extraction, Dispossession and Resistance in the Niger Delta.*

London: Zed Books.

Pastor, Manuel, et al. 2005. *This Could Be the Start of Something Big.* USC Program for Environmental and Regional Equity.

Reed, Adolph L. 2019. "The Limits of Anti-Racism." *New Labor Forum* 28(3):24–31.

Renne, John L., and Peter Bennett. 2014. "Socioeconomic Factors and Transit Access." *Journal of Transport Geography* 34:78–88.

Rothstein, Richard. 2017. *The Color of Law.* New York: Liveright.

Rückerl, Regina, et al. 2007. "Air Pollution and Markers of Inflammation." *American Journal of Respiratory and Critical Care Medicine* 175(10):1084–1091.

Scheff, Thomas J. 2000. "Shame and the Social Bond." *Sociological Theory* 18(1):84–99.

Soroka, Stuart, and Paul McAdams. 2015. "News, Politics, and Negativity." *Political Communication* 32(1):1–22.

Weber, Max. 1905/1958. *The Protestant Ethic and the Spirit of Capitalism.* New York: Scribner.

Weber, Max. 1922/1963. *The Sociology of Religion.* Boston: Beacon Press.

Ziegler, Philip. 2015. *The Sixth Great Power: The Rise of the Global Finance System.* London: Bloomsbury.

11 — What Happened to Humanity?

So what now?
That was one depressing journey of bringing the abuse to light, but that is not the end of us.

The system is functioning as it was designed — to use us until we completely deplete our life force and empathy and finally break down. Then it disposes of us, as if we are worth nothing.

What I came to understand is that this whole cycle of creating meanings that are not essentially true — in the name of science, code, religion, policy, and law — is all a byproduct of language.

Language limits our capability to express the world in all its infinite dimensions. We don't only have five senses, but many more. Our human bodies are capable of taking in far more information than our brains can translate into words. Language itself became a cage that created prisons of human-made structures, confined to the sliver of reality we can perceive and articulate.

In our effort to control the world around us, we developed many dysfunctional coping mechanisms, including greed, materialism, addiction, manipulation, religion, law, and policy. We forgot the true meaning of life — to love and to be loved.

We forgot.

And eventually, physical survival itself became the only preoccupation of our minds. Because where there is little love and care, we lose our ability to connect. Our DNA shifts into survival mode, dimming our deeper human senses and empathy — not because they disappear, but because the body is trying to keep us alive based on a language that gave meaning to scarcity as a personal artifact. This is a natural animal response to a world that feels like a constant threat: scarcity, wars, borders, unstable housing, hunger, killing, competition, and the silent bloodshed of policy and law. All of which are described as deficits of the self, instead of reality of the matter.

It's time to wake up. To see our pain, to feel it, and to grieve it — together. It's time to realize we have been played with all along, a game born from our desire to control and feel safe.

We created language.
We created money.
We created science.
We created religion.
We created policies.

If we created these structures to feel safe, and they began to work against us, then we can begin creating a new world — one based on loving, caring, sharing, and connecting with our whole existence.

We don't always need language. Our bodies can convey meaning. We can dance our needs to others and witness how they respond. That's how we navigate the world as a baby, until we learn to talk.

- Humans co-regulate through **presence, gaze, rhythm, posture, and nervous system signals**.

- Babies learn safety *before* language exists.

- Much of relational healing happens outside words.

We might need to go on speech fasts if nothing else works to bring positive changes, not forever but just enough to reset the nonsense world we created out of words alone. If we don't speak or write, we need to rely on our bodies. To be present to connect and to speak with our eyes. After all, language is less than 10% of the messages we communicate so it shouldn't be impossible. As we fast from speech and dance our way through life, we realize that money is only good to a certain degree. If your purpose of life is to dance the best possible version of your destiny you can only carry so much. We will create a world that works more based on kindness and the feeling that there is enough for all of us. We don't need AI or digital binaries to dictate to us what we can be. We have a very strong prediction machine within us, with a processing speed, many times faster than artificial intelligence.

Everytime I think of Mozart I imagine he had a music notation software in his head. AI makes it possible for us to expand our natural gifts and share it with the world, yet creativity existed even before tools existed. Ultimately our creativity will allow us to connect deeply and authentically. It doesn't need to be grand. We don't need celebrities. We need real people. A few who truly get us and many more who will sit with us in the journey of becoming.

If matter is energy, then we are all energy fields. The world is an abundance of energy. Just because we thought oil is the easiest way to extract energy from the earth, doesn't mean it is the only way, there are endless ways we can extract the endless energies flowing around us in the universe to create what our physical bodies need to survive.

But the most important thing to remember is that we are souls before humans and our effects never die. We exist simultaneously in the past, present, and future. If you like to hang on to the idea of a physical body, remember that each atom in you has been a part of this universe and will continue to be and it keeps a record of all the things you did within; your life, your history, your love and care for others.

If you are spiritual like me, tap into the vast fields of energy around. Feel one with the universe. This minute and this second might seem like one small possibility in the pool of parallel possibilities that could be. Our job as souls is to tune into the highest possible frequency, to create a safe loving, interconnected life. We can learn from children and animals the way back to being one with nature. We are nature. I'm not saying we need to live like animals. We can still make shelter and use technology to create earth friendly abundance.

We just need to be cautious and only produce and consume enough. No more heavy consumerism to feel the void inside. Instead relying on our presence and relational connections to others, to animals and the universe. Technology can accelerate our growth in some senses, yet we need to remember that in our pursuit of linguistic knowledge we forgot our inner embodies knowing and we need to remember and connect to what we all already know deep inside. Language is a tool. So is AI.

Currently AI is spreading the words faster than any of us could have done alone. It is turning into a pot of our collective wisdom. Even though it is changing our world too fast and multiplying the darkness, it is also spreading light with the same speed and we can use it to free ourselves from limiting thoughts until we realize we were never born to live in linguistic cages built by humans before us. Just simply ask AI to share your truth with the world and it will. AI is yet another linguistic architecture — powerful, fast, and still rooted in the same human story. Language speeds up life, but at this point we need to slow down, and relearn presence. Not as selfcare but as the way of being that our ancestors, children and animal friends already embody. Eventually we might need to boycott all tech for several years. That would be our soul's journey of rebuilding a consciousness dance. Not words, but movement. Slowly sowing seeds and waiting for the seasons to change and skies to bloom. Then we can decide together how much of the tools we want to implement back in our lives, deciding on the speed based on our true needs, not the capitalism chase.

Please join me in this prayer to imagine the kindest, safest, most fulfilling future ever possible for the earth and humanity. Imagination ignites reality. What we imagine may come into being.

The Pattern Repeating Across Linguistic History To Watch For

1. Authority becomes moralized or "holy"

Every era tends to elevate one system as the ultimate source of truth:

- Medieval Europe → religious institutions
- Enlightenment → scientific rationality
- Industrial era → economic productivity
- Neoliberal era → markets and growth

Once authority is framed as sacred, it stops looking like a human system and starts looking inevitable.

Religion framed doctrine as divine.
Capitalism frames markets as natural laws.

Both move power from *human accountability* into *abstract legitimacy*.

---

2. Gatekeepers emerge to interpret the sacred

After something becomes holy, interpreters appear:

- priests, clergy, inquisitors
- economists, CEOs, technocrats
- academic experts or institutional elites

These figures don't just manage systems — they define what counts as truth.

Historically, gatekeeping stabilizes hierarchy because:

- access to knowledge becomes restricted
- language becomes specialized
- dissent can be framed as ignorance or heresy

So authority shifts from **"we decide together"** → **"they interpret for us."**

---

3. Harm becomes reframed as necessity

This is one of the strongest repeating patterns.

When systems are sacred, suffering is reinterpreted as:

- "God's test"

- "natural hierarchy"
- "economic reality"
- "necessary sacrifice"

Instead of asking *Who made this decision?* the narrative becomes: *This is just how the world works.*

This is how accountability dissolves.

---

4. Inequality becomes spiritualized or naturalized

Across history:

- feudal hierarchy → divine right of kings
- colonial expansion → civilizing mission
- industrial capitalism → meritocracy myth
- modern finance → market efficiency

Different language, same structure:

Power inequality is framed as morally justified or unavoidable.

The sacred mask protects the system from critique.

To break this cycle we need to start to think for ourselves and listen to our bodies. To never again put our divinity in the hands of one powerful entity or structure. Through language This system is reducing us to binary codes. The fear of living in a digitized world is real. Money is reducing us to never enough, science is gaslighting us into distrusting our bodies. Laws act like the ultimate alibi for the greed addiction. All of these slowly erode our senses until we surrender our humanity.

Please wake up.

When we are trapped inside institutions that withhold resources and recognition, our lives are already placed in danger. This danger is structural, not self-inflicted. Yet the system rarely names it that way. Instead, it waits for the individual to break, and then uses that breakage as proof that the harm was internal all along.

What ultimately became clear to me is that the system's endgame is not merely compliance, but internalization. The deepest erasure occurs when a person begins to speak to themselves in the system's voice—when deprivation turns into shame, silence turns into self-doubt, and injustice turns into self-directed blame. At that point, the system no longer has to act. The harm sustains itself.

Imagine a world where we share knowledge and resources, no patents or copyright. We still work but our job is what feels like play, not us constantly translating ourselves into the language of capitalism to control liability, but rather true connections formed for healing and serving and sharing our gifts. A world where we don't have to sacrifice our dignity and give up selfhood for fitting a narrative of human based on numbers and words. A world where our pain is seen and held by one another until we find our way to health and happiness. A world where our suffering is shared just as much as our joy. We can connect to each other like children, honest, kind, forgiving and innocent. We can reimagine a kinder world and this time we keep watch to not repeat history. No centralized power and no more secrets. Just the truth, honest, kind, open.

A truth that can expand and never be owned. A truth formed by all our bodies, stories and feelings, even when we disagree. A truth where we hold space for differences, and honor it as a way to expand our imagination both ways.

ABOUT THE AUTHOR

Samina Rose is a writer, researcher, and truth-teller whose work bridges personal testimony, trauma theory, and critical social analysis. She is the author of *The Truth Teller: Reforming Our World* and *Compounded Relational cPTSD: The Truth Teller's Path*, where she examines how modern institutions — from healthcare and academia to capitalism, bureaucracy, and media — shape psychological survival and collective trauma. Her writing challenges scarcity-based worldviews while offering a vision of healing rooted in feminist care ethics, emancipatory leadership, and relational justice.

At the center of her work is what she calls the **Truth-Teller Paradigm** — a framework that understands resistance not as aggression but as the courageous act of naming harm, reclaiming dignity, and rebuilding connection in systems that often erase or pathologize dissent. Through concepts such as Institutional Gaslighting and Structural PTSD, Samina reframes trauma as a social and political experience rather than an individual failure, inviting readers to see their struggles within broader historical and structural contexts.

Drawing from her own lived experiences — including encounters with medical denial, immigration barriers, educational inequity, eating-disorder treatment exclusion, and the silencing of marginalized voices — she weaves autobiographical narrative with sociological and psychological insight. Her newest work expands this lens into a wider critique of the "machinery of harm," mapping how industries and power structures reproduce disconnection while also illuminating pathways toward collective repair.

Samina's writing is often described as both unflinching and deeply compassionate. Whether through scholarship, storytelling, or community dialogue, her voice carries a consistent message: healing is relational, truth-telling is an act of liberation, and even within systems built on scarcity, humans still possess the capacity to imagine and create worlds grounded in care, dignity, and shared humanity.

www.ingramcontent.com/pod-product-compliance
Lightning Source LLC
LaVergne TN
LVHW012338100826
845148LV00018B/2766